DATE DUE

WOMEN'S STUDIES ON THE EDGE

A DIFFERENCES BOOK

Edited by **JOAN WALLACH SCOTT** ————

WOMEN'S STUDIES ON THE EDGE

DUKE UNIVERSITY PRESS

Durham and London   2008

© 2008 Duke University Press
All rights reserved
Printed in the United States of America
on acid-free paper ∞
Designed by Amy Ruth Buchanan
Typeset in Dante by Achorn International
Library of Congress Cataloging-in-
Publication data appear on the last printed
page of this book.

CONTENTS

INTRODUCTION:

FEMINISM'S CRITICAL EDGE

Joan Wallach Scott

In a 1984 seminar at Brown University's Pembroke Center for Teaching and Research on Women, the French philosopher Jacques Derrida speculated about the institutionalization of women's studies in the academy. There would be a double effect, he said. When women's studies became what he playfully described as "just another cell in the university beehive," its legitimacy would be established, its future secured. At the same time, he warned, such triumph was not without its costs. These involved above all the disciplining of the field, the imposition of a certain orthodoxy, and so the dulling of its critical edge.

> Do the women who manage these programs, do they not become, in turn, the guardians of the Law and do they not risk constructing an institution similar to the institution against which they are fighting? . . . It is certain that the range of work in women's studies is enormous, and that there are already a considerable number of problems to pose, of bodies of work to study, of objects to define, and that women's studies has a great future. Nevertheless, if this future is of the same type as that of all other departments, of all other university institutions, is this not a sign of failure of the principles of women's studies? ("Women," *differences* 142)

The discussion that followed pushed on many points, among them whether the increase in the numbers of women teaching and in the knowledge they were both producing and transmitting was not itself subversive in an institution that had been (to use one of Derrida's words) "phallogocentric" (male in composition; masculine in focus; and committed to protecting the Law—that is, the foundational premises of the university). Would not the sheer presence of more women itself be a rebuke to male dominance? Were we not, as teachers and researchers, challenging what counted as knowledge and who counted as knowers? Did that not imply exactly the revolutionary transformation feminism sought? Did it matter whether the revolution was achieved by means of separate women's studies programs or by infiltrating the disciplines, "feminizing the curriculum," integrating women everywhere: in history, philosophy, economics, sociology? (144–45). Either way, did we run the risk of affirming a system we sought radically to alter?

Derrida conceded the risk; indeed, he saw no way out of it. "So a problem arises: if you keep the philosophical axiomatics, implying that *women* are subjects, considering women as subjects, then you keep the whole framework on which the traditional university is built. If someone tries to deconstruct the notion of subjectivity within women's studies, saying 'well, woman is not a subject . . . ' this would have two consequences, one radically revolutionary or deconstructive, and the other one dangerously reactive" (145). On the one hand, to say women are not subjects is to question the idea of the subject as it applies to men and women, to the rights-bearing individual in our culture; on the other hand, to say that women are not subjects can be heard to confirm their exclusion from citizenship (whether in the state or the academy), to accept the very terms of their inferiority to men. This tension between revolution (a refusal of the prevailing "philosophical axiomatics," whether of gender or capitalism or liberal democracy), and reform (working within the terms of those axiomatics to improve the lot of women or workers or other "others") is not peculiar to feminism; it was at the heart of the great movements for change in the nineteenth and twentieth centuries. Although the terms *reformist* and *revolutionary* were often used as epithets among factions in these movements, in fact the tension was evident in all camps. To what extent would tactical decisions compromise strategic goals? What was the relationship between long-term and short-term strategy? Would change in one arena necessarily bring about change in another? How could revolutionaries bring down a system by operating within it? How would you know when the revolution had happened?

The discussion with Derrida took place at a heady moment for women's studies. In the mid-1980s foundations and university administrations were recognizing the need for such programs, in part under pressure from students and faculty, in part in response to the richness and relevance of the work being done, and in part because (despite the defeat of the campaign for an Equal Rights Amendment to the Constitution) some feminist principles had been incorporated into national political agendas. Still, women's studies was hardly a full-fledged partner in the university curriculum, so the sense of engagement and the need for vigilance remained. We were embattled, yet on the verge of success. Those were amazingly productive and exciting years.

It is true that the 1980s were also the Reagan years, the beginning of the conservative reaction that has steadily gained ground. But at the same time, they marked the coming of age of second-wave feminism and what, in hindsight, could be called the last stand of the liberal university. Affirmative action not only remained in place but had begun to yield some of its intended results: more women and minorities were gaining admission to higher education as students and faculty; "diversity" was considered a desirable goal; and the quest for new knowledge was challenging the teaching upon which systems of white male privilege were based. In that context, women's studies gained institutional footing and funding in the form of faculty lines and/or joint appointments, student majors, and even degree-granting graduate programs.

How times have changed! On the eve of the new century, the sense of open-ended, utopian possibilities was fast disappearing, replaced by nostalgia for an increasingly idealized past. The only millennial expectations many of us had were anxieties about computer failures. Affirmative action was under attack even by some of its presumed beneficiaries, and feminism had become a dirty word. Not for everyone, of course, but the numbers of young women who wanted to "have it all" and yet swore they were not feminists were distressing to those of us who knew better. After all, Title IX let girls dream of playing sports seriously, the fierce battles to protect Roe v. Wade made pregnancy a choice, and the knowledge produced by legions of psychologists, biologists, anthropologists, historians, political theorists, sociologists, and even economists had undermined gender stereotypes and so granted access to professional careers once closed to women. The desire to "have it all" is a *feminist* fantasy; the possibility of even entertaining that desire exists because of all the agitation the women's movement engaged in, especially during the 1970s and 1980s. Today's young women are the beneficiaries of the women's movement, whether they know it or not.

The turn away from feminism—still evident as I write these lines—is part of a historic development that achieved fruition in the 1990s. It is best characterized as the ascendancy of ideologies of individualism and of corporate management, the apparent contradiction between them resolved within a framework of neoliberal economics. There were many converging factors, among them Supreme Court decisions that gave less credence to class action law suits against discrimination, requiring instead proof that individuals had been harmed; campaigns against affirmative action programs that took the form of law suits on behalf of "victims" of these programs (most often white men with higher test scores than those minorities given preferential treatment in university admissions); and the replacement of analyses of the structural causes of discrimination by emotional appeals to the experience of victims. The restructuring of universities is yet another development. This includes the turn to corporate models of administration and governance and, increasingly, to former CEOs to lead the academy; the redefinition of ideas as commodities and of students as fee-paying clients; the substitution of vocational ends for humanistic ones; and the emphasis on acquiring factual information rather than learning to think critically. Indeed, it was the university's role as the crucible of critical thinking that was most worrisome to the radical Republicans whose reign ushered in the twenty-first century.

The last few years have seen an onslaught by politicians, their self-appointed publicists, and organizations of conservative alumni against the supposed biases of teachers and the "political correctness" that is said to prevail on our campuses. Women's studies programs, with their commitment to feminist goals of equality and social justice, have been among the primary targets. Their agenda is said to be political, not scholarly, and hence not worthy of a place in the curriculum. The insistence on a separation of politics and scholarship is a direct assault on the claims of feminists and others in the 1970s and 1980s that there were connections that needed to be explored between politics and scholarship, that knowledge and power were intimately (though not necessarily directly) linked. Whether in the form of student bills of rights (which would place the opinions of students on the same plane as the learned authority of teachers), of testimonials by students who are "offended" or feel excluded by materials taught in a course, of Internet watch-lists designed to intimidate professors with "radical" views from expressing them, or of outright pressure by Israel's lobbyists to deny tenure to those considered too sympathetic to the Palestinian cause, the attacks are meant not only to silence critics of specific policies but also to rid the university of its long-standing association with critique. The effects of these campaigns have been to intimidate administrators who do not want to offend the politicians and donors upon whom the financial health of the university increasingly depends (state and federal monies have been dramatically reduced—one of the many disastrous consequences of the tax-cut "revolution") and to promote self-censorship, especially among faculty. Yet another effect is the unwillingness of many students to identify themselves in terms of a particular political or social outlook—as feminists, for example.

There is, though, another side to this story, another set of parallel developments I have not yet mentioned. These were more internal to women's studies: at once an autonomous process of institutionalization and a defensive reaction to the changes the university was undergoing. The results were a new emphasis on detail—the administration of programs, the implementation or adjustment of curricular offerings, the supervision of undergraduate majors, the placement of doctoral students, the expansion of budgets—and the emergence of an orthodoxy that set often inflexible standards of admission for the field. The orthodoxy was not without its critics, but the requirements of institutionalization had a force and a logic of their own. There is some truth to the charge that "political correctness" has had a stifling effect on the production of feminist knowledge, setting tests of loyalty and "patroling" the boundaries of what counted and didn't count as acceptable work. Orthodoxy was about defining the terrain of women's studies, elaborating its methods and theories like those of other disciplines. It was also about consolidating support for programs that were always on the verge of diminishment or extinction. Would the budget be granted for another year? How many lines could be secured? Would enrollment be large enough to claim new resources? Would joint appointments work with departments whose criteria were different or for whom women's studies was not a serious undertaking? Difficult negotiations with deans and department chairs often made women's studies faculty ever more protective of the ground they held. Differences among feminists, in this context, were tantamount to heresy. The tendency was to close ranks and attribute criticism exclusively to external forces: to biases of entrenched (male) faculty, or to a political animus against feminism, or to a backlash evident in society at large. In the process, feminism began to lose its critical edge.

The loss of that edge has led to disillusionment for some. One form of this disillusionment is an outright rejection of feminism: personal disenchantment becomes the basis for complaint, which is nonetheless offered as if it were dispassionate analysis. It is as if the slogan "the personal is political" were taken literally; one's feelings are defined as political, rather than (as the slogan intended) the basis for the scrutiny of power relationships. Another form of disillusionment is nostalgia, a cry of longing for a return to the good old days. That nostalgia was apparent in many of the articles published on the eve of the millennium; when asked to contemplate the future of women's studies, most respondents could only look back. The yearning for an idealized past is still evident in more recent articles and books.

The essays in this book, although some evince impatience and even anger, refuse both rejection and nostalgia. Instead they embrace feminism, not as a set of prescriptions but as a critical stance, one that seeks to interrogate and disrupt prevailing systems of gender, one that assumes that what worked in the 1980s might not work in the early years of the new millennium, one that is committed to self-scrutiny as well as to denunciations of domination and oppression, one that is never satisfied with simply transmitting bodies of knowledge but that seeks instead to produce new knowledge. This is feminism not as the perpetuation and protection of orthodoxy but feminism as critique.

THIS COLLECTION IS AN ATTEMPT to restore feminism's critical edge, even to sharpen it. We recognize that this is a difficult moment in which to seem to criticize women's studies programs. They are under siege from the right, ridiculed and reviled by those who want to undo the great gains of the affirmative action years and the analyses of links between power and knowledge that accompanied them. And the attack on feminism goes beyond the borders of the academy; it is evident in the United States in evangelical Christian attempts to defend as God's teaching traditional marriage, the preeminence of paternal rule, and the maternal duties of women. It is evident, too, internationally, in politicized Islamist movements that equate women's liberation with the materialism of the imperial West; in many states in the world where rightist parties seek to dismantle gender equity policies; in nationalist parties in some postcommunist states that define a return to "normalcy" as the restoration of male domination in the political and domestic spheres. To defend feminism in this context requires more than the assertion of women's abilities and accomplishments, the support of women candidates for political office (and the celebration of their victories in Chile, Liberia, and elsewhere), the writing of exemplary histories of women in the past, and the analysis of obstacles women continue to face. It also demands that we exercise critique—still feminism's most potent weapon.

By critique I mean not just criticism but the exposure of the contradictions and inadequacies of any system of thought. The blind spots that insure coherence and stability by ignoring or denying contradictions are probed by critique. It is the question posed to democracy about why inequalities persist, the challenge posed to universalism by those excluded on the basis of their difference, the refusal to accept nature as the common-sense explanation for women's oppression. Critique makes supporters of any system uncomfortable because of its relentless effort to destabilize orthodoxies and its refusal to accept the comforts (and discomforts) of the status quo. The point of critique is not to tear down or destroy but, by bringing to light the limits and inconsistencies that have been studiously avoided, to open up new possibilities, new ways of thinking about what might be done to make things better. Critique does not offer a map that leads to a guaranteed future; rather, it disturbs our settled expectations and incites us to explore, indeed to invent, alternate routes.

Feminists have not only wielded critique (against patriarchy, the nation-state, capitalism, socialism, republicanism, science, canons of literature, all the major disciplines) in the name of ending discrimination against women; they have also interrogated the premises of their own beliefs, the foundations of their own movement. This impulse to self-critique has been present from the inception of feminism as a social-political movement. The critique I refer to is not the same as factional fights or different identity or strategic positions (difference versus equality, liberal versus socialist, straight versus queer, white versus women of color, first world versus third). Instead, it is an examination of the very terms that organize our actions: What does it mean to make "women" the object of our studies? What are the exclusions performed by insisting on a homogeneous category of "women"? When inclusion is the aim, are there alternatives to the endless proliferation of specific (racial, ethnic, religious, geographic, national, sexual, class) identities? Is there such a thing as feminist theory or feminist methodology? What counts as emancipation and for whom?

THE ESSAYS IN THIS BOOK turn feminism's critical edge upon itself. In so doing, they aim to open women's studies to different futures than were either imagined "at the beginning" (in the 1970s and 1980s) or are envisioned now by defenders of the status quo. *Women's Studies on the Edge* had its first incarnation as a special issue of the journal *differences* in 1997. Looking ahead to the millennium, we aimed to take stock of the field of women's studies, evaluate critically what had taken place, and try to think about what the future might hold. The issue became one of the journal's bestsellers, quickly exhausting its imprint. Tattered copies are still in use today; Xeroxed copies of its articles circulate widely.

The reasons for its popularity are clear: there is nothing like it in print, nothing that raises from within feminist thought the tough questions that need to be considered about the impact of institutionalization on this once radical field of inquiry; about how orthodoxy has taken over some parts of the field; about the ongoing difficulties of articulating women's studies with ethnic, queer, and race studies; and about the limits of liberal concepts of emancipation for understanding non-Western women. The essays refuse to be polite about the problems faced by women's studies; they believe that the future of feminist work depends on acknowledging and addressing those problems.

In this book we have retained the most topical and controversial—the edgiest—of the original essays; we've also added others. Some of the added pieces were written in direct response to the original essays; others take the argument further than it went before. There is no single line presented here; rather, there are conflicting interpretations that sometimes overlap and sometimes stand in opposition to one another. The result is a book that embodies the best aspects of critique, the stance at once intellectual and political that, while not peculiar to feminism, characterizes what we take to be feminism's ethos and its aim.

Part I of *Women's Studies on the Edge* begins with two different assessments of the impact of institutional success on women's studies programs. Wendy Brown's explosive essay, "The Impossibility of Women's Studies," argues that the initial impetus for women's studies—the need to end the exclusion of women as objects of knowledge, politics, and policy—is now exhausted, leaving confusion and incoherence in its wake. She takes the proliferation of categories of women—by race, ethnicity, religious affiliation, and sexual preference (to name only a few possibilities)—as evidence of the limits of "any field organized by social identity rather than genre of inquiry" (23). "Women's studies as a contemporary institution," she writes, "may be politically and theoretically incoherent, as well as tacitly conservative—incoherent because by definition it circumscribes uncircumscribable 'women' as an object of study, and conservative because it must resist all objections to such circumscription if it is to sustain that object of study as its raison d'être" (21). As long as women's studies programs remain the site of identity politics, she concludes, their once radical influence is doomed to impotence.

Robyn Wiegman's essay places Brown's piece in the context of debates about the relationship between feminist academic work and feminist politics. Institutionalization has meant different things to different writers, she says. Some have insisted that women's studies programs now suffer from their loss of an earlier connection to practical politics. In this reading, institutionalization is equated with depoliticization. Others—Wiegman puts Brown in this group—insist that institutionalization has fixed the early connection between politics and scholarship in ways that stifle creative thinking, whether academic or political. From either perspective, Wiegman argues, institutionalization has been associated with failure and, she adds, failure with feminization. Her essay seeks to disentangle those associations, to think a future for women's studies programs outside the boxes in which Brown says it has been caught.

Part II offers a set of essays that illustrate some of Brown's points by looking at those who have been "edged out" by the category of "women" or one of its subsets (Middle Eastern women in the first two essays, lesbian and transgender people in the third). Afsaneh Najmabadi recounts her frustration with the available categories of identity for teachers of women's studies: "As a feminist from a country [Iran] that was never colonized and never a colonial power, as a feminist from an Islamicate culture with a strong experience of secular modernity, I find myself speaking from a doubly contaminated zone" (77). She cannot invoke the category of postcolonial identity or of Muslim woman, and yet, to reject these seems to put her either in opposition to some form of authentic experience or outside the hearing of most women's studies scholars. "Hybrid categories" do not solve the problem; they at once intensify it with more adjectives and misrepresent the position of the person being described. Najmabadi's solution is "to refuse to claim categories or to settle for any multiplicity of identities," instead disclaiming them all in a form of "affirmative resistance" (78).

Saba Mahmood comes at the question from a different angle, analyzing the emergence of a new genre of Muslim women's autobiographical accounts of patriarchal abuse. Since September 11, 2001, these accounts have gained widespread popular and academic attention, and they have confirmed a vision of Islam as violent and abusive to women. Mahmood questions the appeal to the Western notions of emancipation that inform these autobiographies, and she tracks the way in which they have been used to clinch arguments about a "clash of civilizations," drawing support for the United States' war against terrorism and its mandate to bring democracy to the Middle East. She asks: How has gender inequality become a justification for the war on terror? How has a particular conception of "religious patriarchy" helped garner popular support for the U.S. war in Iraq? Her essay serves as a warning to those who assume that liberal individualist ideas of women's freedom—those that are often the founding values of women's studies programs—are universal. Such assumptions blind us to the importance of religiosity in creating forms of women's agency, and they obscure the complexities both of religious belief and of gender relations in societies unlike our own. Like Najmabadi, who reminds us that categories of identity are inevitably involved in the construction of mutable relations of power, Mahmood insists on the historicity of values: they acquire meaning only in specific political contexts and it is these contexts that the feminist critic must examine.

Transgender offers another kind of challenge to the established gender categories of women's studies and to its underlying individualism. As Gayle Salamon puts it, "Genders beyond the binary of male and female are neither fictive nor futural, but are embodied and lived, and women's studies has not yet recognized this" (115). Salamon suggests that transgender studies belongs in women's studies programs (rather than in sexuality or queer studies) because it is gender categories that are being challenged. "Without the systemic understanding that women's studies provides—of the structures of gender and the relations of power that underlie those structures—trans studies is unable to understand gender as a historical category and is powerless to account for how the present state of gender emerged" (116). If trans studies needs women's studies, Salamon argues, women's studies also needs trans studies. Even as it works with feminist theories of gender, transgender pushes them beyond their current articulations, not only challenging the equation of gender with biological givens of male and female but also refusing ideas of individual choice as an explanation for identity. As Salamon conceives it, there is a symbiotic relationship between the two fields of study. "The task of theory is not to dismantle gender identity, nor to rob people of their experience of gender. . . . Rather, theory is perhaps uniquely suited to show us how present configurations of gender are contingent and to imagine its possible future articulations differently. It is only through merging the concerns of transgender studies with the historical analysis of women's studies that a new, less contracted space for gender might be created."[1] Feminist critique of the kind Salamon practices opens the way for new, unthought possibilities, and so, different futures.

We have called the set of essays in Part III "edging in" because each in its own way makes the case for the continued importance of women's studies. Ellen Rooney's piece, written in 1990, might at first reading be taken as ancient history: it provides the vision of women's studies that Wendy Brown argues institutionalization has destroyed. Rooney offers the politically motivated critique of disciplinary knowledge production that she associates with women's studies as a model for programs in cultural studies. For her, "feminist theory in the academy is constituted by the discovery that a politicized, theoretical intervention with the disciplines is unavoidable" (147). Women's studies, says Rooney, is driven by political concerns that inevitably lead to a critique of the way knowledge is *produced*. "The feminist students who choose to major in women's studies *construct* their choice as a political one. I believe this is always true (though I write that phrase with a certain dread)" (146). Exactly what that dread is she never explains, though it is perhaps the "always" that gives her pause. Rooney does not anticipate the hardening of categories and political outlooks that other essays in this book argue have dampened the optimistic radicalism of early women's studies scholarship and teaching. But rather than a vision of a world we have lost, her essay serves as an example of what the initial impetus for women's studies programs was: the practice of critique—critique that is not limited to "women" as an object of study or to the consolidation of women's identity but that instead addresses "the production of disciplinary knowledge." This kind of critique, Rooney reminds us, requires "painstaking construction and reconstruction, 'with no end in sight'" (146).

Evelynn M. Hammonds's interview with Beverly Guy-Sheftall offers important insight from a pioneer of black women's studies into the complexities of negotiating issues of gender and race and into the ways in which black women's studies has broadened the scope of feminism. "I think black women's studies really reinvigorated and reconceptualized feminism in such a way so that now it is not a narrow, culturally specific manifestation of one group of women's experiences" (159). As Guy-Sheftall responds to Hammonds's probing questions, we see the ways in which institutionalization (a funded, recognized program) becomes *the* locus for addressing practical and theoretical tensions produced by feminist work.

> Women's studies can force these students [at a historically black women's college] to question their values and the ways in which they have been socialized, which I think would produce students who are more critical, more willing to engage in activist projects that would propel them out of the classroom, and would push them out of their "comfort zone" to engage a broader range of questions instead of having a narrow focus on race. (166–67)

Here is testimony for the continuing operations of critical thinking *within* the parameters of existing women's studies programs.

We end with Biddy Martin's call to rethink women's studies not as a parochial matter confined to one field, but "in the context of larger discussions about the organization of knowledge and of learning in universities and efforts to change the forms of disciplinary and intradisciplinary balkanization that constrain our intellectual vision and prevent us from providing students a more integrated education" (170). Martin provides an overview of the transformations that have affected the academy, touching on fields such as biology that are usually not part of women's studies. She also reviews a variety of proposals to fix what many perceive as the broken promise of humanistic education. She ends by suggesting that the tradition of critique that once inspired feminist study (as Rooney describes it) can be reactivated to address current problems.

> If feminist studies of gender are to remain vital, or even to take the lead in reorganizing our approaches to knowledge and learning, we have to recognize and resist defensive refusals to be moved out of entrenched positions, whether disciplinary or political. Where in our universities and in our professional worlds is the *not known* treated

creatively? . . . Where does Thought appear to unsettle dogma or to set aside disciplinary turf wars, yet remain engaged in the risk of the political? Where, when, under what conditions does the demand for excellence and visibility give way to an effort to interact and build the intellectual connections, with all their pleasures, that women's studies once promised, and at times, has even delivered? (195)

With these questions, we end this book, leaving readers—we hope—on the edge. This edge is defined as a place of indeterminacy, at once exciting and precarious. Exciting because to be on this edge is to be on the verge of discovering new possibilities for a field that may only seem to be exhausted and new ways to disrupt prevailing arrangements and relationships of power. Precarious because in the quest for an as-yet-unimagined future, there are never any guarantees.

NOTES

On behalf of all the contributors to this volume, I would like to thank Denise Davis, editor par excellence, for her careful and rigorous attention to every detail in the production of this book.

　　1. Salamon, e-mail to the author on August 17, 2006.

Part I. **OVER THE EDGE**

THE IMPOSSIBILITY OF WOMEN'S STUDIES

Wendy Brown

There is today enough retrospective analysis and harangue concerning the field of women's studies to raise the question of whether dusk on its epoch has arrived, even if nothing approaching Minerva's wisdom has yet emerged. Consider the public arguments about its value and direction over the past half decade: Is it rigorous? Scholarly? Quasi-religious? Doctrinaire? Is it anti-intellectual and too political? Overly theoretical and insufficiently political? Does it mass-produce victims instead of heroines, losers instead of winners? Or does it turn out jargon-speaking metaphysicians who have lost all concern with Real Women? Has it become unmoored from its founding principles? Was it captured by the radical fringe? The theoretical elite? The moon worshipers? The man-haters? The sex police? Perhaps even more interesting than the public debates are the questions many feminist scholars are asking privately: Why are so few younger scholars drawn to women's studies? Why are many senior feminist scholars, once movers and shakers in the making of women's studies programs, no longer involved with them? How did women's studies lose its cachet? Is it a casualty of rapidly changing trends and hot spots in academe, or has it outlived its time or its value in some more profound sense? Does it continue to secure a crucial political space in male-dominated academia? What is the relationship between its political and its intellectual mission?

I want to consider a problem to one side of these questions that might also shed light on them. To what extent is women's studies still tenable as an institutionalized domain of academic study, as a circumscribed intellectual endeavor appropriate as a basis for undergraduate or graduate degrees? Given the very achievements of feminist knowledge about foundations, identities, and boundaries over the last two decades, what are the intellectual premises of women's studies now? What are the boundaries that define it and differentiate it from other kinds of inquiry? These are not abstract questions, but ones that issue from the very real conundrums currently faced by those of us in women's studies. Consider the following examples from my own program,[1] one that is formally strong and robust with its five full-time faculty, two hundred majors, and introductory courses that annually enroll more than seven hundred students (and hence reach nearly one quarter of the undergraduate population of the university as a whole).

In the early 1990s, women's studies at the University of California, Santa Cruz, undertook that frightening project of self-scrutiny known as curriculum revision. What brought us to this point is itself interesting. For a number of years, we had maintained a set of requirements for the undergraduate degree that comprised an odd mix of the academically generic and the political, requirements that were not coined all at once as a coherent vision of a women's studies curriculum, but rather had been pieced together in response to various and conflicting demands as the program developed. *The generic:* students were required to take a three-term sequence consisting of "Introduction to Feminism," "Feminist Theory," and "Methodological Perspectives in Feminism," a sequence marked by category distinctions notably at odds with the expansive understanding of theory, the critique of methodism, and the challenge to a meaningful divide between the humanities and social sciences that are all putatively fundamental to feminist inquiry. This meant that quite often our first project in these courses was to undo the very distinctions we had given ourselves, thus repeating our founding rebellion against disciplinary distinctions, this time in our own house. *The political:* the only other content-specific requirement for the major was a course called "Women of Color in the United States," in which students gained some exposure to the histories, literatures, and cultures of Asian American, African American, Latina, and Native American women, and white students in the course learned to "decenter themselves" while women of color spoke.

This strange combination of genres in the curricular requirements schooled our students in the isolated intellectual (and putatively nonracialized) character of something called theory, the isolated (and putatively nontheoretical) political mandate of race, and the illusion that there was something called method (applied theory?) that unified all feminist research and thinking. Most of the students loved the experiential and issue-oriented introductory course, feared theory, disliked methods, and participated somewhat anxiously in the "Women of Color" class. Hence, most women's studies students regarded the requirements as something to be borne and the major as having its rewards in the particulars of the elective courses they chose or in the feminist community of students the major harbored. Moreover, the limited and incoherent nature of these requirements as a course of study meant that our students were obtaining their degrees on the basis of rather impoverished educations, something women have had too much of for too long.

But what happened when we finally sat down to revise the curriculum is even more interesting than the desires symptomatized by the existing curriculum—in particular, the desire for disciplinary status signified by the claim to a distinct theory and method (even as women's studies necessarily challenges disciplinarity) and the desire to conquer the racialized challenge to women's studies' early objects of study by institutionalizing that challenge in the curriculum. In our curriculum revision meetings, we found ourselves completely stumped over the question of what a women's studies curriculum should contain. Since, in addition to trying to produce a curriculum that would express the range, depth, and problems occupying women's studies scholarship, we were also trying to address faculty frustration about students not being well enough trained in anything to provide rewarding classroom exchange in the faculty's areas of expertise, we focused intently on the question of what would constitute an intellectually rigorous as well as coherent program. We speculatively explored a number of possibilities—a thematically organized curriculum; pathways that roughly followed the disciplines; more extensive requirements in each domain of feminist scholarship that the faculty considered important—but each possibility collapsed under close analysis. Each approach seemed terribly arbitrary, each featured some dimension of feminist scholarship that had no reason to be privileged, each continued to beg the question of what a well-educated student in women's studies ought to know and the tools

with which she ought to craft her thinking. We also found ourselves repeatedly mired by a strange chasm between faculty and students in the
program: a majority of our majors were interested in some variant of feminist sociological or psychological analysis—experientially, empirically, and
practically oriented—or in studies of popular culture. Yet not one of our
core faculty worked in sociology, psychology, community studies, commu-
nications, or film/video. Many of our students wanted to think, learn, and
talk about body image and eating disorders, gender and sexuality in the media, sexual practices, intimate relationships, sexual violence, how children
and adolescents are gendered, and survivor identities ranging from alcohol
to incest. Our five core and three most closely affiliated faculty were trained
respectively in American literature, American history, Chinese history, English literature, Renaissance Italian and French literature, Western political
theory, European history, and molecular biology. As feminist scholars, we
have clearly strayed from the most traditional boundaries of these fields,
just as we have learned and taught material relatively unrelated to them,
but even this reformation of our training and scholarly orientation could
not close the gap between the students' interests and our own.

If the practical project we set for ourselves in revising the curriculum
was running aground, certainly we were in the grip of an important historical-political problem. Why, when we looked closely at this project for
which we had fought so hard and which was now academically institutionalized, could we find no there there? That is, why was the question of
what constituted the fundamentals of knowledge in women's studies so
elusive to us?[2] We were up against more than the oft-discussed division
between "women's studies" and feminist theory, the political insidious-
ness of the institutional division between "ethnic studies" and "women's
studies," a similarly disturbing division between queer theory and feminist
theory, or the way that the ostensibly less identitarian rubric of "cultural
studies" promised but failed to relieve these troubling distinctions. And we
were up against more than the paradox that the disciplines that have been
so radically denatured in recent years are also apparently those that we
cannot completely do without, if only to position ourselves against them
within them. We were also up against more than the dramatic fracturing
of women's studies as a domain of inquiry during the last decade—the fact
that contemporary feminist scholarship is not a single conversation but is
instead engaged with respective domains of knowledge, or bodies of theory, that are themselves infrequently engaged with each other. And we

were up against more than the ways that this decade's theoretical challenges to the stability of the category of gender, and political challenges to a discourse of gender apart from race, class, and other markers of social identity, constituted very nearly overwhelming challenges to women's studies as a coherent endeavor. We were up against more than the fact that many of the intellectual impulses originally formative of women's studies have now dispersed themselves—appropriately, productively, yet in ways that profoundly challenged the turf that women's studies historically claimed as its own, especially the terrains of sexuality and of race.

We were up against more than any one of these challenges because we were up against all of them. And together, they called into question the quarter-century-old project of institutionalizing as curriculum, method, field, major, or bachelor of arts what was a profoundly important political moment in the academy, the moment in which women's movements challenged the ubiquitous misogyny, masculinism, and sexism in academic research, curricula, canons, and pedagogies. Indisputably, women's studies as a critique of such practices was politically important and intellectually creative. Women's studies as a contemporary institution, however, may be politically and theoretically incoherent, as well as tacitly conservative—incoherent because by definition it circumscribes uncircumscribable "women" as an object of study, and conservative because it must resist all objections to such circumscription if it is to sustain that object of study as its raison d'être. Hence the persistent theory wars, race wars, and sex wars notoriously ravaging women's studies in the 1980s, not to mention the ways in which women's studies has sometimes greeted uncomfortably (and even with hostility) the rise of feminist literary studies and theory outside of its purview, critical race theory, postcolonial theory, queer theory, and cultural studies. Theory that destabilizes the category of women, racial formations that disrupt the unity or primacy of the category, and sexualities that similarly blur the solidarity of the category—each of these must be resisted, restricted, or worse, colonized, to preserve the realm.[3] Each, therefore, is compelled to go elsewhere, while women's studies consolidates itself in the remains, impoverished by the lack of challenges from within, bewildered by its new ghettoization in the academy—this time by feminists themselves.

If uncertainty about what constitutes a women's studies education is a persistent whisper in all undergraduate program development, it positively howls as a problem at the level of graduate training. Since our program has regularly been invited by our administration over the past decade to submit a plan for a graduate program, we have struggled repeatedly to conjure the intellectual basis for a Ph.D. program in women's studies. In what should the graduate student in women's studies be trained? What bodies of knowledge must a women's studies doctoral candidate have mastered and why? Which women should she know about and what should she know about them? Which techniques of analyzing gender should she command and why? Ethnography or oral history? Lacanian psychoanalysis? Quantitative sociological analysis? Objects relations theory? Literary theory? Postcolonial criticism? Neo-Marxist theories of labor and political economy? Social history? Critical science studies? There is a further question: who are we to teach these things simply because we are interested in feminism and feminist analysis from our own scholarly perspectives?

The unanswered question of what women's studies is also manifests itself in day-to-day concerns about what may count as a women's studies course and who may count as an affiliated member of a women's studies faculty. Almost all women's studies programs rely on faculty and curricular offerings in other departments, both because they are too small to do otherwise and because of the proud interdisciplinarity undergirding the intellectual project of women's studies. But if political devotion to the cause (once the main criterion for who is in women's studies and who is not) no longer serves as the measure for what constitutes a women's studies course, what does? Must such a class be focused solely or primarily on women? (What of feminist courses on other topics, such as feminist science studies or studies in masculinity, and what of nonfeminist courses concerned with women?) Must the class be taught from a feminist perspective? (What counts as such a perspective and who decides?) Is it a class that potentially contributes to feminist theory and research? (Don't most well-conceived courses in the social sciences and humanities potentially make such a contribution?)

For many women's studies programs, the difficulty of deciding these things leads to some strange curricular formations: Chaucer taught by one faculty member may count for women's studies, but not when it is taught by another; "Introduction to Sociology" does not count, but a course called "The Chicano Experience" does; philosophy courses on phenomenology are excluded, but courses on Saussure and Derrida are included; "Early Modern Europe" taught by a feminist historian counts, but "Modern Europe" taught by a nonfeminist does not; similarly, Lacan taught by a lesbian feminist semiotician counts, while Lacan taught by an avant-garde art historian and filmmaker does not; an anthropology course called "Queer Political Cultures" counts, but one called "Peoples and Cultures of the American Southwest" does not. And then there is the endless petitioning. A student wants to know if her invertebrate biology course, in which she focused intensely on biological discourses of mating, might count—and why not? Another student wonders whether he can include his history of political theory courses—and what better background for grasping the antecedents of feminist political theory? A third student complains that her "Psychology of Women" course, listed as a women's studies elective, mostly trafficked in unreconstructed psychological behaviorism and was not feminist at all. Yet another petitions to have her passion for psychoanalytic feminism certified as legitimate by letting her count all her studies in Freud and Klein as part of her feminist education. Especially given the strange routes by which most faculty arrived at women's studies, and given the diverse materials we draw upon to vitalize our own research, who are we to police the intellectual boundaries of this endeavor? And how did we become cops anyway?

CERTAINLY WHEN PEERED AT CLOSELY, the definitions of all disciplines wobble, their identities mutate, their rules and regulations appear contingent and contestable. Most disciplines, founded through necessary exclusions and illusions about the stability and boundedness of their objects, have reached crises in their attempts to secure their boundaries, define an exclusive terrain of inquiry, and fix their object of study. And in most cases, the desire to persist over time has resulted in a certain conservatism, or its close cousin, methodism. Thus for sociology to sustain the radicalism that was one strain of its founding, rather than becoming nominalist and positivist, it had to connect with political economy, politics, semiotics, and history, as a small branch of it did. Similarly, the contemporary battles in literary studies can be understood, in part, as turning on the question of whether literature's object of study shall remain fixed and narrow or shall become much more indeterminate and broad in scope, up to and past the point where the objects constituting the identity of the discipline—literary texts—are regarded as contingent and even dispensable.

There is something about women's studies, though, and perhaps about any field organized by social identity rather than by genre of inquiry, that is especially vulnerable to losing its raison d'être when the coherence or boundedness of its object of study is challenged. Thus, paradoxically, sustaining gender as a critical, self-reflexive category rather than a normative or nominal one, and sustaining women's studies as an intellectually and institutionally radical site rather than a regulatory one—in short, refusing to allow gender studies and women's studies to be disciplined—are concerns and refusals at odds with affirming women's studies *as* a coherent field of study. This paradox will become clearer as I turn to what I take to be one of the central problematics of feminist inquiry today and one of the central conundrums facing women's studies: how to come to terms with the problem of the powers involved in the construction of subjects.

This problem is also shaped by a paradox. On the one hand, various marked subjects are created through very different *kinds* of powers—not just different powers. That is, subjects of gender, class, nationality, race, sexuality, and so forth, are created through different histories, different mechanisms and sites of power, different discursive formations, different regulatory schemes. On the other hand, we are not fabricated as subjects in discrete units by these various powers: they do not operate on and through us independently, or linearly, or cumulatively. Insofar as subject construction does not take place along discrete lines of nationality, race, sexuality, gender, caste, class, and so forth, these powers of subject formation are not separable in the subject itself. These powers neither constitute links in a chain nor overlapping spheres of oppression; they are not "intersectional" in their formation (Crenshaw); they are not simply degrees of privilege (Hurtado); and they cannot be reduced to being inside or outside, or more or less proximate to, dominant power formations (Collins).[4] As so many feminist, postcolonial, queer, and critical race theorists have noted in recent years, it is impossible to extract the race from gender, or the gender from sexuality, or the masculinity from colonialism. Moreover, to treat various modalities of subject formation as additive in any of the ways suggested by the terms above is to elide the way subjects are brought into being through subjectifying discourses. We are not simply oppressed but *produced* through these discourses, a production that is historically complex and contingent and that occurs through formations that do not honor analytically distinct identity categories.[5]

For feminist theory, the most problematic dimension of this paradox pertains to the fact that grasping subject construction for different forms of social subjection (class, race, etc.) requires distinctive models of power, yet subject construction itself does not unfold according to any one of these models precisely because we are always constructed by more than one, even if we participate in the norms of some and the deviations of others. Not simply the content but the modalities of power producing gender, race, or caste are specific to each production—the mode of production and dimensions of state power that produce class and the discourses and institutions of normative heterosexuality that produce gender are largely noncomparable forms and styles of power. Thus, for example, understanding the way in which class and gender are regulated by various discourses of class and gender is not a matter of applying a neutral "apparatus" of regulation to the specific problem of class and gender. There is not, as Judith Butler has remarked, first gender and then the apparatus that regulates it; gender does not exist prior to its regulation.[6] Rather, the gendered subject emerges through a regulatory scheme of gender—we are literally brought into being as gendered subjects through gender regulation. From this perspective, the very idea of a regulatory "apparatus" appears as a kind of structuralist Althusserian hangover clouding the Foucauldian insight into the radical reach of subject production through regulatory discourse. In Foucault's understanding of the power that circulates through the subject of regulation, there can be no actual apparatus because there is no sharp distinction between what is produced and what is regulating—we are not simply targets but vehicles of power.[7] Thus, to paraphrase Nietzsche awkwardly, we must be able to conceive regulation without the regulator, to understand regulation as only and always materializing in its effects, and to understand these effects as specific to that which is being regulated.

This problem can be put the other way around: the forms of power that produce gender or class are themselves saturated with that production—they do not precede it. Indeed, it is this element of subject production that makes intelligible the very notions of masculinist power, or bourgeois power, as opposed to speaking about gender and class power simply in terms of rule by one group of people and the oppression of another. In the more conventional way of speaking about power as an instrument of domination interchangeable among groups and even individuals, power is cast as a (gender, class, and race) neutral means of achieving privilege and domination. Power is conceived as something held by particular individuals or groups, and this commodity status gives it independence from the bearer of it and the subject of power. It is this (mis)conception of power that allows various forms of oppression to be spoken of in additive and interchangeable terms. Power in this pre-Foucauldian view is seen to locate subjects in a field of power, but the field itself is not seen to produce the subjects it locates; it is not regarded as the very medium of emergence of those subjects.

Law is one quite fertile place to see the effects of the conundrum that distinctive models of power are required for grasping various kinds of subject production, yet subject construction itself does not transpire in accordance with any of these models. I want to ponder this domain at some length in order to shed light from outside the field of women's studies on the problem of the subject that it faces. Through a consideration of the ways that different kinds of marked subjects appear in law and legal studies, we can reflect on the difficulties that women's studies encounters in its simultaneous effort to center gender analytically and to presume gender's imbrication with other forms of social power.

Bracketing the sphere of formal and relatively abstract antidiscrimination law, where discrimination on the basis of a laundry list of identity attributes and personal beliefs is prohibited, it is unusual to find the injuries of racism, sexism, homophobia, and poverty harbored in the same corners of the law. These injuries are rarely recognized or regulated through the same legal categories or redressed through the same legal strategies. Consequently, legal theorists engage with different dimensions of the law depending on the identity category with which they are concerned—for example, feminists might focus intently upon family law while working-class activists might be more closely engaged with contract and labor law. In addition, they often figure the law itself in quite incommensurate ways. Consider, as an example of the latter, the debate about the value of rights between critical legal theorists, concerned with the function of property rights in producing the very existence of workers, tenants, the poor, and the homeless, and critical race theorists, concerned with enfranchising historically rights-deprived members of subordinated racial groups. While critical legal theorists tend to regard rights as entrenching and masking inequality, many critical race theorists have figured rights as vital symbols of personhood and citizenship, as the very currency of civic belonging in liberal constitutional orders. More interesting than brokering this debate in terms of the relative validity of the arguments is recognizing what each argument makes visible that the other does not. The neo-Marxist perspective of the critical legal theorists emphasizes the convergence of formal legal equality with the tendency of other liberal and capitalist discourses to naturalize class inequality and the social powers constitutive of class, including those powers conferred by legal rights. The histories of slavery and the civil rights movement out of which arises the critical race theory position, in contrast, emphasize the extent to which rights discourse historically has designated who does and does not count as a member of human society: if rights signal personhood, then being without them is not merely to be without a concrete asset but to lack the less tangible but equally essential degree of civic belonging they confer.

Both claims are important and compelling, but can both be true? Can the same juridical discourse both obscure and articulate social inequality, that is, serve both as an instrument of entrenching inequality and as a means of redressing it? This question appears less paradoxical when it is recognized that what the critical legal theory position makes visible are certain mechanisms of socioeconomic inequality in liberal and capitalist societies, while the critical race theory claim about the symbolic value of rights highlights discursive strategies of marginalization and dehumanization.[8] These are two different forms of power and subjection, sometimes converging in a common subject and injury, sometimes not. While both are relevant to class as well as race, the former probably has a heavier bearing for class and the latter for race. Because the powers formative of class and of race are so different, it should not surprise us to discover that they bear different relationships to crucial legal categories. What is difficult, of course, is determining how to navigate these differences when one is dealing with race and class subordination in a single subject. Indeed, it is in the place where race and class converge (in a poor, racially stigmatized population) that the operation of rights becomes deeply paradoxical. This problem becomes even more complex when one considers the category of gender, where both socioeconomic deprivation and dehumanization operate as part of what constitutes women as such: clearly women need the "rights of man" in order to establish their place in humanity, yet, as countless feminist theorists have pointed out, these same rights not only fail to address but also mask many of the substantive ways in which women's subordination operates.[9]

Consider other examples of the ways the law itself is figured differently by those invested in different social categories and social identities. The sodomy statutes that quite literally constitute the homosexual legal subject, and constitute it as an always already criminal subject, have no obvious parallel in the making of race, gender, or class.[10] There are no similarly taboo practices that both identify and criminalize the racialized, gendered, or class subject. Nor is there, in the production and regulation of these other subjects, an analogy to the prohibition on same-sex marriage or the lack of a secure legal status for homosexual parenting. On the other hand, the equality/difference dilemma faced by feminist legal reformers has no parallel in theorizing about race or class and rarely surfaces in discussions of gay rights. There would appear to be no equivalent, in the operation of homosexual, racial, or class subjection, to the conundrum of maternity, or even of sexual and physical violability and vulnerability, in defining the central problematic and central paradoxes of feminist legal reform. More generally, there is no equivalent to the crucial place of reproductive rights for women's equality in defining the parameters of racial freedom or ending the stigma for minority sexual orientation.[11] Within liberal legalism, no distinctive domain of control equivalent to that of women over reproduction stands as a *condition* of freedom and equality for homosexual and racially marked subjects. Beyond liberal legalism, it was Marx, of course, who argued that collectivization of the means of production was exactly such a condition for the working class, but even this possible parallel breaks down when the importance of collective ownership and control for workers is contrasted with women's need for individual control over their reproductive bodies.

The heated debate among advocates of lesbian and gay legal reform about whether gayness is immutable (genetically rooted) also has no parallel in other domains of identity-based critical legal theory. While there is certainly much discussion about gender's mutability among feminist theorists and activists, and much controversy about hypothesized racial differences, these discussions have not entered the legal fray in the same way as the "gay gene" debate, nor could one imagine them occupying the place that the mutability debate has in queer theory and legal reform. The central question in the legal version of the immutability debate is not simply about whether sexual preference is genetically coded and hence determined prior to the emergence of desire. Rather, the debate revolves around whether it best serves homosexuals to represent themselves as unable to be other than what they are, and hence as discriminated against if they are subjected to unequal treatment, or conversely, whether it is strategically wiser to concede not only the mutability but even the temporal contingency and ambiguity of sexual preferences and practices and to root antidiscrimination claims in a program of sexual freedoms relevant to all sexualities. It is hard to imagine a parallel to this debate in other domains of legal politics, such as those concerned with race or gender, since it has never become part of popular consideration to imagine that we have a choice in these identities or that the markers of these identities are radically contingent or ambiguous.

Given such differences in the formation and legal inscription of different marked subjects, it is unsurprising that concern with securing certain legal terrains does not simply vary, but often works at cross purposes for differently marked identities. Earlier I offered the example of conflicts over the general value of rights. Privacy functions in a similar way. For many feminists, the legal and political concept of privacy is a highly ambivalent one insofar as, historically, "the private" has functioned to depoliticize many of the constituent activities and injuries of women—reproduction and caring for children, domestic violence, incest, unremunerated household labor, emotional and sexual service to men. Yet for those concerned with sexual freedom, with welfare rights for the poor, and with the rights to bodily integrity historically denied to racially subjugated peoples, privacy appears as an unambiguous good. Indeed, the absence of a universal right to privacy constitutes the ground on which Hardwick's bedroom was invaded in *Bowers v. Hardwick*. This absence was also the legal basis for decades of surprise visits by social workers to enforce the "man in the house rule" for welfare recipients. Like rights themselves, depending upon the function of privacy in the powers that make and position the subject, and depending upon the particular dimension of marked identity that is at issue, privacy will sometimes be regarded as advancing emancipatory aims, sometimes deterring them; in some cases it will be seen to cloak the operation of inequality, while in others it will be seen as assisting in the elaboration of equality doctrine.

Nor is it only categories, problems, and domains of law that vary across different modalities of social subjection. Approaches to law vary as well, depending upon the modality in question, since law is understood to carry and deploy these different powers in disparate ways. Thus racism, understood by most critical race theorists as omnipresent in legal argument yet less frequently explicit in legislation and adjudication, has necessitated the development of a critical practice for excavating the racism in legal textual narrative. Much critical race theory involves close readings of the narrative strategies and devices—including symbol, metaphor, metonymy, and analogy—upon which judicial opinion draws when discussing race or racialized cases. This is an analytical practice, however, that neither feminist jurisprudence, nor critical legal theory concerned with class, nor most queer legal theory has followed: each has been more inclined to expand or rework the formal legal categories that overtly carry the power of gender, class, and homosexuality.[12]

I have chosen critical approaches to the law as a way of highlighting diversity in the production and regulation of different marked subjects because law's formal purpose in liberal constitutional orders is to redress the injuries occasioned by unjust distributions of power, and the purpose of critical theoretical engagements with legal doctrine has been to more closely specify such power. Consequent to this attention to power, the ensemble of critical practices aimed at reforming juridical practices of justice vis-à-vis particular identities highlights something often mentioned but rarely followed for its implications in feminist theory: formations of socially marked subjects occur in radically different modalities, which themselves contain different histories and technologies, touch different surfaces and depths, form different bodies and psyches. This is why it is so difficult for politically progressive legal reformers to work on more than one kind of marked identity at once. This is why it is nearly impossible to theorize a legal subject that is not monolithic, totalized by one identity category, and cast as identical with other subjects in that category. We appear not only in the law but in courts and public policy as (undifferentiated) women, or as economically deprived, or as lesbians, or as racially stigmatized, but never as the complex, compound, internally diverse and divided subjects that we are. While this could be seen as a symptom of the law's deficiency, a sign of its ontological clumsiness and epistemological primitivism, more significant for purposes of this essay is what it suggests about the difficulty of analytically grasping the powers constitutive of subjection, a difficulty symptomatized by the law's inability either to express our complexity or to redress the injuries carried by this complexity.

In other words, the problem of representing and redressing the construction, the positioning, and the injuries of complex subjects is not just the law's problem with power, but ours. It is a problem that can only be compounded by programs of study that feature one dimension of power— gender, sexuality, race, or class—as primary and structuring. And there is simply no escaping that this is what women's studies does, no matter how strenuously it seeks to compensate for it. Indeed, the notoriously fraught relationship of women's studies to race and racism can be understood as *configured* by this dynamic of compensation for a structural effect that can never be made to recede, even as it is frantically countered and covered over. Insofar as the superordination of white women within women's studies is secured by the primacy and purity of the category gender, guilt emerges as the persistent social relation of women's studies to race, a guilt that cannot be undone by any amount of courses, readings, and new hires focused on women of color. Indeed, consider again the curriculum I describe earlier in this essay in which "women of color in the United States" is the sole group of women our students are *required* to learn about. Consider again that students' experience of this course is intensely emotional—guilty, proud, righteous, anxious, vengeful, marginalized, angry, or abject. And consider, too, that alumnae of the course often relay these feelings, highly mediated, into other women's studies courses as criticisms of the syllabi, the student constituency, or the pedagogy in terms of a failure to center women of color, race, or racism. Faculty, curriculum, and students in women's studies programs are in a relentless, compensatory cycle of guilt and blame about race, a cycle structured by women's studies' original, nominalist, and conceptual subordination of race (and all other forms of social stratification) to gender.

TO REITERATE, the paradoxical moment in the problem I have been discussing comes with the recognition that despite the diverse and often even unrelated formations of the subject according to race, class, nation, gender, and so forth, subject construction itself does not occur in discrete units as race, class, nation, and so forth. So the model of power developed to apprehend the making of a particular subject/subjection will never accurately describe or trace the lines of a living subject. Nor can this paradox be resolved through greater levels of specificity in the models themselves, for example, mapping the precise formation of the contemporary "middle-class Tejana lesbian." This subject, too, is a fiction insofar as there are always significant elements of subjectivity and subjection that exceed the accounting offered by such lists. There will always be those who feel misdescribed by such descriptions even as they officially "fit" them. Perhaps even more important, this kind of excessive specificity sacrifices the imaginative reach of theory, inevitably moving toward positivism, and in this way repeats the very eclipse of sociohistorical powers it was intended to challenge: these powers become fixed as categories of analysis, rendered as adjectives and nouns, rather than historicized and theorized. Finally, this kind of specificity in identity description and analysis tacitly reiterates an understanding of power as only domination; the powers named in these supposedly complex appellations or "subject positions" always refer to vectors of social stratification that figure social power in terms of hierarchy. That is, "white middle class" is presumed to convey two lines of privilege while "third world woman" is presumed to convey two lines of subjugation. Power is not seen as producing the subject, but only as privileging or oppressing it.

To conclude this excursus into the question of subject production, as feminism has for many become irreversibly connected to the project of multicultural, postcolonial, and queer analysis, terms such as *multiplicity, intersections, crossroads, borderlands, hybridity,* and *fracturing* have emerged to acknowledge—without fully explaining or theorizing—the complex workings of power that converge at the site of identity. The currency of these terms suggests the limitations of existing theories of both power and history for articulating the making of subjects, and especially gendered subjects. For this work of articulation, I would argue that we need a combination of, on the one hand, analyses of subject-producing power accounted through careful histories, psychoanalysis, political economy, and cultural, political, and legal discourse analysis, and, on the other, genealogies of particular modalities of subjection that presume neither coherence in the formations of particular kinds of subjects nor equivalence between different formations. In other words, what is needed is the practice of a historiography quite different from that expressed by notions of cause and effect, accumulation, origin, or various intersecting lines of development, a historiography that emphasizes instead contingent developments, formations that may be at odds with or convergent with each other, and trajectories of power that vary in weight for different kinds of subjects. The work I am describing involves serious and difficult research, arduous thought, and complex theoretical formulations—it will not be conducive to easy polemics or slogans in battle. And it will add up to neither a unified and coherent notion of gender nor a firm foundation for women's studies. But it may allow us to take those powerful founding and sustaining impulses of women's studies—to challenge the seamless histories, theories, literatures, and sciences featuring and reproducing a Humanism starring only Man—and harness them for another generation or two of productive, insurrectionary work. However much it is shaped by feminism, this work will no longer have gender at its core and is in that sense no longer women's studies. To the extent that women's studies programs can allow themselves to be transformed—in name, content, and scope—by these and allied projects, they will be renewed as sites of critical inquiry and political energy. To the extent that they refuse this task and adhere to a founding and exclusive preoccupation with women and feminism, they will further entrench themselves as conservative barriers to the critical theory and research called for by the very scholarship they incited and pedagogical practices they mobilized over the past two decades.

SOME FINAL THOUGHTS AND REJOINDERS. Among those committed to women's studies who are cognizant of the problems and incoherence of the field, the usual arguments on behalf of sustaining and building women's studies programs are mounted in expressly political language. Women's studies, it is said, remains the primary site for feminist consciousness-raising among students and for feminist agitation in university life as a whole. Moreover, given the historical struggle to institutionalize women's studies programs through the establishment of departments or the procurement of full-time faculty positions, the idea of radically transforming their direction such that they are no longer identified primarily with women or even gender seems as if it could only signal that the opposition was right all along. In other words, most of us assume that women's studies programs continue to have irrefutable political value, that there are intractable political constraints against accepting even friendly challenges to women's studies programs, and that this value and these constraints must override whatever is troubling about women's studies' intellectual aporias.

I share this assumption to a degree, but the problem with allowing it to serve as the justification for maintaining women's studies programs as they are is that it renders dispensable a deep and serious intellectual basis for women's studies, just as it disregards the erosion of that basis as something less than a challenge to women's studies' raison d'être. Indeed, by privileging the political over the intellectual and the institutionally strategic over the intellectually sound, and by effectively conceding that these operate on separate planes, these arguments affirm the status of women's studies as something distinct from the rest of the university's intellectual mission for research and teaching. In effect, by admitting its thoroughly politicized rationale, these defenses replicate the low value that hostile outsiders often accuse women's studies of attaching to the caliber of arguments and to intellectual life as a whole; suspicions about the non- or anti-intellectual dimensions of women's studies are thus confirmed. Equally problematic, these arguments affirm this non-intellectual mission for something wholly and uniquely identified with women, and what could be more detrimental to feminist aims? How, indeed, could such an understanding of women's studies constitute it as a credible basis from which to influence university curricula and life?

I am not arguing that the struggle to establish women's studies programs was misbegotten, nor am I suggesting that women's studies is entirely void of rich intellectual content. Rather, I am making a specific historical argument. There is an unimpeachable importance to the last two decades of developing scholarship, of feminist teaching across the university, and of feminist influences on administrations, all of which were incited by struggles centered on developing women's studies programs. Without doubt we are everywhere now, and without doubt, this "we" was literally brought into being by the fight to establish and legitimate women's studies. But the strategies and ambitions that produced this effect at one historical moment are not necessarily those that will sustain or enhance it at another. Feminist scholars must ask whether the very institutional strategies that once fomented rich and exciting intellectual endeavor now work against it, or work against the currents that might be its most fruitful future.

There is another question to be raised here. If the mission of women's studies is understood as primarily political and as willingly sacrificing intellectual coherence and aims to its political project, who will teach in such programs and what kind of teaching will it be? Without discounting the varied degrees and types of political aims that many of us bring to our academic work, it is one thing to craft and mobilize these aims in the course of one's teaching and research and quite another to function within an intensely politicized space in which intellectual life and standards are often regarded as secondary concerns. Many contemporary feminist scholars currently have limited traffic with women's studies programs—they may cross-list a course or two, or allow their names to be affiliated with the program, but remain peripheral to the curriculum and governance of the program. Conversely, many women's studies programs are staffed by a disproportional number of faculty with an attenuated relationship to academic research and writing but whose political devotion to feminism or emotional devotion to the students is often quite intense. More and more, feminist scholarship is spun from sites other than women's studies programs. And more and more, women's studies faculty are not using this scholarship; sometimes they are explicitly hostile to it.

Rather than assigning blame for this complex and painful dynamic, let us note instead some of its effects. First, the anti-intellectualism discussed above is increasingly codified as the spirit of women's studies work, while the gap widens between the ethos and curriculum of women's studies and the rest of the humanities, arts, and social sciences. Second, while women's studies once served to legitimate and support, in a positive way, feminist scholarship across the academy, it would now seem to legitimate it negatively by allowing feminist scholars in other disciplines to tacitly define themselves and their work *against* women's studies. Women's studies has come to be perversely useful to some academic feminists as "the other" against which respectable feminist scholarship is defined.

Is it possible to radically reconfigure women's studies programs without sacrificing the feminism they promulgate among students and help to keep alive at universities? We might ask this question another way, by asking whether teaching feminist courses, including basic courses such as "Introduction to Feminisms," "Introduction to Feminist Theories," and "Histories and Varieties of Women's Movements," must be done in the context of a degree-granting program or whether the discussions we had long ago about "mainstreaming" (moving these courses into the general curriculum of other disciplinary and especially interdisciplinary programmatic sites) might be revived. To retain such course work without containing it within women's studies might allow us to reconfigure women's studies programs without such a move appearing as a neoconservative return to "traditional curriculums." And it might allow us, too, to insist that students of feminism and feminist theory learn the appropriate antecedents and cognates to these topics, for example, the emergence of the struggle for women's emancipation in the context of democratic and socialist revolutions in the West, or the relevance of Rousseau, Marx, Freud, and more recent philosophical and literary thinkers to feminist thought and practice. In this regard, consider how difficult it is to teach contemporary feminist theory to students who share none of the intellectual referents of the feminist theorists they are reading. What a difference it would make to develop those background knowledges as part of students' work in philosophy, cultural studies, literature, anthropology, or critical theory so that they would actually be armed to engage and contest the arguments they encounter in feminist theory and in postcolonial, queer, and critical race theories as well.

Still, am I, in the end, suggesting that we never should have developed and institutionalized women's studies programs? Absolutely not. Without doubt, women's studies constituted one of the most vibrant and exciting contributions to the American academy in the 1970s and 1980s. Moreover, I believe there are large and complex lessons to be developed—about institutionalizing identitarian political struggles, about conflating the political with the academic, and about late modern forms of disciplinarity—from the process of watching women's studies falter in the 1990s. The story of women's studies suggests that our current and future contests over meaning and knowledge, and for freedom and equality, should probably avoid consolidating victories in the form of new degree-granting programs in the university. But it does not tell us what to do instead. Perhaps the present moment is one for considering where we have been so that we might, in a Nietzschean vein, affirm our errors. Perhaps it is a moment for thinking.

NOTES

For their critical engagement with a draft of this essay, I am indebted to Judith Butler, Gail Hershatter, Valerie Hartouni, and Joan Wallach Scott. None of them should be held responsible for, nor associated with, the criticisms and positions it tenders.

1. When this article was written, Wendy Brown was teaching at the University of California, Santa Cruz.

2. While it is true that debates about "fundamentals" pervade many disciplines, I think that in most it is possible to both acknowledge the fictional character of the field *and* to venture arguments about what constitutes a good undergraduate education in it. For example, I would argue that any undergraduate obtaining a bachelor of arts in politics or political science in this country should have a basic grasp of (1) international relations in the era of nation-states and globalization, (2) U.S. political institutions, (3) one or two other political systems, (4) political economy, (5) social movements as sources of modern political upheaval and change, and (6) the history of political theory. This is a contestable list, and it also does not specify how this basic grasp is to be procured. However, what concerns me here is the disconcerting fact of my inability, and my colleagues' inability, to even conjure a similar list for women's studies about which to begin arguing.

3. Two recent anecdotes from feminist colleagues at other universities sharpen this point. (1) A feminist scholar at a public university was asked to remove her course, "Introduction to Sexualities," from the women's studies curriculum on the grounds that its subject matter was sex, not gender. (2) The director of women's studies at a research university was seeking to convert her steadily declining

program into one on gender and sexuality, for which there was abundant student demand and faculty interest. But in the process, she met with intense resistance from colleagues who feared a loss of focus on women, and especially women of color, in the revamped program.

4. The formulations offered by Kimberle Crenshaw, Aida Hurtado, and Patricia Hill Collins are extremely useful in thinking about the difficult place of entry for black women into legal discourse (Crenshaw), the difficulty of making feminist political coalitions among women of color and white women (Hurtado), and the distinctiveness of black women's thought and political practice (Collins). Nonetheless, these projects should not be confused with the project of offering an account of subject formation.

5. Thus, to consider the making of gender through sexuality without reference to the more general regime of sexuality Foucault depicts in *The History of Sexuality* (MacKinnon's mistake [*Feminism Unmodified*]) is just as myopic as formulating the terms of that regime with little or no reference to gender (Foucault's mistake).

6. See "Gender Regulations" in *Undoing Gender*.

7. "The individual is an effect of power, and at the same time . . . it is the element of its articulation. The individual which power has constituted is at the same time its vehicle" (Foucault, "Two Lectures" 98).

8. It should be underscored that not all who travel under the sign of "Critical Race Theory" subscribe to the view of rights articulated by Patricia Williams in *The Alchemy of Race and Rights* and by Robert Williams in an earlier article, "Taking Rights Aggressively."

9. For a more complete development of this point, see Brown, "Rights and Losses" (in *States of Injury*) and "Suffering Rights as Paradoxes."

10. Some might argue that miscegenation laws functioned in this way. However, miscegenation laws did not criminalize the racially marked subject as such but rather regulated the sexuality of such subjects.

11. It should be noted that the monological axes of analysis I am deploying here both underscore and fail the point made above, that modes of subject production operate through different trajectories and modalities of subjection, and must be subjected to distinctive modes of analysis, yet cannot be extricated from one another in living subjects. Thus, to say as I did here, that "there is no equivalent to the place of reproductive rights for women's equality in defining the parameters of racial freedom, or ending the stigma for minority sexual orientation," elides the fact that racism and heterosexism operate in part through a distinct lack of reproductive freedom for peoples of color and homosexuals. Yet to presume that this lack functions in the same way *as* racism and heterosexism as it does *as* sexism is precisely to colonize racism and heterosexism with a feminist analysis, a colonization feminists have been engaging in for too long. This is the move that Catharine

MacKinnon makes with regard to thinking about the place of women of color and racism in pornography, presumably to establish that her feminist analysis is also an analysis of race and racism (*Only Words*). But it strikes me as an argument that is in bad faith as well as analytically impoverished.

12. Janet Halley and Kendall Thomas, for example, in their respective readings of *Bowers v. Hardwick,* are notable exceptions in the field of queer jurisprudence.

FEMINISM, INSTITUTIONALISM, AND THE IDIOM OF FAILURE

Robyn Wiegman

Essays that come into being in the utopian idiom of contemporary cultural critique often take a great risk when they arrive at the moment of producing proper evidence. Instead of approximating the language of disciplined knowing, they tend to turn to coincidence and conjecture; instead of taking refuge in method and procedure, they make their cases according to ideals of political success and failure. Critical activity of this kind is born in disjuncture, if not disidentification: the present time of writing is never the future the critic strains to think. What, then, serves to guarantee knowledge as political progress? The *nothing* that persists as the haunting answer to this question makes legible the anxiety at the heart of academic feminism's chief rhetorical strategy, the critical claim, which generates value by promising to carry thought beyond the failure of the present. In its function to transport feminism into the future, the critical claim generates for academic work a positive political use value, and in this the anxiety over knowing and doing—over politics and academic production—is seemingly eased.

Throughout the 1990s, the opposition recorded here has settled most contentiously in debates about the category of *women* and its saliency as a guarantee for knowledge and political movement. For such feminist scholars as Judith Butler, Joan Scott, and Denise Riley, it is the refusal of *women* as a foundational referent that gives to feminism the internal critique necessary to rethink its own historical emergence within modern forms of liberal governmentality. Such rethinking functions to revise accepted notions of power, politics, and subjective agency, thereby challenging the foundational assumptions of certain activist agendas common to feminism's earlier practices. It is this challenge that numerous scholars—Susan Gubar, Susan Bordo, and Martha Nussbaum, for instance—find unproductive if not damaging for feminism, as theoretical considerations are seen to overwhelm the imperative for a public political voice and feminism's ability to define and inhabit social change is jettisoned in favor of academic insularity. These debates have constituted much of the claim-making in academic feminism in the 1990s, and there is no good reason to think that a resolution is necessary; surely the end of such claim-making is not in sight.

For women's studies, that institutional domain that first named the imperative toward interdisciplinary feminist analysis, the debate over the category of *women* has been particularly momentous, in part because of the field's distinct function in establishing woman as a legitimate object of study and in fighting for the legibility of "her" epistemological importance in knowledge production more widely. To the extent that *academic feminism* as a term describes this historical project of challenging the university by institutionalizing new knowledge formations, it indicates something quite profound about the indivisibility of politics and academic institutional intervention. And yet, to conjoin academic to feminism today is almost always a distinct insult, an accusation that draws its blood precisely because politics and academics have come to be so firmly opposed. It is this opposition between the political as a set of social movement ideals and the institutional as a project of academic transformation that underlies to a great extent the mood swing in academic feminism in the 1990s, where feminist articulations of the political agenda that impelled it into the academy have been held in check by a diagnostic analysis that seeks to understand the tenor of bad feeling (and hurt feelings) of feminism's current institutional success.

I use the language of mood and feeling to indicate the depth of the attachment that feminism inculcates in the subjects who organize themselves under its sign. From such attachment a great deal has been won, and yet feminism's inability to predict, much less inhabit, its radical future has meant that disappointment, and sometimes intense feelings of betrayal, have been both the persistent accompaniment to attachment and its persistent detractor. It is in this context that the hegemony of the critical claim arises, for it is the strategic function of the claim to give to cultural critique a world-making use value, and in this, the tension between critical analysis and social protest is, if not settled, at least momentarily relieved. Feminism, in particular, has struggled over the dynamic of knowing and doing, over the difference that each constitutes to the other, weighing one over the other, at times defending real world politics as a culmination of both. Much of the mood swing in the 1990s has been self-consciously cast as a consequence of academic feminism's lost relation to activist practices, with theoretical know-how having very little understanding of what the *how* could possibly be. The pressure on certain theorists—think here of Judith Butler—to define in practical terms what her work compels feminists *to do* brings the political imperative embedded in the rhetoric of the claim into definitive view. Butler's refusal to render her utopianism in a language that manages the anxiety her work now symptomatically evokes has led to a number of bitter attacks, including those that hold her responsible for bringing feminist politics to a crashing halt. I will take up some of the issues surrounding Butler's work shortly, but for now I want to register how unsure, even insecure, academic feminism has become about the meaning, practices, and goals of its own project of institutional intervention.[1] Indeed, *academic feminism* as a term registers today a series of internal contradictions, most of which collate around the perceptible disparity between feminism's academic success and its loss of "real" world revolutionary political power.

This essay works within the tensions described above between the academic and the "real," knowing and doing, and institutionalization and politics in order to interrupt the temporality of the critical claim by inhabiting the specter of failure that haunts contemporary academic feminism. My conversation will be less thesis-driven than meditative, and it will begin not in the present argument but in a slightly prior moment of academic feminist contention, when a great deal of debate was centered on understanding what domestication and sentimentality meant to women's political efforts to make a claim on public institutions in the unfolding political economy of nineteenth-century industrial life. I return briefly, then, to Ann Douglas's now classic argument in *The Feminization of American Culture*, where the specter of political failure drove her central claim about women's feminization in the marginalizing realm of a commodified and hence paradoxically privatized public sphere. That *feminization* could stand as the descriptive term for the social transformations that Douglas tracked and that she could at times be so harsh toward the women she studied provides an unpredictable, even skewed angle from which to consider current discussions about academic feminism by a very unlikely pair, Martha Nussbaum and Wendy Brown, who collectively if contradictorily read failure as the primary characteristic of academic feminism's present tense.

For Nussbaum in "The Professor of Parody," academic feminism as embodied in the work of Judith Butler is seen as interrupting feminism's historical continuity by luxuriating in theoretical pleasure and thereby abandoning practical politics. Calling for a return to "old-style" feminism that aims toward the transformation of "laws and institutions," Nussbaum depicts Butler's ambivalence toward institutional intervention as a collaboration with "evil" and in doing so rejects the academy as an institution to be grappled with in the politics of the "real" (38, 37, 45, 37). Poststructuralist theory, in her terms, has domesticated the feminist enterprise, leading to narcissistic performances that parody real feminist struggle. In contrast, Brown marshals some of the keenest insights of poststructuralism to consider the very political project—the academy—that Nussbaum's rendering of the real so symptomatically excludes. By defining "The Impossibility of Women's Studies" as a consequence of its anti-intellectual political affect, Brown critiques the privileging of the political over the academic that has accompanied the "institutionalization of identitarian political struggles" and turns to law as a mirror (not, as in Nussbaum, as an escape) for understanding the failure that haunts women's studies: an account of complex subject formation. From these two essays, academic feminism emerges as a deeply conflicted arena; it is at once too theoretical and not theoretical enough, too political and not political enough. By analyzing each essay's narrative of present failure, I explore one of the most paradoxical features of feminist academic discourse in the 1990s: its struggle with "academic feminism" itself.

NOW AND THEN

Feminism is by definition as well as by historical fact a reactive force; it is most generally an argument *against* political and social systems, ideological practices, and cultural discourses that subordinate women and the feminine, on one hand, and that arrange human potential, roles, and qualities through binary apparatuses, on the other. In this, its project remains temporally constrained: coming after, forging a response, being responsive to whole worlds and histories of freedom's oppressive failure. For feminism in the academy in general and for women's studies in particular, this problem of origins has always strained against the imperative to originate—to construct our own curriculum, define its core knowledge, and inaugurate a field that can do more than correct the partialities of traditional knowledge formations. Feminist scholars have thus sought feminist antecedents and repeatedly managed the problem of origins and originating intentions by defining the scope and subjectivity of contemporary academic feminism through a progressive historical narrative that proceeds from U.S. social movements. Thus defining its drive toward institutionalization as a consequence of resistant politics, women's studies has been able to found itself on a claim of innovative insurgency, and it has ridden this wave of self-defined insurgency until institutional development and incorporation have become visible enough to compel a critical reassessment of what it means to be self-located on "the edge."

I have no wish to argue here with the narrative of women's studies' becoming as a consequence of social movement.[2] But I am interested in how feminist scholars understand the *process* we operate in the middle of: crafting a knowledge formation for feminism from an originating identification with social movements whose profound political force had a great deal to do with their ethos of anti-institutionalism—that is, their critique, in method and political content, of state practices and functions (segregation, imperialist war, domestic wage discrimination, anti-immigrationism). This contradiction—between state critique and intervention in the institutions of the state—was not for feminism a founding contradiction. Rather, it has emerged as one of the central features of feminism's *academic* legibility, and it speaks to what is for academic feminism a problem: having institutional power.

In my role as the director of a women's studies program that has earned in the 1990s the "right," as our own documents have called it, to hold full-time faculty appointments and therefore to judge the credentials of feminist scholars, the problem of institutional power has been a haunting one. The responsibility of "building the program"—which means increasing enrollments, fighting for campus space, enhancing library holdings, hiring and retaining faculty, extending the intellectual domain of curricular projects (into areas such as biological and natural sciences long untouched by women's studies)—is overwhelming in its time consumption and profoundly constitutive of a subjective focus that threatens to become overdetermined by the goals of institutionalization as ends in themselves. It was in this subjective space, in this context of affect and exhaustion, that I returned, for the first time since graduate school, to Ann Douglas's *The Feminization of American Culture* and its deep lament that educated middle-class white women in New England would find themselves by the end of the nineteenth century further unmoored from the established domains of political life, which is to say more entrenched in the realm of a sentimental privacy that tried to make powerlessness into "influence" and disenfranchisement into the occasion, if not the condition, for the production of social and moral good.

From one perspective, Douglas's despair over the sentimentalizing process, which she saw as a consequence of consumption and hence as a failure of political clarity and nerve in the face of the industrial development of consumer capitalism, was a predictable feminist response to a certain kind of social marginalization. But the language of her analysis was overlain with judgment and blame toward those women (and the ministers who came to need them) who directed their energies into sentimentalism's primary domain: mass market literary culture. Let me quote at length:

> Sentimentalism provides a way to protest a power to which one has already in part capitulated. It is a form of dragging one's heels. It always borders on dishonesty. . . . Many nineteenth-century Americans in the Northeast acted every day as if they believed that economic expansion, urbanization, and industrialization represented the greatest good. It is to their credit that they indirectly acknowledged that the pursuit of these "masculine" goals meant damaging, perhaps losing, another good. . . . Yet the fact remains that their regret was calculated not to interfere with their actions. We remember that Little Eva's beautiful death, which Stowe presents as part of a protest against slavery, in no way hinders the working of that system. The minister and the lady were appointed by their society as the champions of sensibility. They were in the position of contestants in a fixed fight: they had agreed to put on a convincing show and to lose. The fakery involved was finally crippling for all concerned. (11)

Douglas was quite aware of her own harsh assessment. Shortly before the above passage, she defends her position as a necessary one: "It does no good to shirk the fact that nineteenth-century American society tried to damage women like Harriet Beecher Stowe—and succeeded. . . . To view the victims of oppression simply as martyrs and heroes . . . is only to perpetuate the sentimental heresy I am attempting to study here" (11).

Subsequent studies of sentimental culture, such as Jane Tompkins's *Sensational Designs* (1985), have turned against Douglas's interpretation to seek the sentimental collaboration. Where Douglas ascribed agency to the women she studied who failed to resist in ways that spoke to structure and not sentiment, Tompkins and others countered with a vision of agency found in the very strategy of "influence." From their perspective, women resisted their social marginalization by elevating the realm that consigned them to secondary status; hence sentimental culture became an important intellectual site for feminist analysis by providing a context for thinking about how power operates outside of and in opposition to its sanctioned channels. This is not to say that scholars after Douglas found nothing amiss in the sentimental culture they explored, for certainly "influence" rarely survived the critique of its contradictory and often passive abolitionism.[3] But their interest in sentimental culture was a powerful attempt to position it as an antecedent for contemporary feminism, not as in Douglas to write it as the inaugural cooptation, the feminization that would lead to feminism's seemingly transhistorical lack of effectivity. As Douglas wrote about her project, "I expected to find my fathers and mothers; instead I discovered my fathers and my sisters. The best of the men had access to solutions. . . . The problems of the women correspond to mine with a frightening accuracy that seems to set us outside the process of history" (11). In the scenario of the family drama that Douglas uses to characterize her study, "sisters" emerge in the rightful place of the mother, and anger becomes the palpable register for history's failure to unfold for women a progressive narrative. In the eight years that came to separate *Feminization* from *Sensational Designs,* feminist scholars would find the mother in sentimental culture, and they would indeed love and admire her. But for Douglas, sentimentality remained too contemporary; it was repetition and sameness, not historical-political difference. This is why her book reads today as a betrayal: she could not admire the women she studied, nor could she explain them without blaming them; she most certainly did not want to be one of them.[4] And yet, in the context of her own literary commitments (her love, as she says at the outset, of Little Eva's decorousness), she could not find in historical distance an adequate guarantee that she had fully escaped being one of them.

The complex identification and disidentification that motivated Douglas's feminism had a great deal to do with her refusal to accede to the category of woman as a representative figure for either women or feminists. What she seems to have found most dismaying about nineteenth-century white middle-class women was their embrace of the feminine as the content of woman's categorical designation and hence their acceptance of the limited social orbit to which women were consigned. Like Mary Wollstonecraft and other feminists in the Anglo-American tradition, Douglas would risk "siding with the enemy" (11), as she put it, in order to critique the feminine as the site and source of feminism's transformative historical possibilities.[5] I am tempted to say that she wanted for herself as for the women she studied, all sisters, "real" institutional power, even as that description risks the binary constitution of gendered domains that Douglas found lamentable for nineteenth-century white middle-class women. Cast outside official domains of national political life, white middle-class women, Douglas asserts, substituted the pleasures of consumer culture for the harder work of structural transformation. While they "advocate[d] important reforms," they "pursued partially feminist goals by largely anti-feminist means; genuine success was hardly possible" (51). *The Feminization of American Culture* thus stands as a meditation on political failure, on the way that class privilege had consumed radical intentions and given marginality a feminized and in Douglas's terms faulty cache. It is to Douglas's own credit, to use a bit of her language, that she found herself implicated in their pleasures, not just an inheritor but a critical agent trying to figure out what women in her own day seemed unable to do and know.

THEN

Douglas's critical strategy is an interesting counter to second-wave historiography, which has tended to rest its self-understanding, indeed its very sensibility of the political, on an ideal of subversion (if not outright dissent) that offers reconnection and retrieval as the means for overcoming the contemporary feminist subject's monumentalized alienation. History for Douglas carried the weight of "not" and "never yet"; it held forth the ideology of change but seemed unable to engineer it. The continuity history yielded thus reconfirmed the omnipresence of feminization's social entrapments, which meant that for Douglas a sentimentalized attachment to the category of woman worked against feminism at every turn. It is this rendition of feminism as undone in its nascency that finally renders *The Feminization of American Culture* such an eccentric text—and even more so when read in the context of recent critiques that cite the present as the tense in which feminism has gone wrong.[6] Martha Nussbaum's "The Professor of Parody" is exemplary in this regard, offering a vision of "old-style" feminism to counter the "naively empty politics" of those who follow Judith Butler and her theoretical *detachment* from the category of woman. While Nussbaum is not alone in her postulation that poststructuralism has ruined feminism's good health, it is certainly the case that her *New Republic* essay gave to media culture a new interpretive frame for *Time*'s 1997 front-page query "Is feminism dead?" While in the 1980s feminists might have read *Time*'s query as evidence of the recuperative project we now call "backlash," today it calls forth an answer that locates the undoing of feminism from within.

Written as a manifesto for a return to "old-style feminist politics," "The Professor of Parody" defines Butler's work as lacking "a fierce sense of the texture of social oppression and the harm that it does" (42). This is Nussbaum's final statement:

> Hungry women are not fed by [Butler's theory], battered women are not sheltered by it, raped women do not find justice in it, gays and lesbians do not achieve legal protections through it. . . . The big hope, the hope for a world of real justice, where laws and institutions protect the equality and the dignity of all citizens, has been banished. . . . Judith Butler's hip quietism is a comprehensible response to the difficulty of realizing justice in America. But it is a bad response. It collaborates with evil. Feminism demands more and women deserve better. (45)

In trying to resuscitate, in her terms, a feminism dedicated to "working for others who are suffering" (44), Nussbaum repeatedly turns to the real as the register of the truth that Butler abandons: "the material conditions of real women," "real bodies," "real struggles," the "real issue of legal and institutional change" (37). To be trained on the real is feminism's historical inheritance and academic feminism's critical, at times distinctly moral, imperative. "For a long time now," the essay opens, "academic feminism in America has been closely allied to the practical struggle to achieve justice and equality for women" (37). In finding in the past a historical means for achieving justice in the future, Nussbaum deploys the critical claim in its most familiar temporal construction, overriding the differential of the present in order to make continuous the past and the future. In this imposition of historical continuity as the already known truth of political struggle, Nussbaum offers poststructuralism in general and Butler in particular as spectacular deflections of what might otherwise be understood as contemporary feminism's own complex entanglement with failure. That this is a convenient strategy for repressing the possibility that feminism may not already know how to counter the political problems that called it into being is surely obvious. But such obviousness has not weakened the enthusiasm for situating poststructuralism as the locus of failure, the means for abandoning both politics and the real. In this increasingly celebrated strategy, certain academic feminists renegotiate their relation to both the university and knowledge production—a renegotiation that gives to critical thought a use value by claiming its justice in the real.

In "The Professor of Parody," Nussbaum achieves her own self-presentation as an undisputed agent of justice by casting the "institutional" as the antithesis to Butler's collaboration with "evil" while paradoxically writing the academy as itself other to the real: "Feminist theory has been understood by theorists as not just fancy words on paper; theory is connected to proposals for social change. . . . Indeed, some theorists have left the academy altogether, feeling more comfortable in the world of practical politics, where they can address . . . urgent problems directly" (37). Here, the academy functions to disestablish feminism's political relation to the real by exchanging a focus on legal routes of redress for theoretical and highly linguistic accounts of the social constitution of subjects. In the context of this newly wayward and overtly "symbolic" feminism, "young feminists" have been led to believe "that the way to do feminist politics is to use words in a subversive way, in academic publications of lofty obscurity and disdainful abstractness. . . . They can do politics in [the] safety of their campuses . . . making subversive gestures at power through speech" (38, 45).[7] What Douglas found in the feminization of American culture—a political quietism that abandoned political assaults against institutions in favor of the pleasures of influence in literary culture—Nussbaum seems to find in academic feminism, an emphasis on the manipulation of words and the cultivation of a kind of domesticated, because privatized self: "The great tragedy in the new feminist theory in America," Nussbaum writes, "is the loss of a sense of public commitment" (44).

While feminization as a process of political domestication circulates in both Nussbaum and Douglas, the category of "theory" marks their critical difference from one another. For in seeking an arena of possibility that did not entail women's enmeshment in sentiment, in feeling as the primary motive and defining feature of their social subjectivity, Douglas rejected the imposition of a vocabulary of pain and its triumph, preferring in her own terms "theorizing" as that which the "Victorian lady" avoided and that her twentieth-century descendents, even the "overtly politicized" ones, were likely to avoid as well (199). Douglas's "theory," of course, operated without the overdeterminations of poststructuralism's inauguration of a humanities subfield, *critical theory*, which is today both the source and figure for defining feminism's abandonment of the real. With theory as the interloper in a contemporary context that tends to wager the symbolic against the real and writes abstraction as antithetical to practical politics, "The Professor of Parody" engages the sentimental formulation by transforming suffering into "real" knowledge and making pain the defining feature of feminism's relation to and understanding of the construction of female subjects. Intended as a counter to Butler's narcissistic entrapments in the self, Nussbaum's language for social change—working "for others who are suffering" and "for the public good"—posits feminism in a modality of identification that arises at the scene of women's disempowerment and loss. Coupling such identification with a definition of the public good as "building laws and institutions" (44), Nussbaum gives to "old feminism" an unquestioned relationship of justice to women.

In defining for old feminism this relation of justice, Nussbaum produces the critical claim that in turn operates as a political guarantee for feminism's futurity. Where Douglas resisted this guarantee, in part by defining both past and present as the failed ground of feminism's coherent relation to the future, Nussbaum reorganizes, through rhetorical excision, the political imaginary of the present in order to make past and future coincident. In the process, she resolves through declaration and repression the crises of institutionalism that have arisen within feminism since its second-wave inception. I would define these crises as the functional institutionalization of a normative woman as the referent for women within feminism; and the institutionalization of feminism as a structural and discursive form of power in the academy. Nussbaum negotiates the first by defining old feminism's agenda of the real as the way "feminist theory still looks . . . in many parts of the world" (37). Her specific example is India, where

> academic feminists have thrown themselves into practical struggles, and feminist theorizing is closely tethered to practical commitments such as female literacy, the reform of unequal land laws, changes in rape law (*which, in India today, has most of the flaws that the first generation*

of American feminists targeted), the effort to get social recognition for problems of sexual harassment and domestic violence. These feminists know that they live in the middle of a fiercely unjust reality; they cannot live with themselves without addressing it more or less daily, in their theoretical writing and in their activities outside the seminar room. (38; emphasis mine)

By defining the project of Indian feminism as akin to the work of "the first generation of American feminists," Nussbaum produces simultaneously the third world woman of color as a referent for the real *and* the trajectory of feminism in the United States and its state-based tactics of intervention as feminism's accepted global form. The shift from *woman's* normative white, middle-class, heterosexual, and first world referent to that of the Indian feminist, in short, enables a kind of critical repression of the political dynamics of naming and annexation that accompany U.S. feminism's enunciation.[8] In this move, Nussbaum tags Butler with the charge of U.S. provincialism and produces a global feminist future attendant to "the real situation of real women" (38), one in which "old feminism" in the United States evinces no complicity with power because its referential object—suffering women—exists as the public counter to academic feminism's privatized narcissism and abandonment of the real.

Nussbaum produces "old feminism" as the authentic and authenticating project of social transformation, one whose real world legibility relies on a tacit privatization of the university as a public political institution in its own right. Through her retrieval of a sentimental discourse as the affective foundation for global feminist agency, Nussbaum reclaims the very notion of the liberal humanist subject that Butler and other poststructuralist feminists have been trying to think without. She thus dismisses as narcissistic the profound anti-institutionalism that accompanies certain theoretical attempts to consider the subject as an effect and not an origin of institutional practices and discourses. In thus expelling anti-institutionalism as a political question about subject formation, "The Professor of Parody" can dismiss any imperative to register the feminist critical genealogy that has critiqued Western feminism's alliance with the state and modernity, especially as that alliance has reiterated a secular humanism that fashions U.S. feminism *as* the privileged discourse of global feminism.[9] Nussbaum offers us instead MacKinnon and Dworkin as central figures in a tacitly national history of late-twentieth-century feminism, thereby bypassing those discourses that challenge the United States as the subjective and political content of both feminist knowledge *and activism*.[10] In doing so, Nussbaum is able to assert as an unquestioned truth legal institutional intervention, but the force of her critical claim as the production of continuity between past and future rests on the eradication of both the critical and political contexts of past and present. That is, she banishes the late-twentieth-century feminist tradition of critiquing the state as the end logic of political reform (giving to poststructuralism alone the critical honor of this offense) and jettisons consideration of the institution within which she finds herself: the academy.

The second crisis of institutionalism is found here, in the transformation that the academic institutionalization of feminism has created in both the structural production of knowledge and in intradisciplinary and transdisciplinary modes of analysis—which is to say, the transformation that has enabled feminism in the academy to both claim and inhabit institutional power. While Butler has demonstrated an increasing ambivalence about feminism's relation to institutionalized power, especially old feminism's dedication to institutional apparatuses as the counter to various kinds of social exclusion, it is certainly the case that her own critical stature is part of, if not evidence for, feminism as an academic institutional power. Herein lies the reason that Nussbaum opens her essay by citing those academic feminists who have left the academy to pursue directly the real: real feminists do not openly inhabit institutional power in the name of feminism, for *that* name, as I have discussed, has as its real referent "those who are suffering." This is the moral judgment that underlies Nussbaum's critique (or should we call it her criminalization?) of Butler, which functions as an indictment against academic feminism in the 1990s, whose relation to power can no longer (if it ever could) be claimed as a wholly oppositional one.[11] To reclaim the oppositional formulation and write feminism on the side of women without contradiction or complicity, Nussbaum must forfeit the analytical opportunity that her anger at failure makes intellectually palpable: a consideration of how feminism's institutionalization in the academy has given not only depth and texture but a lengthy archive to a difference previously unperceived between *thinking about feminism as a politics* and *thinking about politics through feminism*.[12] Being wed to the former, Nussbaum produces the latter as a kind of betrayal and in doing so sacrifices insight into the processes of institutionalization through which feminism has become a knowledge formation, one whose relation to politics lacks the assurance of an "old-style" political guarantee.

My reading of Nussbaum is not a defense of Judith Butler per se, though readers no doubt sense my considerable lack of sympathy with the strategy of "The Professor of Parody" for guaranteeing feminism's futurity. *That* future of feminism as a monotheistic politic, narratively equipped with its own fallen angel and moralistically dedicated to pain as an agenda for both knowledge and social change, is finally too allergic to the possibility of any future that second-wave feminism has not already imagined. In this regard, Nussbaum's characterization of contemporary feminism is yet another contribution to the growing list of generational laments that invest in accusation and attack to rescue feminism's future from certain academic feminists. That these apocalyptic narratives, as I call them, always find the specter of feminism's political end in the academy is one of the paradoxical features of "old feminism" today: it has come to define itself against the very project of institutional intervention it inaugurated and hence against those women who inherited from it a feminism animated by the questions, contradictions, and complicities of academic feminism's relationship to both politics and knowledge.

NOW

In her postulation of a referential real as the defining feature of feminist politics, Nussbaum tacitly establishes a model for feminist knowledge production that is familiar to anyone currently working in women's studies. It views feminism in the academy as fulfilling its political mission by reproducing social activism, and in this it sets as the standard of political judgment a trajectory of movement (of knowledge, bodies, and practices) into and out of the academy, from the so-called ivory tower to the real. In this system of value, women's studies garners its value by reproducing within the academy the social organization of *women* as a political sign outside of it, which thereby defines the field as a site of belonging in the social identitarian sense. For many feminist scholars, belonging to women and belonging to women's studies are thus completely compatible, if not seemingly identical, as the field's object of study and the subjects who study "her" are (politically speaking) one.

The costs of this configuration of knowledge and politics—and the structure of belonging it has generated—are at the heart of Wendy Brown's incisive and controversial essay "The Impossibility of Women's Studies." Reading the history of feminism's institutionalization in the academy as a necessary error, Brown writes at the end of her essay: "The story of women's studies suggests that our current and future contests over meaning and knowledge, and for freedom and equality, should probably avoid consolidating victories in the form of new degree-granting programs in the university" (36). Where Nussbaum reads the academy as the site for the depoliticization of feminism through a turn to theory, Brown critiques the institutionalization of "identitarian political struggles" as producing a conflation of the political with the academic (36).[13] Brown's call for the end of degree-granting women's studies programs is not, however, a diagnosis that the work of academic feminism is itself at an end. Indeed, she tries to avoid the temporality of the apocalyptic formulation by writing the present as incommensurable with the past, and the future as an open question: "[The faltering of women's studies] does not tell us what to do instead. Perhaps the present moment is one for considering where we have been so that we might, in a Nietzschean vein, affirm our errors. Perhaps it is a moment for thinking" (36). In this hesitant arrival at her essay's final word *thinking*, Brown offers a striking reversal of the temporal promise of the critical claim, engaging feminism's generational battle at its most theoretical pitch by interrupting the transportation of the past's utopianism into the definitional shape of both the present and the future. The importance of this defense against continuity as the precondition for both assessing and challenging the various problematics that animate women's studies as a field cannot be underestimated, as it enables us to take seriously what "old feminism," as Nussbaum calls it, has come to disavow: feminism's complex and contradictory entanglement in academic knowledge production.

And yet, even as Brown compels us into a rigorous consideration of this entanglement, her essay's extrapolation of the content of the present that interrupts the critical claim's linkage between past and future comes to figure critical thought as outside, indeed other to women's studies as an institutional site. In the context of *this* essay, any formulation that aligns women—as political category or strategic academic endeavor—with an immunity to thought recalls Ann Douglas's explication of the conundrum of feminization in which feminism's failure was founded on its excision of rigor in favor of women's affect-bound social circumscription. For Brown, women's studies seems to be a contemporary analogy to the nineteenth century's domestic enclosure, with affect overwhelming its internal organization and the intellectual faltering, as she describes it, on the grounds of its object of study's inescapable demand for a faulty coherency. "Indisputably, women's studies . . . was politically important and intellectually creative," she writes at the outset. "Women's studies as a contemporary *institution,* however, may be politically and theoretically incoherent, as well as tacitly conservative—incoherent because by definition it circumscribes uncircum-scribable 'women' as its object of study, and conservative because it must resist all objections to such circumscription if it is to sustain that object of study" (21; emphasis mine). In this passage, Brown aims her analysis at the "contemporary institution of women's studies" which, as she describes it, must defend its chosen object of study, even (perhaps especially) against feminist scholarship's own transdisciplinary critique of the category of *woman.* If Nussbaum implicitly posits "academic feminism" as constituted by an opposition between theory (the academic) and politics (suffering in the real), Brown relocates this axis wholly within the university and reverses its assessment. Affect is thus immobility, not as in Nussbaum the very engine of political movement, and critical thought is not only constituted by theory but the very force of feminism's political intervention in the academy.

To trace Brown's remapping of the problematic of "academic femi-nism," I want to return to the departmental scene that she uses to open her essay, where the difficulty of efforts to reform the undergraduate curricu-lum in her own department provides the first evidence of the impossibility of women's studies. She writes:

> We found ourselves completely stumped over the question of what a women's studies curriculum should contain. . . . [W]e focused intently on the question of what would constitute an intellectually rigorous as well as coherent program. We speculatively explored a number of dif-ferent possibilities. . . . Each approach seemed terribly arbitrary, each featured some dimension of feminist scholarship that had no reason to be privileged, each continued to beg the question of what a well-educated student in women's studies ought to know and with what tools she ought to craft her thinking. . . . Why, when we looked closely at this project for which we had fought so hard and that was now aca-demically institutionalized, could we find no there there? That is, why was the question of what constituted the fundamentals of knowledge in women's studies so elusive to us? (19–20)

Brown lists a number of crucial issues that contributed to this impasse: the multiple divides that have emerged within women's studies between eth-nic studies, feminist theory, and queer studies; the proliferation of feminist scholarship into methodologically incompatible domains of knowledge where no "single conversation" emerges; and the inability of gender to adequately configure the complexity of social identity (20–21). "We were up against more than any one of these challenges," she writes, "because we were up against all of them" (21). These intellectual challenges bring to crisis "the unanswered question of what women's studies is" (22).

While Brown acknowledges that "the definitions of all disciplines wobble," she finds that "there is something about women's studies . . . and perhaps about any field organized by social identity rather than by genre of inquiry, that is especially vulnerable to losing its raison d'être when the coherence or boundedness of its object of study is challenged" (23–24). She thus turns to law to trace the core intellectual problem that haunts all identity-based academic endeavors: their reduction of "the powers involved in the construction of subjects" into singular identitarian domains (24). Where Nussbaum cites law as the political enterprise that, in linking gendered, racial, sexual, and class-based discriminations, can provide the answer for feminism as a project of justice, Brown finds law powerfully lacking, unable to speak to "the difficulties that women's studies encounters in its simultaneous effort to center gender analytically and to presume gender's imbrication with other forms of social power" (26). This is the case, she writes, because "the injuries of racism, sexism, homophobia, and poverty . . . are rarely recognized or regulated through the same legal categories, or redressed through the same legal strategies. Consequently, legal theorists engage with different dimensions of the law depending on the identity category with which they are concerned" (26). Such fragmentation within the legal apparatus demonstrates for Brown two crucial points: first, that the social powers at work in subject formation are neither compatible nor evenly distributed across the social field, which means that "formations of socially marked subjects occur in radically different modalities, which themselves contain different histories and technologies, touch different surfaces and depths, form different bodies and psyches" (30); and second, that this problem "can only be compounded by programs of study that feature one dimension of power—gender, sexuality, race, or class—as primary and structuring. And there is simply no escaping that this is what women's studies does, no matter how strenuously it seeks to compensate for it" (30). As a consequence, "the model of power developed to apprehend the making of a *particular* subject/subjection will never accurately describe or trace the lines of a living subject" (31; emphasis mine).

This last statement is one that would receive little rebuttal in contemporary academic feminism, as it defines the very problematic that has animated feminist theory for over a decade. Why, then, does Brown turn the problematic that occupies the field into that which necessitates its dissolution? And why must an object of study and a field formation be repeatedly figured as structurally, which is to say inescapably, the same? To answer these questions, we need to examine not only how women's studies comes to be inhabited, in Brown's account, by affect and not intellect, but how this inhabitation functions to conceal competing forms of identity in the contemporary academy: that between identity studies on one hand and the disciplines on the other.

In her description of the various imperatives that led her department to seek curricular reform, Brown analyzes the incoherency that structures the core requirements of the major: "Introduction to Feminism," "Feminist Theory," "Methodological Perspectives in Feminism," and "Women of Color in the United States." These courses, which produced in students, respectively, pleasure, fear, dislike, and guilt, evince a split between generic inquiry (theory and method) and political inquiry (women of color), thereby installing the intellectual need for an analysis that exceeds gender's particularist logic in an emotional register, as a "compensatory cycle of guilt and blame" (31). For Brown, this cycle is "structured by women's studies' original, nominalist, and conceptual subordination of race (and all other forms of social stratification) to gender" (31), which means that women's studies cannot *not* be inhabited by the powerful pain of racial wounds. As she writes, "Insofar as the superordination of white women within women's studies is secured by the primacy and purity of the category gender, guilt emerges as the persistent social relation of women's studies to race, a guilt that cannot be undone by any amount of courses, readings, and new hires focused on women of color" (30–31). As one of the crucial last sentences in her essay's section on law, this "insofar" functions as a kind of relay in which the theoretical explanation of the category of gender is transformed into a social relation, one that cannot be retrieved for articulation in an intellectual register, as no "amount of courses, readings," and so on can undo the founding problem of the field. Under these terms, no resignification, no performative rearticulation, indeed no possible difference in the deployment of *women* is possible. The critique launched by feminists of color against the reduction of women to white women can never hit its target, as the category of women remains structurally predetermined to yield an exclusionary result "insofar as the superordination of white women within women's studies is secured by the primacy and purity of the category gender" (30).

Brown's response to this impasse, to the structural impossibility (in her terms) of rearticulating women to yield anything but an exclusionary effect, is to call for teaching the women's studies curriculum in something other than its own degree-granting site. Might we, she asks, move such "basic courses as 'Introduction to Feminisms,' 'Introduction to Feminist Theories,' and 'Histories and Varieties of Women's Movements' . . . into the general curriculum of other disciplinary and especially interdisciplinary programmatic sites" (35)? And yet, in talking about her own department's failure to find the "there there" for a coherent women's studies undergraduate curriculum, Brown's focus on the faculty demonstrates how their distinct disciplinary identities have come to compete for intellectual and pedagogical priority within women's studies as a field. "Our five core and three most closely affiliated faculty are trained respectively in American literature, American history, Chinese history, English literature, Renaissance Italian and French literature, Western political theory, European history, and molecular biology" (20). While Brown notes that all these scholars "have strayed from the most traditional boundaries of these fields, just as we have learned and taught material relatively unrelated to them," the faculty nonetheless experience the women's studies classroom as the scene of intellectual disappointment as students are not simply unprepared in "the faculty's areas of expertise" but drawn to "some variant of feminist sociological or psychological analysis—experientially, empirically, and practically oriented—or . . . studies of popular culture. Yet not one of our core faculty worked in [these areas]" (20). The "gap" thus created between student interest and faculty expertise is the gap between two forms of identity production: the social relation of identity that produces political belonging in women's studies and the intellectual formation of identity that proceeds from disciplinary training and the academic construction of "expertise" (19). Where Brown diagnoses the problems of installing the former as the faulty coherency of a women's studies curriculum, she leaves the latter identity structure of traditional disciplinarity in place. In this way, her essay privileges disciplinary identity over corporeal identity, which reverses the political imperative but not the organizing structures within which knowledge and bodies, identities and thought, in the university now move.

It is in this broader context that I want to resituate the impossibility of women's studies that Brown so cogently cites. For while identity studies in general have sought to intervene in the university by critiquing its practices of excluding particular groups of subjects, they have been less successful in establishing the study of identity as a knowledge project that distinctly challenges the identitarian form of the university's intellectual reproduction in the disciplines. This is the case, it seems to me, regardless of the earliest intentions of programs in identity studies that organized themselves as critical interruptions into disciplinary practices through a foregrounded discourse of interdisciplinarity. Through interdisciplinary frameworks, identity studies sought to overcome the professionalized divide between knowledge domains in the university (between, for instance, the study of literature and political economy).[14] And yet, given the academy's own political economy of knowledge production, identity studies have relied and continue to rely on faculty both trained and located in traditional disciplines, which means that intellectual subject formation as well as intellectual belonging are predicated on the identity and authority conferred by disciplinary structures. This is not to say that scholars experience no abjection in their relation to disciplinary structures, but it is to foreground the fact that knowledge identity is today disciplinarily based, which often has the powerful effect of rendering identity studies solely as domains of belonging in a corporeal identitarian sense. In this dynamic where one may *be* a woman, one also *is* a literary critic, political scientist, sociologist, or critical theorist, which means that knowledge production as we know it today is also an identitarian project, one articulated around privileged objects of study and their equally privileged modes of inquiry. That these intellectual identities have come to rest in enlightened modernity on their dis-establishment from the corporeal does not make them less identitarian; rather, it reveals how profoundly shaped by structures of identity is the domain of academic knowledge production on the whole.

Brown's notion that other academic sites are adequate to feminist knowledges in ways that women's studies is not reads finally as an attempt to escape the feminized "wounded state" that the institutional location has become in her analysis.[15] It is for this reason that the courses she lists for integration into the existent organization of the university by necessity omit "Women of Color." That referent—and the problematic of a "notoriously fraught relationship" it cannot help but bring (30)—is rendered wholly internal to women's studies; indeed, it seems to have no living trace once women's studies as an institutional unit has been critically undone.[16] But to teach "Introduction to Feminisms" in English, political science, or history—or in American studies, cultural studies, or other underfunded interdisciplinary sites—will not in the end give complexity to our students' understanding of the present that "The Impossibility of Women's Studies" so cogently charts, nor will it make possible the radical refashioning of feminist scholarship as an interdisciplinary domain attentive to the complexities of power and subject formation. This is the case because the evacuation of identity as the primary object that organizes an institutional site in favor of other interdisciplinary and disciplinary projects presents no opportunity to radically reconfigure the intellectual constitution of academic feminist subjects, those who might through new practices of doctoral training and new modes of inquiry articulate a "there there" for women's studies by critically engaging the problems that the study of identity presents in its present tense. After all, it is precisely the existence of women's studies today as an interdisciplinary institutional domain defined in relation to identity that makes productive the movement of courses and knowledge from women's studies to other institutional arenas, for it is only under the auspices of women's studies that feminism can emerge as a legitimate object of study embroiled in rethinking and remaking identity as a critical category of inquiry.

This does not mean, however, that I think Brown is wrong to suggest that academic feminism mobilize itself by teaching what we think of as basic women's studies courses in various sites throughout the institution. To offer "Introduction to Feminisms" in the sociology or English department, instead of such discipline-based mainstay courses as "Sociology of Gender" or "Women and Literature," does introduce a radical reconfiguration of feminist knowledge. It allows for a different kind of intellectual circulation and the displacement of the stable unity of *women* and gender in multiple domains. Such mobility, however, cannot substitute for the continued reshaping of objects and modes of inquiry within women's studies, which is to say that the mobility that Brown calls for can only be sustained in relation to the continued function of women's studies as an extradisciplinary domain for thinking about identitarian projects. Why assume, after all, that feminism's knowledge project can be reinvigorated and rescued from within the apparatus that has produced practitioners who admit to being "completely stumped over the question of what a women's studies curriculum should contain"? The present that Brown calls into thinking as an interruption of the assumptions of the past provides the necessary first move in the reanimation of feminist knowledge production in the academy, but such a move begets another: a theoretical investigation of the organization of knowledge that structured the field's inaugurating understanding of its object of study and that continues to consign identity-based studies to their most reduced and realist referential function as affect and not intellect, as particularity and not complexity. When Brown calls for thinking to interrupt the past's temporal determination of the future, it is this that must be interrupted as well: the particularist reduction whereby the university's distillation of bodies from knowledge yields an understanding of identity studies as the sole institutional domain within which the complexity of power cannot possibly be thought.[17]

To say that the study of identity needs more critical thinkers like Wendy Brown might appear contradictory in the context of my criticisms, but it is precisely because "The Impossibility of Women's Studies" allows us to understand so much that one feels compelled to labor over what remains obscured.[18] Women's studies does "need a combination of, on one hand, analyses of subject-producing power accounted through careful histories, psychoanalysis, political economy, and cultural, political, and legal discourse analysis, and, on the other, genealogies of particular modalities of subjection that presume neither coherence in the formations of particular kinds of subjects nor equivalences between different formations" (32). But this does not mean that, because "the work I am describing . . . will add up neither to a unified and coherent notion of gender nor to a firm foundation for women's studies," it will "no longer [be] women's studies" (32). Why refuse the possibility that attention to the issues she defines will productively contribute to the redefinition, resignification, and redeployment of the intellectual force, frame, and function of the field? If it is *women* that we must let go of, as along with Brown I believe we must, then we must also refuse the assumption that intellectual domains and their objects of study are referentially the same.

In this present that is not possibly the same as the past nor a simple predictive platform for the future, academic feminism's attachment to the institution is decidedly insecure. Political failure haunts us on all sides, and we have very little vocabulary outside accusation and injury for understanding the institutionalizing process of feminism's transit from the street to the university. While Brown comes closest to offering us the object lessons that identity-based studies might be made to yield, she is finally, paradoxically, too optimistic, as the contemporary university offers quite literally "no there there" for the study "of the powers involved in the construction of subjects" (24). The present of *thinking* that Brown calls for needs to register *this* institutional failure, not as preamble to dismissing women's studies as an academic endeavor, but in order to extend the critique of identitarian belonging to the disciplinary formations that currently structure women's studies' own knowledge production.

UN-BELONGING

In "The Impossibility of Women's Studies," Brown argues that a mode of social belonging has been installed as the political rationale for the field, thereby rendering it an intellectually domesticated site. In doing so, she makes two central claims: first, that the most important contemporary force inhibiting critical thought about power and the living subject is identity studies; and second, that the mobilization of feminist knowledge will be possible, indeed more probable, in the absence of women's studies as an institutional entity. I have sought to counter these two assumptions by positing that the critical diagnosis of the field offered by Brown is not intellectually possible from outside it, that indeed it is the productive disparity between the field's own critical horizons and its internal critique that have rendered "The Impossibility of Women's Studies" possible as a critical project. In addition, I have defined a second and equally formidable identitarian project in the academy, one whose effect of fragmentation is no less intense than the structural incommensurabilities that Brown finds in law: the disciplines. In doing so, I have tried to emphasize that within the disciplinary apparatus of knowledge production, one does not simply study literature, politics, or social organization. One is constituted as belonging on an identitarian basis, where the imperative to *be* a biologist, philosopher, political scientist, even a critical theorist is to partake in an identitarian project. My purpose in these moves is to define the idiom of failure within feminism as a condition and consequence of the problematic of identity as an object of knowledge, and hence I have interrupted Brown's determination of an end to the project of institutionalization by placing institutionalization itself at the center of consideration of feminism's own struggle with the specter of failure.

Am I, then, trying to rewrite the idiom of failure I have unsystematically tracked? Not exactly. Failure, it seems to me, is the unavoidable consequence of imagining political transformation, especially in the context of the differentials that collate around investments in institutions, social practices, and various kinds of critical agencies and projects. I have been interested in these investments in the work of three very different kinds of critical thinkers—Ann Douglas, Martha Nussbaum, and Wendy Brown—in part because of what they strangely share: the somewhat tortuous suspicion that feminism is itself the victim of processes of feminization, which means that feminism has been (or in Douglas continues to be) undone by narcissistic and indulgent approaches to the political. For Brown, the institutionalization of feminism's presumption of social belonging within the category of *women* structures this foundational association, making women's studies a domain of anti-intellectualism in its dedication to modes of guilt and pride or what we might understand as the psychic economy of racialized pain. Nussbaum, on the other hand, splits the affective economy of suffering from a critical narcissism that dominates her rendering of academic feminism's intellectual obsessions in order to retrieve a humanist subject animated by the "suffering of others," a subject who sees the future in a "real" world now disarticulated from the academy's illusory attachment to abstraction. For Douglas, feminization is a process that fully counters institutionalization of any kind; it is both a mode of affect and a set of social practices that distance and differentiate women from the realm of politics and power.

In their permutations of the relationship among feminism, failure, and the feminizing specter of different kinds of institutionalization—of women's relation to the domestic (Douglas), of critical theory (Nussbaum), of race as the labor of affect underlying *women*'s identity production (Brown)—these texts cannot be said to constitute a critical taxonomy, nor do they assemble anything as solid as a history of feminist use of the idiom of failure. They are linked rather by a certain coincidental reading, one animated by the desire to un-belong to the reproductive mechanics of the critical claim's inhabitation of time. On this score, each of the texts I have examined provide importantly different renderings of feminism's relation to past, present, and future, interrupting or consolidating the binary apparatus of knowing and doing that I have defined as the motivating anxiety for the critical claim's contemporary deployment. As a kind of exercise in un-belonging to both the normative notion of the category of *women* and to the critical claim's utopic assurance that knowledge production can find a real-world guarantee in political activity, this essay seconds Brown's suggestion that we engage more deeply with what it means to be where we think we are.

NOTES

My thanks to a group of generous readers of drafts of this essay: Rey Chow, Inderpal Grewal, Susan Gubar, Caren Kaplan, Donald Pease, Leonard Tennenhouse, and Philip Gould.

1. This insecurity is regularly demonstrated by faculty debates over departmentalization, Ph.D. programs, and other features of institutionalization. A recurrent expression is that interpellation into the institution's traditional forms of production will imperil distinctly feminist knowledge projects, and hence marginality (in unit structure, size, and resources) is necessary to guarantee academic feminism's political futurity. The escape from marginality and downright exclusion that marked the historical impulse toward academic intervention is thus turned on its head, as the process of institutionalization now signifies as a source of political corruption, if not the very mechanism for feminism's academic domestication.

2. In "Feminism's Apocalyptic Futures," I take up some of the problematic consequences for academic feminism's future that arise from the narrative of revolutionary transit from the street to the university.

3. See Sánchez-Eppler for an important reassessment of the sentimental form's relation to abolition.

4. Toward the end of *The Feminization of American Culture,* Douglas devotes a chapter to Margaret Fuller, who is the only fully formed female figure in the book to warrant the author's admiration. Tellingly, Fuller's life is described as "an effort to find what she called her 'sovereign self' by disavowing fiction for history, the realm of 'feminine' fantasy for the realm of 'masculine' reality. . . . Fuller protected and sanctioned herself by commiserating profusely with the cost her life exacted of her; but she never thought she had done, could have done, or should have done, otherwise. Self-pity never became sentimentalism: it never seriously sapped her boldness" (317). Even here, Douglas's distaste for the feminine and for the strategies of political reform and response that arose from the symbolic and social location of traditional women puts her on the side of masculine accomplishment.

5. See Gubar's "Feminist Misogyny" for a compelling discussion of the impulse toward "misogyny," as she calls it, in Wollstonecraft's work.

6. See especially Gubar, "What Ails Feminist Criticism?" For a direct response to Gubar, see Wiegman, "What Ails Feminist Criticism? A Second Opinion."

7. Nussbaum's tactic in reading across the range of Butler's work—from *Gender Trouble* to *Excitable Speech*—is to argue that little is new. Defining Butler's main idea as "gender is a social artifice" (40), Nussbaum proceeds to find in Plato, John Stuart

Mill, and a host of contemporary feminist thinkers (Andrea Dworkin, Catharine McKinnon, Nancy Chodorow, Gayle Rubin, and Susan Moller Okin) ideas that Butler claims as her own. In Nussbaum's account, Butler's difference from her predecessors is her refusal not only to write in a clear and coherent language but to link her insights to "realizing justice in America" (45).

8. In her letter to the editor in a subsequent issue of the *New Republic,* Gayatri Spivak challenges Nussbaum's turn to Indian feminism to secure U.S. feminism's political guarantee. Spivak writes, "This flag waving championship of needy women leads Nussbaum finally to assert that 'women who are hungry, illiterate, disenfranchised, beaten, raped . . . prefer food, school, votes, and the integrity of their bodies.' Sounds good, from a powerful tenured academic in a liberal [U.S.] university. But *how* does she know?" (Letter 43).

9. For a discussion of U.S. feminism's increasing status as the hegemonic discourse of global feminism, and hence its complicity with a whole set of practices around development and first world rescue of the nonsecular world, see Grewal's and Kaplan's introduction to *Scattered Hegemonies* and their essays "Warrior Marks" and "Transnational Feminist Cultural Studies."

Nussbaum also represses the critique from within the national domain concerning the state as the arbitrator of rights. Most recently, this critique put forward by Janet Halley and Gayle Rubin, who trace how feminism's hard-won legal remedies for sexual harassment and antipornography have become the means for policing nonnormative sexualities in both the workplace and public sphere. Nussbaum's use of gays and lesbians in her list of those in need of legal protection is the figural trace of this particular repression. It functions strategically to cast Butler as a traitor to her own—to both women and queers. My thanks to Janet Halley and Gayle Rubin for sharing their work in progress with members of the University of California Humanities Research Institute group, of which I was a part in fall 1998.

10. In giving centrality to MacKinnon and Dworkin, Nussbaum also virtually silences those who have long challenged the political projects of both thinkers. See, for instance, the debate now referred to within feminism as "the sex wars" in Freccero; King; and Rubin, "Thinking Sex."

11. In saying this, I am not upholding the model of power that has attended the theorization of the liberal state, one that sees power in the stark terms of domination and oppression, complicity and oppositionality. Rather, I am indexing how feminism's initial movement into the academy brought with it *this* particular understanding of power and in such a way that the growth of academic feminism has existed in tension, if not at times contradiction, with this originating conception of the political.

12. It is not clear to me whether this difference has emerged as a consequence of institutionalization or whether institutionalization makes it newly legible.

13. While women's studies and ethnic studies typically function as the common referent for identity studies, it is important to articulate the interdisciplinary project of American studies, inaugurated in the 1930s, as the U.S. academy's first form of identity-based knowledge. Indeed, what is compelling about the case of American studies is that it was the identity projects of the 1960s that served as its structural "other" and initiated the kind of crisis over its object of study that Brown tracks in the domain of women's studies. For more on American studies, see Pease and Wiegman.

14. As Lisa Lowe has discussed, it is the organization of the disciplines that bifurcates the realms of culture and political economy, which in turn produces structural antagonisms for accounting for subject construction across various social domains. She writes: "The traditional function of disciplinary divisions in the university is to uphold the abstract divisions of modern civil society into separate spheres: the political, the economic, and the cultural. The formation and reproduction of the modern citizen-subject is naturalized through those divisions of social space and those divisions of knowledge" (38).

15. In *States of Injury,* Brown argues that a discourse of injury has replaced a discourse of freedom in leftist political projects in the past two decades, and in doing so she offers a compelling way to understand how civil rights reform has itself been reformulated to yield laws that protect the privileges of the majority. In "The Impossibility of Women's Studies," she seems to reiterate her reading of injury as the primary formulation of difference in the public sphere by defining it as the discourse that organizes women's studies as an academic field.

16. My point in locating the way "The Impossibility of Women's Studies" seems trained on figuring out for feminists some kind of escape from this situation should not be read as an accusation that Brown hopes to dismiss altogether the significance of race. *That* reading would be deeply inaccurate. And yet, while I agree with Brown that the women of color rubric within women's studies has a problematic history and political construction, I would base my argument against its placement in a core curriculum not on the affect that it generates, but on the various intellectual displacements that it provides: how it reduplicates but does not reveal its complicity with the university's broader association of race with particularist bodies; how it reinscribes a national political horizon for thinking feminism's relation to race and racialization by constraining the question of "color" within the referential framework of the United States; and how this constraint produces both intellectual and political difficulties for thinking through the challenge of international/transnational/postnational knowledges in the field. For important new work on the problems and complexities of the women of color course, see both Lee and Moallem.

17. In her 1981 essay "Archimedes and the Paradox of Feminist Criticism," Myra Jehlen provides important directions and caveats for my own thinking in this essay.

She talks about the critical difference between "feminist thought" and "thinking about women" (76), and she uses her own disciplinary training and location—literary study—to reconsider that discipline's "fundamental axioms" (76, 77). Such a project propels her into the heart of feminist literary criticism's interest in sentimental culture and moves her to critique the project of heralding women's sentimental resistance by noting that "the map of an enclosed space describes only the territory inside the enclosure" (80). To the extent that my essay calls for an interrogation of women's studies in the wider space of the university—and of the organization of knowledge in the university more widely—it seeks a larger map on which to chart the implications of feminist knowledge. But it also risks encasing the question of feminist knowledge in its own enclosed space, the academy, which cannot possibly stand in as an adequate representation of the production of knowledge in the social formation as a whole. My hope in drawing attention to issues of academic production and thereby of failing to heed what is now a popular call to academic feminists (that we write for popular audiences and seek translations between scholarship and the public sphere) rests on the necessity of an interrogation that has been avoided for too long.

18. Brown's essay, it seems to me, is the most important discussion of women's studies as an academic field since the 1983 publication of Gloria Bowles's and Renate Duelli Klein's edited volume, *Theories of Women's Studies*. It is certainly the most rigorous challenge to the institutional operation of the field ever written by someone who labored there for years.

Part II. **EDGED OUT**

TEACHING AND RESEARCH IN
UNAVAILABLE INTERSECTIONS
Afsaneh Najmabadi

In spring 1997 I was asked by an organizer for a conference titled "The Politics of Interdisciplinary Location" to speak on one of its panels. An earlier talk about the challenges of teaching a broad survey course, "Women, Islam, and Nationalism in the Middle East and North Africa," at a college like Barnard in a city like New York had apparently generated the interest that produced this invitation (see "Secular"). I was asked to send a talk title and a brief paragraph describing my presentation.

Ambivalent about participating in the conference and unclear about its agenda, I missed the deadline. In July, I received the preliminary program for the conference. My talk title was specified as "Where Have We Gone in Postcolonial Studies?" and I was identified as a speaker who would present "the perspective of a Muslim woman teaching in a U.S. university." I was shocked by both the talk title and the identification attributed to me. There was a double misrecognition at work here: I had never written or spoken on postcolonial studies, a field that I try, without much success, to keep up with as a reader. Nor had I ever written, spoken, or identified myself in public as a Muslim woman. I instantly imagined my colleagues who in fact do postcolonial studies as justifiably angry that a total outsider would engage in an evaluation of their field. More seriously, I was in a panic thinking of my Muslim feminist friends' reaction to my opportunistic misappropriation of their identity. Even worse, my Iranian secular feminist friends and colleagues, critical of my recent appraisals of Islamic feminism in Iran, would now feel confirmed in their skepticism about my allegiances.[1] Not only had I sown illusions about possibilities for political alliances with Islamic feminists, not only had I suggested a rethinking of the history of feminism in the light of these developments in Iran, but, my secular feminist friends would conclude, I had fallen victim to my illusions and gone through a conversion experience.[2]

Once I had overcome my initial irritation and panic, however, I became deeply intrigued by the meaning of these misidentifications: What did this double misrecognition mean? What had gone into its production in the first place? How did I come to be marked as a postcolonial scholar and a Muslim?[3] The invitation to speak at this conference clearly indicated a genuine attempt to include difference; yet it was an inclusion that assumed recognizability. A place was made for me on the assumption that I belonged to a definable category. It is this combined move—an inclusion of difference that assumes, if not demands, recognizability—that concerns me here.

The emergence, consolidation, and resources of women's studies have undoubtedly made available to me a zone from which I can speak, teach, and do research as a feminist.[4] In particular, the more recent (though no longer very recent!) hybridization and fracturing of this zone have enabled me to speak as a multiply marked subject. This hybridization was itself a product of intersections, among them intersections of critiques of feminism by women of color with critiques of Orientalism, initiated by Edward Said's *Orientalism* and the kind of scholarship and politics that it helped to generate in academia. This intersection has in fact produced an almost privileged platform from which to speak: that of a postcolonial feminist.

Yet it is that very definition, postcolonial feminism, that has also produced the conditions for the kind of misrecognitions with which I am concerned and the desire to occupy "unavailable spaces" I continue to crave. Though we have fragmented and multiplied the zones from which we can speak, opening up marginal spaces, changing margins from the end walls of central spaces into centers of new zones, this process of multiplication and hybridization is not simply a paradise of speaking possibilities; it also makes particular "speaking-as" demands on us.

The speech demand that concerns me here arises from the obliteration of particular locations in a by now dominant historical narrative: the narrative of a world once-upon-a-time divided into the colonizer and the colonized. Though this narrative has become more complex with the emergence of two other categories, neocolonial and postcolonial, these are clearly derivative categories, presuming the previous division of the world.

My problem, however, begins with that original division. That vision already obliterated vast geohistorical spaces, societies that were neither colonizers nor colonized. Already in this very formulation there is a problem: this is a zone defined by a neither-nor, a negatively defined space. I happen to come from one such zone, Iran, but Iran is by no means a unique oddity of the imperial age. Thailand was never colonized, for instance, nor were many of today's nation-states that emerged out of the disintegration of the Ottoman domains. Though some (such as Lebanon, Syria, and Iraq) experienced brief periods of protectorateship, others (such as Albania, Bulgaria, and Romania) directly established nation-states.[5] In the colonial/colonized division, countries like Iran were sometimes called semicolonial, but this was a derivative category, marking what an entity was not rather than what it was and reminiscent of earlier histories that attempted to analyze why, for instance, capitalism did not develop here or there, rather than what did develop here or there.

The challenge of "unavailable intersections"—itself a negative concept, an unsatisfiable desire—is not only a matter of space, but also a question of time.[6] In the colonial versus anti-, neo-, post-colonial narrative of history, there is a zero-time set at the moment of colonization. In important ways, history begins at this zero-time. The subsequent shift to neo- or post-coloniality does not challenge this zero-time of the narrative, but within that time matrix marks a turning point. The people populating the in-between zones become people with uncomfortably unlocatable places and uninitiable times. Not only do their geopolitical locations become defined as a neither-nor space—neither in the domain of the British Empire, nor in the domain of czarist Russia, for instance—but writing the history of modernity in these neither-nor spaces looks like a narrative with disjointed time, a history out of synch with the zero-time established by the colonial/anticolonial narrative. Given the hegemony of that narrative, a historian of the neither-nor lands is suspected of producing timelessness: her or his history seems marked by a lack, a lack of the zero-time, of a big bang moment of colonial conquest that effaced all dynamics prior to that moment and set in motion all subsequent history. Doing history of the neither-nor lands seems to sink into a time zone with no beginning, or it seems to follow a periodization that suspiciously claims temporal frames outside of the zero-time set by colonial clocks. It is an uncomfortable not-time.

Teaching from and doing research in these detemporized neither-nor zones, these unavailable intersections, is an enterprise born under marks of suspicion and complicity. Such a historian is suspected of doing "organic history" or of being trapped in a search for authentic history. Yet the very categories of organic and authentic belong to the colonial/anticolonial space-time zone.

In a sense, the historical narrative of the colonies follows the footsteps of the colonizers; it moves from the outside in. This narrative framework makes the historian of the neither-nor lands appear to be engaged in an act of reversal: writing history from inside out. This makes her historical enterprise immediately suspect of "denying" colonialism as the central fact of modernity. The historian of the neither-nor lands may find the out-in and in-out movements an irrelevant frame but nonetheless remain implicated in colonialism's master narrative by denial.

Thus the neither colonial nor anticolonial zone, even in our postcolonial world, is not simply a nonexistent zone. Attempts to carve it out, to generate it as a third time-space (but one different from Lavie's and Swedenburg's third time-space), efforts to engage in some sort of dezoning of the colonially marked time-spaces are always already—if I may use that charged phrase—a suspected enterprise. To the extent that such efforts may in fact succeed in dezoning, in generating any small corner of a third time-space, that space is always already a suspected and contaminated zone. It is suspected of complicity with the colonizers through the blurring effects that it may produce in the border zones between the colonial and anticolonial domains.

I suspect it is the intellectual weight of this historical zoning that makes it difficult to imagine a teacher-scholar of some part of the non-West as a not-postcolonial subject in any positive sense. The currently zoned spaces and temporalities require me to speak as a postcolonial. The problem is that neither the geopolitical matrix of that category nor its temporal demarcations are analytically productive in my teaching and research in the ways that they are for many other places and historical experiences.[7] The presumption of their universal relevance for the non-West makes different imaginings of spaces and temporalities "unavailable intersections."

Since the late 1970s, a second "zoning" problem has emerged. In the wake of political and intellectual radicalization of the U.S. academy, dissident academics from those lands perceived as colonized were in a privileged position: they were courted to speak, incited to speak. But the incitement came with expectation of what one was to speak as. When, in the late 1960s, I would talk about the Iranian state and economy, I more often than not disappointed those expectations.[8] The most frequent first question I would be asked from the audience was a variation of "where is imperialism in your scheme of things?" The anxiety expressed in this question followed from the fact that I had not spoken of Iran in terms of a world divided into colonized and colonizer. My analysis of Iran as a rentier state seemed dangerously to defamiliarize the then-dominant script of imperialism.

Then came the 1979 revolution in Iran and after that a new speech-demand emerged. Now when I present my work on constructions of gender and modernity in late-nineteenth-century Iran, the first question I am asked has become a variation of "where is Islam in your scheme of things?" As a scholar from an Islamicate culture, doing research and teaching courses related to Islam, I seemed to gain what I had lacked in the colonial/postcolonial narrative: a time and place of my own.[9] In fact, I was required always to own the time and place that has come to define Muslimhood: seventh-century Arabia. The originary narrative of Islam and of the Islam most often defined as scripturally determinate—that is, Qur'an says so, or Muhammad said or did such and that is why things are so in Muslim societies—sometimes can take a comic turn. For instance, Geraldine Brooks, in her *Nine Parts of Desire,* begins by noting that as a single woman she "couldn't check [her]self into a Saudi hotel room in the 1990s *because* thirteen hundred years earlier a Meccan named Muhammad had trouble with his wives" (3; my emphasis). What a remarkable man Muhammad must have been, I thought upon reading this passage, to set off a causal chain that has lasted so many centuries! How many other cultures or religions are there these days about which such a casually causal statement could be made?

Serious scholarship often reproduces the effects of Brooks's journalism by piecing together information from diverse sources and historical periods. For instance, in an influential book, *Women in Islam: From Medieval to Modern Times,* Wiebke Walther not only assumes an unproblematic reflexivity of literary sources (42) but uses twentieth-century anthropological reports on central Arabia and northern Morocco, modern works of fiction by Lebanese and Egyptian novelists, medieval Arabic works of medicine, tenth-century *adab* (belles lettres) literature, twelfth-century theological treatises, eighth-century commentaries and narratives, and eighteenth-century and nineteenth-century European travelers' writings as if they could all be unproblematically culled for facts on women in Islam from medieval to modern times. The result is profoundly ahistorical, the production of a conception of Islam marked by timelessness and spatial homogeneity.[10]

Challenging the dominant production of Islam poses enormous problems, especially for a feminist who comes from a region where the majority of the population is Muslim, from Iran, a country that has been ruled as an Islamic republic for the past nineteen years, who is now located in the United States, and who teaches courses on women and Islam. In a concluding note to his essay "Ethnography, Literature, and Politics: Some Readings and Uses of Salman Rushdie's *The Satanic Verses*," Talal Asad posed my dilemma succinctly (260). To paraphrase, a major question for those concerned with the West's Other *in* the West is this: how do our discursive interventions articulate the politics of difference in the spaces defined by the modern state? His implicit answer to this question is to place himself on the side of the immigrant minority under cultural and political siege in the West. He speaks from the vantage point of "most Muslims," "many Muslims" (who were hurt by the novel). That minority *within* the minority community who identified with the book and considered it expressive of *their* immigrant experiences as hybrids and exiles are in Asad's judgment "some of the most Westernized," "anglicized," and so on. Asad's discursive choice is not attractive to me as a feminist, because more often than not I find myself in that minority within the minority position.[11] This position, however, does not relieve me of the dilemmas posed by Asad's question: how do I speak, write, and teach about Islam within the circumstances set by the larger dominant anti-Islamism?

I face this dilemma at least twice a week in my class "Women, Islam, and Nationalism in the Middle East and North Africa." On the first day, I ask the students to write briefly what the words "women" and "Islam" bring to their imagination. The answers are wonderfully varied, yet they always tend to include statements such as "veil," "unfair," "suppressed," "no freedom," "repression," "oppression," "submission," "not too many rights," "inequality," "subordination," "segregation," "fundamentalism," "polygamy," "denied sexuality," "subjugation," "lesser beings," "not respected," "living according to some sort of a dress code," "puritanical way of life," "living for pleasure of men," "circumcision" (even "sati" has made an occasional appearance!), and most tellingly, "completely different from US." (I have often contemplated whether the apparent pun on US—capitalized us or U.S.?—is ever intentional.) But Barnard (where I then taught) is a rather diverse community. So, on the other side of the spectrum, students from families that originated in Islamicate cultures provide me with another set of challenges; they often uncritically or defensively embrace a religion, heritage, and culture they feel is under siege. I face the challenge of how I should teach about women and Islam in a way that is neither apologetic nor culturally defensive of misogyny and at the same time does not regenerate the kind of images that have been received from contemporary cultural constructions of Islam (as "the West's Other" in Asad's formulation and as "completely different from US" in the words of some of my students).

What I find most troubling is the persistent production of a single-voiced Islam, the Islam of rulers, of men of state and men of religion, of men of cultural and political power, as the only Islam, which is, of course, what these producers of Islam would like it to be. When the Islamic Salvation Front (FIS) in Algeria kills unveiled women, it is their way of making sure unveiled is synonymous with un-Islamic. Never mind that millions of unveiled women across the Islamicate world continue to consider themselves Muslims. When an Islamic theologian says wives ought to be obedient to their husbands, that at once defines his Islam and becomes a representation of something inherent to all Islam. We rarely, if at all, hear of women (and men) who challenge, also in the name of Islam, that injunction.

But there are dissident voices from feminists in Islamicate cultures. One such voice is that of Fatima Mernissi. In her book *The Veil and the Male Elite,* Mernissi uses the technique (used by Islamic reformers since the nineteenth century) of historicizing and contextualizing Qur'anic verses and other material from the commentaries and narratives. She produces a particular logic of time and place for each of the texts she analyzes and then comments on them from a woman's point of view. Her project produces an almost feminist Prophet and an egalitarian Islam that was corrupted by Umar and by later caliphs and Islamic commentators. In the process, many conflicting narratives and stories are told that do challenge dominant versions.[12] Yet the overall project remains hostage to some notion of a Golden Age of Islam, which is also the same ground that many of the Islamist political groups she opposes lay claim to. They, too, consider actually existing Islams as corrupt, and they aim to recreate the lost early spirit of Islam. Need we compete by trying to produce an alternative feminist golden age for Islam? Is that our most effective strategy?

Another dissenting voice comes from Farida Shaheed (of Women Living under Muslim Law, an international network of women that has been doing invaluable work bringing information, campaigning, and analysis together across many national boundaries). Shaheed introduces a distinction between Islamic, as that which is ordained by religious scriptures, and Muslim, as that by which Muslims define themselves as a community. The distinction has the obvious advantage of allowing her to argue that much of what Muslims practice is not really Islamic (that is, ordained by scriptures). Despite a space opened up again between actually existing Islams (Muslim) and some true essence of Islam (as ordained by a set of texts), this move has the disadvantage of locking itself into the search for the truly Islamic.

What I am seeking is a way out of authenticity through the now widely accepted notion that all readings are acts of interpretation and thus any claim to what is ordained by any text, including the Qur'an itself, is already a "contaminated" claim. We have learned to view all such claims to authenticity and truth as power claims. But why contest power on its terms? The powerful have reason to present their claims as the truth of the faith, but those who want to contest that power can perhaps make a more persuasive case by presenting theirs not as *the* authentic version of Islam, but as another version that they would work to make powerful. Instead of a search for an original Islam, for the Islam ordained by scriptures, for true Islam, we may be better off producing alternative versions of Islam *without* any claims to authenticity. There are in fact a number of women and men across the Islamic world who have in recent years moved in that direction: Amina Wadud-Muhsin and Sisters in Islam from Malaysia, a group of women and men writers in the pages of the Persian journal *Zanan,* and the Egyptian intellectual Nasr Hamed Abu Zeid come readily to mind.

Back in my classroom, this approach relieves me of trying to argue that what my students have read and heard is not truly Islamic. Instead, I can concentrate on offering alternative readings of Islamic texts—religious, literary, and historical (including the meanings of actually existing commentaries and interpretations)—and examining the cultural work done by their gender constructions.

But even with this resolution of the "authenticity" problem, the current divisions among secular feminisms and religious Muslims produce a sense of incredulity toward any project that claims feminism but refuses anti-Islamism. I can speak as a feminist, but the minute I say something that indicates any empathy for Islamicate cultures, it is interpreted as a "defense of Islam," thereby bringing my feminist credentials under scrutiny. The current division between Islam and anti-Islam demands contrary speaking positions: I must either speak as a Muslim woman or as a secular, anti-Islamic feminist. Most scholars and activists put the term Islamic feminism in quotation marks—indicating some original meaning for the two categories that presumably has trouble containing the combination.

Parallel to the unavailability of a noncolonial/noncolonized time-space, dezoning in this realm is also under suspicion for complicity—either with Islamic retrogression or with anti-Islamic xenophobia; any success at dezoning produces a space contaminated by both. As a feminist from a country that was never colonized and never a colonial power, as a feminist from an Islamicate culture with a strong experience of secular modernity, I find myself speaking from a doubly contaminated zone.

To refuse to speak as a Muslim, or as anti-Muslim—similar to the refusal to speak as an anticolonial or colonial—is of course a risk. Repeatedly, my refusal to speak anti-Islam has become translated into pro-Islam, if not Islamic apologia, and I am myself marked as a Muslim woman, a category unavailable to me in any case.[13] Similarly, my feminist critique of Islam in its dominant "actually existing" variations becomes appropriated into anti-Islamic discourse. Both as a teacher and as a scholar I face these risks constantly. Yet, like many other risks discussed in feminist theory, these are risks I cannot afford not to take.

Nor can these risks be averted by constructing new hybrid categories. For one thing, making categories acquire new meanings is not arbitrary. Individual willful self-naming does not work. If I were, for instance, to rename myself a secular Muslim feminist, it would only work if other Iranian Muslims and other secular feminists were willing to accept that naming by recognizing me, and themselves, in those terms—an unlikely event since the overwhelming majority of Muslims continue to consider some notion of faith, rather than empathy or cultural belonging, necessary and required for such naming, and the overwhelming majority of secular feminists consider secular and Muslim inherently incompatible categories.

Moreover, trying to use old categories with new connotations and meanings also reinvigorates the old meanings. For instance, much literature has argued quite persuasively that women's voluntary veilings in contemporary political contexts have produced new meanings for the veil. But have they reconfigured its meaning as marking a woman's body as site and source of social contamination and chaos, or have they at once also reproduced that meaning?[14] In fact, are the two not dependent on each other for either to work?

Second, despite the attraction of provisional positionalities, of "temporary marriages," the meanings read in a certain social context onto a particular performance are unpredictable and often out of the control of the performer. This is an especially risky business when performed under suspicion and from zones of double contamination.

Finally, new categories—no matter how many times hybridized and how provisionally performative—continue to construct (new) zones that produce the kind of confining pressures from which I have been trying to escape by arguing for the desirability of unavailable intersections, by resisting acts of inclusion premised on recognizability.

To end on a note of refusal to claim categories or to settle for any multiplicity of identities may feel intellectually unsatisfactory and politically irresponsible. But if we can accept the offer of "disclaiming, which is no simple activity . . . as a form of affirmative resistance" (Butler, "Imitation" 15), then disclaiming categories as identities need not become politically paralyzing. The unboundedness of intellectual space is not a reason for fear and insecurity.

NOTES

An earlier version of this essay was presented at the conference "The Politics of Interdisciplinary Location: Teaching and Learning in the Intersections," organized by the Coalition of Programs in Gender and Women's Studies in the Greater New York Area, held at the Institute for Research on Women and Gender, Columbia University, November 7, 1997. My thanks to the organizers for inviting me to this conference. Susan Shapiro offered me a deeply appreciated listening ear, as well as empathic and insightful responses in the initial stages of developing some of these ideas. Her critical comments, as well as those of Elizabeth Weed and Judith Weisenfeld, on an earlier draft, in addition to conversations—vocal and electronic—with Joan Scott, Kathryn Gravdal, and Zohreh Sullivan, were crucially productive for writing this paper. I am grateful to them all; needless to say, they are not responsible for any views expressed here.

1. The debates have appeared most directly in the Persian periodical *Kankash*. See Najmabadi, "'Salha-yi'" and "'Years of Hardship'"; Moghissi; Tohidi. See also Mojab.

2. My overreaction has a history. Subsequent to public comments I made in October 1991 regarding the then heated debate in Iran on the issue of temporary

marriage (*Haeri*), I received a phone call from a friend in Paris who had heard I had become Muslim and veiled. When I first began to speak publicly in winter 1994 on the emerging current of Iranian Muslim women who were doing innovative reinterpretations of Islamic sources, including the Qur'an, a friend from Los Angeles called me and inquired nervously: "I've heard you've become Muslim." Despite the literal meaning of the query in both instances, neither was a question about any experience of religious conversion on my part. Rather, the concern was: had I abandoned feminism? But any identification of me as speaking from "the perspective of a Muslim woman" would connote religious conversion in this context.

3. I want to thank the organizers of the conference for immediately changing, upon my request, my identification and my talk title to "Teaching and Research in Unavailable Intersections." My talk was part of a panel, "Locating Postcolonial Knowledge," which in a sense continued the initial misrecognition. Some of the other panels, such as "Epistemological Contests," or "Repeated Disappearances," would seem to have been—with hindsight!—more appropriate locations.

4. In the rest of this essay I will use "speak" to stand for speak/teach/do research.

5. Ottoman disintegration was a very slow process, with many provinces gaining autonomies of various kinds and degrees, some eventually establishing independent states.

6. By a "negative concept," I do not mean to imply an unwanted valuation of the "unavailable intersections." Rather, I mean to draw attention to the fact that these intersections are shaped by what they are *not* rather than by positive definition. In fact, as Susan Shapiro insightfully pointed out to me, in the whole essay, beginning with "the unavailable" in its title, many negatives—uns, nors, and nots—perform a great deal of productive rhetorical work. By linking the concept of unavailable intersections to desire, I am of course invoking a psychoanalytic meaning for this zone as a concept "the power of which lies in the fact that it NEVER can be satisfied because it doesn't have AN origin that can be recapitulated in some kind of return" (e-mail from Elizabeth Weed to the author, 21 Jan. 1998). It is this unsatisfiability that perhaps demands the repeated rhetorical uses of the negative in this essay in order to refuse recognizable identities as well as to form my not-so-hidden pleasure at being unable or unwilling to.

7. At this point in the development of feminism internationally and the development of interdisciplinary knowledges, more scholars and activists than those from the third time-spaces have a stake at dezoning efforts. I suspect that at least some inhabitants of the anticolonial zone may also be fatigued (and the pull of postcoloniality may be seen as one indication of that fatigue) by the constraints of the current zoning.

8. At the time I was working on the political economy of modern Iran.

9. I use the word *Islamicate* in the sense first proposed by Marshall Hodgson. Whereas "Islamic," he suggested, would be used to refer to "'of or pertaining to' Islam *in the proper, the religious, sense* . . . 'Islamicate' would refer not directly to the religion, Islam, itself, but to the social and cultural complex historically associated with Islam and the Muslims, both among Muslims themselves and even when found among non-Muslims" (59).

10. I have to say, with hindsight, that for a number of years I found myself implicated in this kind of production through the structure of my course syllabus. I would start the course with seventh-century Arabia and the rise of Islam and follow a primarily linear historical narrative to the present time. For most students this did in fact produce a causal chain between seventh-century Arabia and the twentieth-century Islamicate world.

11. I say not attractive, rather than not available, because in fact some feminists from Muslim societies located in the West have opted for that choice. If feminist critiques of things Islamic, e.g., the veil, can be used to produce anti-Islamism, one must remain silent.

12. These include some contradictory statements by Mernissi herself, which to my mind only display the problems of the original body of texts that she works with, mirror their contradictory statements and historiographies that we may no longer notice because of the weight they have acquired through centuries of repetition and clerical authorization.

13. This current unavailability is in contrast to the availability of such categories as secular Jewish, or even atheist Jewish. I have asked myself many times: is it possible / desirable to construct another hybrid category; something like secular feminist Muslim? One problem is that although Muslim communities in many European and North American countries may feel under siege, we have Islamic governments and powerful social and political Islamic movements in a number of countries that define themselves as totally opposed to secularism and feminism. So this is not a situation in which a powerless group can straightforwardly appropriate a category by which the powerful have previously designated it. The appropriation at once energizes contemporary structures of oppression. Moreover, the kind of appropriations of Jewishness that Laura Levitt has elaborated are possible in part because of the existence of a secure secular tradition in American Jewish culture—a possibility that seems blocked to many secular feminists from Islamicate cultures for fear of being sucked back into the sacred since the secular feels so flimsy!

14. For an insightful discussion of some of these issues, see MacLeod.

FEMINISM, DEMOCRACY, AND EMPIRE:

ISLAM AND THE WAR OF TERROR

Saba Mahmood

The complicated role European feminism played in legitimating and extending colonial rule in vast regions of Asia, Africa, and the Middle East has been
extensively documented and well argued for some time now.[1] For many of us
raised on this critical tradition, it is therefore surprising to witness this older
colonialist discourse on women being reenacted in new genres of feminist
literature today with the explicit aim of justifying the United States' war of
terror upon the Muslim world. It seems at times a thankless task to unravel
yet again the spurious logic through which Western imperial power seeks to
justify its geopolitical domination by posing as the "liberator" of indigenous
women from native patriarchal cultures. It would seem that this ideologically
necessary but intellectually tedious task requires little imagination beyond
repositioning the truths of the earlier scholarship on Algeria, Egypt, Indo-
nesia, and India that has copiously and rigorously laid bare the implicated
histories of feminism and empire.

Despite the sense of intellectual exhaustion I share with many friends and
colleagues working in colonial and postcolonial studies, I think it is important
for feminists to attend to the specificity of this moment of Euro-American
domination of the Muslim world and its peculiar indebtedness to key tropes
within contemporary feminist discourse. While ordinary Americans and

Europeans seem to have lost their enthusiasm for the Bush-Blair strategy of unilateralist militarism (whether in Iraq, Afghanistan, or Iran), they continue to trust the judgment offered by their politicians and media pundits that Muslim societies are besotted with an ideology of fundamentalism whose worst victims are its female inhabitants. This judgment further entails the prescriptive vision that the solution lies in promoting "democracy" in the Muslim world and Western values of "freedom and liberty" through religious and cultural reform so that Muslims might be taught to discard their fundamentalist propensities and adopt more enlightened versions of Islam. What concerns me most in this essay is the role the tropes of freedom, democracy, and gender inequality have come to play in this story and the ease with which Islam's mistreatment of women is used as a diagnosis as well as a strategic point of intervention for restructuring large swaths of the Muslim population if not the religion itself. How have the tropes of freedom, democracy, and gender equality—constitutive of a variety of traditions of feminist thought—facilitated the current Euro-American ambition to remake Muslims and Islam?[2] What does such an imbrication obfuscate and what forms of violence do they condone?

It is important to state at the outset that my goal is not so much to show how discourses of feminism and democracy have been hijacked to serve an imperial project. Such an argument would assume that democracy and feminism are strangers to the project of empire building and that aspects of liberal thought and practice have little to do with the neoconservative imaginary that informs the policies of the Bush White House. My aim instead is to lay bare a terrain of shared assumptions internal to liberal discourses of feminism and democracy—particularly their normative secularism—that make the Euro-American war on Muslims across the world appear palatable, if not advisable, to people across the political spectrum. While the U.S. administration's ambitious plan to establish absolute military and economic domination in the Middle East might abate in its zeal, as long as the assumptions that link the projects of empire, liberal feminism, and democracy continue to reign, an imperial impulse will continue to corrupt our judgment in regard to Islam and the Middle East. Unless feminists rethink their complicity in this project, which requires putting our most dearly held assumptions and beliefs up to critical evaluation, feminism runs the risk of becoming more of a handmaiden of empire in our age than a trenchant critic of the Euro-American will to power.

The empirical terrain from which I want to think through these issues is the plethora of recently published nonfiction bestsellers written by Muslim women about their personal suffering at the hands of Islam's supposedly incomparable misogynist practices. Pick up any bestseller list in Europe or North America, and chances are that at least one of these accounts will be among the top-selling nonfiction books for the season. Since the events of 9/11, this vastly popular autobiographical genre has played a pivotal role in securing the judgment that Islam's mistreatment of women is a symptom of a much larger pathology that haunts Islam, namely, its propensity to violence. Calls for the reformation of Islam, now issued from progressive, liberal, and conservative podiums alike, are ineluctably tied to its oppression of women. The argument is simple and goes something like this: Women are the most abject victims of the ideology of Islamic fundamentalism. The solution lies in bringing "democracy" to the Muslim world, a project that will not only benefit women but will also make them its main protagonists. In our age of imperial certitude, it seems that the fate of Muslim women and the fate of democracy have become indelibly intertwined.

The autobiographical genre attesting to Islam's patriarchal ills that I will describe in some detail below is significant not only for its extensive reliance on the most exhausted and pernicious Orientalist tropes through which Islam has been represented in Western history but also for its unabashed promotion of the right-wing conservative agenda now sweeping Europe and America, particularly in regard to Islam. Many of the authors of these accounts have been handsomely rewarded by conservative political parties and think tanks internationally, and some have been catapulted into positions of political power, having few qualifications for this mercurial ascension other than their shrill polemic against Islam. Given their public prominence, the authors of this genre perform a quasi-official function in various American and European cabinets today: lending a voice of legitimacy to, and at times leading, the civilizational confrontation between "Islam and the West."

As will become clear, however, the popularity of these authors extends beyond their conservative supporters to liberal and progressive publics. Their work is often reviewed positively by liberal political pundits and literary writers who dismiss the poor writing, lack of imagination, and gross exaggerations characteristic of this genre as incidental to its real merits: the truth of Islamic misogyny that it unequivocally and heroically represents. These authors are now part of an international literati (cavorting with celebrities such as Salman Rushdie, to whom they are often likened), inspiring both anti-Muslim pathos and anti-Muslim chic among their rapt audiences. The popularity and ideological force of this literature owes largely to the ability of the Muslim woman author to embody the double figure of insider and victim, a key subject within Orientalist understandings of women in Muslim societies. These autobiographical works are, however, also distinct from earlier colonial accounts in which it fell to Europeans to reveal the suffering of indigenous women oppressed by the primitive practices of colonized cultures. Here it is the "indigenous woman" herself who provides the ethnographic grist for this bloodied imagination, lending a voice of authenticity to the old narrative that a liberal ear, raised on a critique of colonial literature, can more easily hear and digest.

The fact that this genre of Muslim women's biographies speaks to a range of feminists, many of whom oppose the neoconservative agenda championed by the current Bush White House, is particularly disturbing. A number of well-known feminist critics have endorsed these books, and several of the bestsellers are either taught or widely read within women's studies circles.[3] While the authentic "Muslim woman's voice" partially explains the popularity these books command, it is the emancipatory model of politics underwriting these accounts that provokes such pathos and admiration among its feminist readership. It is this emancipatory model, with its attendant topography of secular politics and desire for liberal freedoms, that I wish to trouble in this essay, drawing attention to the blind spots and omissions it has produced in the collusion of empire and feminism in this historical moment.

In what follows, I will make three related but distinct arguments. First, in the section "Neoconservatism and Women's Suffering," I examine the symbiotic relationship between the authors of this genre of Muslim women's literature and conservative political parties and think tanks in America and Europe, a relationship that should serve to mute the enthusiastic reception these books have received in many feminist circles. Then, in the "Selective Omissions" section, I analyze the particular kinds of elisions and inaccuracies, so characteristic of these autobiographical accounts, that have helped construct an essential opposition between Western civilization and Muslim barbarism (or fundamentalism). This opposition is a necessary step in securing the classical imperial argument for why the burden must fall upon "the West" to enlighten and liberate Muslims from the misogyny of their cultural practices. Finally, in the section "Women, Democracy, and Freedom," I examine current arguments for bringing democracy to the Muslim world and the role the figure of the oppressed Muslim woman plays in these calls. I draw attention to the singular and reductive conception of religiosity underwriting these calls, one that enjoys wide currency among a range of feminists[4] but that needs to be criticized for the forms of violence it entails and the narrow vision of gender enfranchisement it prescribes. In this section I also discuss how the liberal discourse on freedom, endemic to various traditions of feminist thought, blinds us to the power that nonliberal forms of religiosity command in many women's lives. If indeed feminists are interested in distancing themselves from the imperial politics of our times, it is crucial that these forms of religiosity be understood, engaged, and respected, instead of scorned and rejected as expressions of a false consciousness.

ONE OF THE MOST successful examples within this genre of Muslim women's literature is Azar Nafisi's *Reading Lolita in Tehran*. Since its publication in 2003, this book has been on the *New York Times* bestseller list for over one hundred seventeen weeks, has been translated into more than thirty-two languages, and has won a number of prominent literary awards. Although Nafisi's writing exhibits aesthetic and literary qualities that make it unique among the works I discuss here, it shares with these other writings a systematic exclusion of information that might complicate the story of women's oppression within Muslim societies. The author has deep links with leading neoconservative figures and think tanks, as I will show, and her support for Bush's agenda of regime change is well known. Her neoconservative credentials notwithstanding, leading liberal and progressive literati have endorsed and praised Nafisi's memoir, and she is represented by the Steven Barclay Agency, which holds the portfolios of luminaries such as Adrienne Rich, Michael Ondaatje, Frank Rich, and Art Spiegelman.

A second book published to wide acclaim—though it does not have the literary pretensions of the former—is by the Canadian journalist Irshad Manji: *The Trouble with Islam: A Muslim's Call for Reform in Her Faith*. This book has been translated into more than twenty languages, republished in over twenty-three countries, and was on the Canadian bestseller list for twenty weeks during the first year of its publication. Manji's shrill diatribe against Muslims has won her a prominent public profile: she regularly appears on a variety of television networks (including BBC, CNN, FoxNews), her op-eds are published in prominent international dailies (such as the *New York Times,* the *Times* of London, the *International Herald Tribune,* the *Sydney Morning Herald*), and she is invited to give lectures at elite academic institutions despite the fact that her writings and speeches are full of historical errors and willful inaccuracies about Islam.[5] Like Nafisi, Manji has also been championed and supported by the neoconservative establishment (more on this below).

A third sample from this genre, Carmen bin Laden's *Inside the Kingdom: My Life in Saudi Arabia,* is an account of Carmen's marriage to one of Osama bin Laden's twenty-five brothers and the years of claustrophobic (albeit plush) boredom she spent in Saudi Arabia. Translated into at least sixteen languages, with translation rights sold in more than twenty-seven countries, the book was on the bestseller list in France for months after its initial publication as well as on the *New York Times* bestseller list during the first year of its publication.[6]

In France a number of such books reached high acclaim at the time of the passage of the controversial law that banned the wearing of the veil (and other "conspicuous" religious symbols) in public schools. Leading these publications was Fadela Amara's *Ni putes ni soumises,* which received two prominent literary awards (Le Prix du livre politique and Le Prix des Députés in 2004), sold over fifty thousand copies, and was translated into multiple languages.[7] A sequel to the book, *Ni putes ni soumises, le combat continue,* has sold out prior to its publication. An equally popular first-person account attesting to Islam's barbaric customs is *Bas les voiles!* written by the Iranian dissident Chahdortt Djavann, whose quote on the dust jacket exemplifies the enunciative position that constitutes this literary genre: "I wore the veil for ten years. It was the veil or death. I know what I am talking about."

Both Amara and Djavann provided personal testimonies against the veil to the Stasi commission (a government-appointed investigative body that recommended the ban), which reportedly moved the presiding officials to tears. These women's highly dramatized statements,[8] marshaled as "evidence" of the oppressive character of the veil in the Stasi commission's report, played a key role in securing French public opinion against the veil and creating a communitas of shared aversion to Islam's religious symbols and the misogyny to which they give expression. In addition to these prominent memoirs, there are countless other contributions to this genre in France, including Loubna Meliane's *Vivre libre,* Marie-Thérèse Cuny Souad's *Brûlée vive,* Leila's *Mariée de force,* and *Dans l'enfer des tournantes* written by Samira Bellil.[9]

Other European countries, including Holland, Spain, Sweden, and Germany, also lay claim to their own ambassadors of Islam's patriarchally oppressed. In a context where the "Muslim problem" has become a key focal point in debates about European identity, such spokeswomen perform an unofficial but now essential role within the national political culture. They authenticate and legitimize the Islamophobia sweeping Europe today, lending a voice of credibility to some of the worst kinds of prejudices and stereotypes Europe has seen since the rise of anti-Semitism in the 1930s. Culture rather than race is the site through which much of this new hatred of the Other is justified and promoted, invoking in its wake all those stock phrases, images, and representations through which a different Other had been vilified and blamed for Europe's economic and civilizational problems.[10] These authentic Muslim voices have played a crucial role in shoring up support for the passage of a number of anti-immigration laws in Europe targeting the poorest and most vulnerable sections of the population. It is no small task that these female "critics of Islam" perform, and indeed, their service is recognized by the conservative political forces of contemporary Europe and America who have bestowed considerable honors on this group.

NEOCONSERVATISM AND WOMEN'S SUFFERING

Consider, for example, the mercurial rise of Ayaan Hirsi Ali in Dutch politics. A woman of Somali descent, Hirsi Ali had no public profile until she decided to capitalize on the anti-Muslim sentiment that swept Europe following the events of 9/11. Excoriating Muslims for their unparalleled barbarity and misogyny, she scored points with the right wing when she attacked the Dutch government's welfare and multicultural policies for fostering and supporting the culture of domestic violence supposedly endemic to Islam and Muslims. In highly staged public statements, Hirsi Ali has characterized the prophet Muhammed as a pervert and a tyrant, claiming that Muslims lag "in enlightened thinking, tolerance and knowledge of other cultures" and that their history cannot cite a single person who "made a discovery in science or technology, or changed the world through artistic achievement."[11] Soon thereafter, Hirsi Ali acquired rock-star status in the legendarily tolerant Dutch society, and the right-wing People's Party for Freedom and Democracy offered her a ticket to run as a member of the parliament, a seat she won by popular vote in January 2003 despite the fact that she had little or no prior qualifications for such a position.[12]

In 2006, Dutch immigration services discovered that Hirsi Ali had lied to gain entry into the Netherlands and had fabricated her past, including the story of her plight from a forced marriage and a vengeful natal family. Threatened with the repeal of her Dutch citizenship, Hirsi Ali resigned from the Dutch parliament and was immediately granted a position at the prestigious right-wing think tank in Washington, the American Enterprise Institute. In 2005, *Time* magazine hailed her as one of the world's "100 Most Influential People" (along with George Bush) ("Leaders"), and the *Economist* has since described her as a cultural ideologue of the new Dutch right ("Living"). Predictably, Hirsi Ali also published a memoir in 2006 entitled *The Caged Virgin: An Emancipation Proclamation for Women and Islam,* a title highly reminiscent of the nineteenth-century literary genre centered on Orientalist fantasies of the harem.[13] Despite the facts that Hirsi Ali's personal story of suffering under Islamic customs has been discredited and the book is full of absurd statements (such as "[Muslim] children learn from their mothers that it pays to lie. Mistrust is everywhere and lies rule" [25–26]), it has done quite well.[14] *The Caged Virgin* has sold translation rights in fifteen countries, and Christopher Hitchens, the contemporary doyen of "conservative left criticism," deems it an "excellent book" ("Dutch"), adding: "This is an author and a politician who has made the transition from early Islamic fanaticism (she initially endorsed the fatwa against Salman Rushdie) to a full-out acceptance and advocacy of secularism and of Enlightenment ideals. Hirsi Ali calls for a pluralist democracy where all opinion is protected but where the law does not—in the name of some pseudo-tolerance—permit genital mutilation, 'honor' killing, and forced marriage."

While the swell of anti-Muslim sentiment in Europe and America following the events of 9/11 is partly responsible for the immense popularity these personalities command, it is clear that they would never have been able to achieve this success without the formidable support of the conservative political industry in Europe and the United States. The arguments of these authors read like a blueprint for the neoconservative agenda for regime change in the Middle East. In this, the authors do not simply echo but amplify the neoconservative rhetoric, taking liberties and indulging in unchecked bigotry where an administration ideologue might falter.[15] Irshad Manji is a case in point. Her book *Trouble with Islam* is breathtaking in its amplification of neoconservative policies and arguments—all told in the voice of a purportedly self-critical and reformist Muslim woman who wants to bring her lost brethren to the correct path. While inflammatory hyperbole is characteristic of this genre, Manji takes particular pleasure in using language clearly aimed at injuring and offending Muslim sensibilities. Her text is littered with sentences that describe Muslims as "brain-dead," "narrow-minded," "incapable of thinking," "hypocritical," "desperately tribal," and "prone to victimology" (22, 30, 31). She brands Islam as more literalist, rigid, intolerant, totalitarian, anti-Semitic, and hateful of women and homosexuals than any other religion, and its rituals more prone to inculcating "mindless and habitual submission" to authority. Manji's denunciations of Islam and Muslims are matched by the unstinting praise she reserves for the "West," "Christianity," "Judaism," and "Israel." She finds the Western record unparalleled in human history for its tolerance, its "love of discovery," "openness to new ideas," and so on (18, 20, 204–18).

Like Hirsi Ali, Manji supported the U.S. invasion of Afghanistan and Iraq and subsequently the Israeli destruction of Lebanon in summer 2006—all in the name of cleansing the Muslim world of "Islamic fanatics and terrorists" ("Don't Be Fooled"). In her book, Manji, in Manichaean fashion, upholds Israelis as paragons of virtue, capable of self-criticism and tolerance, while Palestinians are condemned for inhabiting a culture of blame and victimhood.[16] (She goes so far as to say that Israel's discrimination against its Arab citizens is a form of "affirmative action" [112]). Manji has been promoted by the pro-Israel information lobby, the Middle East Media Research Institute (MEMRI),[17] and the infamous Daniel Pipes, who reviewed her book in glowing terms and with whom she has appeared at Israeli fundraising events.[18]

Despite the cozy relations Manji enjoys with such Likudite neoconservative luminaries and think tanks, it would be a mistake to underestimate the broad public presence she commands. Not only do her polemical op-eds appear in prominent international dailies, she is routinely invited to lecture at a wide range of liberal arts colleges and universities and asked to comment on political events of international import on major television and radio talk shows. Manji's website claims that *Ms.* magazine cites her as a

"Feminist for the 21st Century."[19] The inaccuracies and willful misrepresentations that pepper her publications and speeches are no impediment to her popularity; if anything, the opposite seems to be the case. Her reviewers often benignly overlook the factual errors and polemical oversimplifications that characterize Manji's work.[20] Consider, for example, Andrew Sullivan's review of her book. Sullivan has published op-ed pieces in the *New York Times* and is a former editor of the *New Republic*.[21] In an early review published in the *Times*, Sullivan writes:

> *The Trouble with Islam* is a memorable entrance. It isn't the most learned or scholarly treatise on the history or theology of Islam; its dabbling in geopolitics is haphazard and a little naïve; its rhetorical hyperbole can sometimes seem a mite attention-seeking. . . . But its spirit is undeniable, and long, long overdue. *Reading it feels like a revelation.* Manji, a Canadian journalist and television personality, does what so many of us have longed to see done: assail fundamentalist Islam itself for tolerating such evil in its midst. *And from within.* (emphasis added)

The last caveat is telling: Manji's identity as a Muslim lends particular force to the Orientalist and racist views she parrots, reaching audiences that ideologues such as Bernard Lewis and Daniel Pipes cannot. Apart from her vitriolic attacks on Islam, what makes Manji so valuable for someone like Sullivan is her "distinct tone of liberalism"—"a liberalism that," he writes, "seeks not to abolish faith but to establish a new relationship with it. If we survive this current war without unthinkable casualties, it will be because this kind of liberalism didn't lose its nerve. Think of Manji as a nerve ending for the West—shocking, raw, but mercifully, joyously, still alive." While later in this essay I will focus in some detail on the liberal imaginary undergirding this literature, here I want to draw attention to the providential role this imaginary is expected to play in the Muslim world. Not only is it supposed to be the harbinger of joy and mercy for Iraqis whose entire country has been destroyed by the U.S. military occupation, but it promises to reorchestrate every Muslim's relationship to his or her faith. The ambitious scope of this liberal agenda is breathtaking in that it is both political *and* religious in character, and as I will argue later, it is this particular combination of the religio-political that distinguishes the current moment of empire from America's traditional project of establishing its geopolitical hegemony in the non-Western world.

SELECTIVE OMISSIONS

In this section I want to focus on how elisions and inaccuracies, so characteristic of these accounts, have helped secure a monochromatic picture of Islam, one that fits neatly into the rhetoric of conquest and reform currently deployed by the Euro-American conservative and neoconservative establishment. I want to use Azar Nafisi's celebrated *Reading Lolita in Tehran* to make this point. Given the vast acclaim bestowed on this book, there is now a substantial body of critical scholarship on Nafisi's writing whose arguments I do not want to rehearse here.[22] My aim is more limited: I want to focus on how the description Nafisi provides of women's lives in postrevolutionary Iran can be complicated by a short recounting of recent developments in Iranian politics to yield a very different picture. Instead of her simplistic view of "gender apartheid," we get a more nuanced understanding of postrevolutionary Iranian politics, one that should lead secular feminists to rethink many of their assumptions about Islam, gender inequality, and political enfranchisement.

Nafisi's *Reading Lolita in Tehran*, with its literary pretensions and invocations of great "Western Classics," stands in contrast to Manji's and Hirsi Ali's books. Indeed, much of its appeal stems from the fact that it plays on Nabokov's subtle masterpiece *Lolita* in a manner that makes Nafisi's narrative palatable to sensibilities critical of the strident opportunism of the other texts. *Reading Lolita in Tehran* is a first-person account told from the point of view of an Iranian professor of English (Nafisi herself) who, after resigning from her post at an Iranian university out of frustration over clerical control of the curriculum, gathers several of her female students to teach them classics from Western literature in the privacy of her home. Nafisi uses these sessions as a means not only to denounce clerical political rule but also to express her visceral distaste for Iranian cultural life—both contemporary and historical. She paints a stultifying picture of life in postrevolutionary Iran, devoid of any beauty, color, inspiration, poetry, debate, discussion, and public argumentation. In this suffocating environment, it is only the Western literary canon that offers any hope of redemption in its irrepressible power to foment rebellion and critique and its intrinsic capacity to incite critical self-reflection.

Despite the difference in tone between Nafisi and authors like Hirsi Ali and Manji, the fundamental message her memoir communicates is not that different: Islamic societies are incapable of thought, reflection, and creativity, and their propensity to violence is most evident in their treatment of women. At one point in the memoir, Nafisi sweepingly declares that Iranian university students are only capable of obsequious sycophantic behavior toward their instructors because "from the first day they had set foot in the elementary school, they had been told to memorize. They had been told that their opinions counted for nothing" (220). Such declarations are coupled with gratuitous statements such as "it is a truth universally acknowledged that a Muslim man, regardless of his fortune, must be in want of a nine-year-old virgin wife" (257). The contempt that Nafisi reserves for Iranians and Muslims stands in sharp contrast to the utter adulation she reserves for the West: from its cultural accomplishments to its food, its language, its literature, its chocolates, and its films. As must be clear by now, this dual theme of abhorrence of everything Muslim and sheer exaltation of all things Western is a structural feature of this genre of writing.

For anyone who has even the most rudimentary knowledge of what has transpired in Iran in the last thirty years, this image of Iranian life is ruthless in its omissions. During this period, not only has Iranian clerical rule faced some of the toughest challenges from a broad-based reform movement in which women played a crucial role,[23] but Iranian universities have been at the center of this political transformation. This is in keeping with Iran's long history of student involvement in almost all protest movements of any significance in the modern period, including the overthrow of the Shah. One of the most interesting accomplishments of the last three decades is the establishment of a feminist press and a critical scriptural hermeneutics that is quite unique in the Muslim world.[24] During the same period about which Nafisi writes so disparagingly, Iran has produced an internationally acclaimed cinema, which is just as fiercely critical of various aspects of contemporary Iranian society as it is reflectively ponderous about the existential meaning of modern life itself. None of this has been easy or without cost for those who have struggled against the absolutist impetus internal to the clerical establishment in charge of the Iranian state apparatus. But it is important to note that dissent has come not only from secular leftists and liberals but from the clerics themselves, many of whom had supported the revolution at its inception but later became the most trenchant critics of the establishment's corruption and totalitarian control.[25] Social and political critique, in other words, has been a deeply integral aspect of postrevolutionary Iranian life.

All this and more is completely erased in Nafisi's life-quenching portrayal of Iran. Instead, the narrative reproduces the presumptions of its audience, convinced by the feat of its own ignorance, that Iran is nothing but a site of religious zeal, hatred of women, and totalitarianism. It is in this respect that *Reading Lolita in Tehran* fits the Orientalist paradigm most faithfully: it reproduces and confirms the impressions of its Western audience, offering no surprises or challenges to what they think they already know about Iran and its rich cultural and political history. Like Delacroix's famous painting *Women of Algiers*, Nafisi's memoir only embellishes the tapestry of anecdotal prejudicial impressions that the spectator brings to her reading of the object at hand.[26] One cannot help but wonder how Nafisi's book would have done had it surprised its readers with social facts that do not neatly fit her readers' structure of expectations, such as the fact that the literacy rate for women shot up dramatically under Islamic rule from 35.5 percent in 1976 to 74.2 percent in 1996, or that over 60 percent of Iranian students in higher education are women, or that postrevolutionary Iran has had more women representatives elected to the parliament than the U.S. Congress? (Bahramitash 235).[27] In addition, the population growth rate in Iran declined from 3.2 percent in 1980 to 1.2 in 2001 as a result of one of the most effective family planning and public health initiatives launched in recent history.[28] How would one reconcile such statistics with the rule of Islamic clerics, who Westerners know with absolute certainty cage and abuse women within the confines of their incestuous homes? If indeed Iranian women have been able to achieve this kind of political and material enfranchisement under conditions of Islamic clerical rule, then how does this complicate the rather simple diagnosis that Islamic rule is always and already oppressive of women?

Nafisi's book had already gained considerable popularity when Iran was declared to be part of the "axis of evil" by President Bush and neoconservative plans to attack were made public.[29] It is hard not to read Nafisi as providing the cultural rationale for such plans, particularly given the praise extended to her by the neoconservative establishment. Bernard Lewis, the Orientalist ideologue of the current U.S. imperial adventure in the Middle East, calls the memoir "a masterpiece," and Nafisi was given a prestigious position at the Johns Hopkins School of Advanced International Studies, where her friend Fouad Ajami, another prominent conservative ideologue, directs the Middle East program. The fact that Nafisi was awarded such a position, even though she had no substantial publishing record or a comparable position at a similar institution, attests to the considerable service she has performed for the scions of the U.S. empire.

Political patronage aside, Nafisi has also been promoted as a cultural icon by corporations eager to showcase their socially responsible side. The manufacturer of the luxury car Audi, for example, promoted Azar Nafisi (along with media figures like David Bowie and the actor William H. Macy) as part of "Audi of America's 'Never Follow' Campaign" to sell the brand to affluent and educated potential buyers. Nafisi has appeared in Audi advertisements for magazines as diverse as *Vanity Fair, Wired, Golf Digest,* the *New Yorker,* and *Vogue* (see Salamon). Insomuch as automobile advertisements sell not simply cars but also forms of social identity, Audi's promotion of Nafisi shows the extent to which a genuine concern for Muslim women's welfare has been evacuated of critical content, whittled down to a commodified token of elite chic. The project of "Saving Muslim Women" is reminiscent these days of the "Save the Whale" campaign: while the latter might have contributed to the well-being of the species the campaign sought to protect, the former, I fear, might well obliterate the very object it champions.

Indeed, this is a conclusion that echoes Hamid Dabashi's assessment in his devastating review of *Reading Lolita in Tehran.* Apart from the political service the text renders, Dabashi criticizes the book cover for the "iconic burglary" it performs. The cover of the book shows two young veiled women eagerly pouring over a text that the reader infers to be *Lolita* "in Tehran." Dabashi shows that this is a cropped version of an original photograph that portrayed two young students reading a leading oppositional newspaper reporting on the election of the reformist candidate Khatami, whose success was widely attributed to votes cast by Iranian women and youth. In censoring the photograph and denuding it of its historical context, Dabashi argues that the book strips these young women "of their moral intelligence and their participation in the democratic aspirations of their homeland, reducing them into a colonial harem." For Dabashi, insomuch as the book cover places the veiled teenage women within the context of Nabokov's celebrated novel about pedophilia, it reenacts an old Orientalist fantasy about the incestuous character of the East, simultaneously repulsive and tantalizing in its essence. It is hard to escape the conclusion that the women whose suffering Nafisi sets out to capture must be obliterated in their particularity, both narratively and iconically, so that they can be reenshrined as the "caged virgins" of Islam's violence. The fact that Nafisi's book has drawn accolades from feminist writers such as Susan Sontag and Margaret Atwood is disquieting in that even vocal critics of the conservatism now sweeping Europe and America remain blind to the dangerous omissions texts such as Nafisi's embody and to the larger political projects they facilitate.[30] It is crucial that feminist writers and cultural critics learn to read such texts more critically, a reading that must ground itself in a familiarity with the complexities and ambiguities that attend even the much-spurned Iranian clerical regime and the politics of dissent it has spawned.

BUT WHAT ABOUT ISLAM'S ABUSE OF WOMEN?

The reader might object at this point that even though accounts of Muslim women's suffering have been opportunistically used to serve a political agenda, is it not the case that Islamic societies exhibit a forbidding record of misogynist practices directed against women, such as "honor killings," stoning women to death for committing adultery, oppressive sexual mores, sex segregation, and so on? How can anyone concerned about women's well-being not criticize and condemn such unspeakable atrocities? By way of an answer, let me begin by stating categorically that I fully acknowledge that women in Muslim societies suffer from inequitable treatment: they are disproportionately subjected to discriminatory acts of violence; many Islamic edicts and practices uphold gender inequality; and women are often held responsible for breaking what are considered to be protocols of proper gendered behavior. Any feminist concerned with improving Muslim women's lot, however, must begin not simply with the scorecard of Islam's abuses but the terms through which an act of violence is registered as worthy of protest, for whom, under what conditions, and toward what end.

In this essay, I have drawn attention to the manner in which Muslim women's suffering is currently being mobilized within disparate fields of argument so as to justify interventions and political projects that have little or nothing to do with the well-being of the women in question. This double-edged use of Islam's abuses, I fear, can only serve to further the violence committed against Muslim women, rather than be a safeguard against it. As colonial and postcolonial history makes evident, attempts to impose "women's freedom" from above have often produced spectacular socio-political disasters. This was true in the Caucasus under the agency of Soviet rule, in Iran and Turkey under autocratic indigenous rule, and in India and Egypt under the auspices of colonial law.[31] A more recent example is Afghanistan, when, once again, feminists and nonfeminists alike cheered the U.S. invasion so as to liberate the "burka-clad" Afghani women from Taliban rule. In the aftermath of the war, as many observers have noted, it is not Afghani women but the warlords and drug and arms dealers who have benefited from the ensuing condition of lawlessness, chaos, misman-agement, and starvation.[32]

Let me flesh these points out by considering the much-publicized issue of "honor killing," a widely condemned practice that received international media attention even prior to the events of 9/11 but has since surfaced more dramatically in the genre of literature I discuss here. "Honor killing" is gen-erally understood to be an "Islamic practice" in which women suspected of engaging in illicit sexual behavior are murdered by male family mem-bers. This practice might be compared to acts of man-on-woman homicide common to many Western societies. Consider, for example, the following comparable statistics: various reports show that in a country of 140 million people, almost 1,000 women are killed per year in Pakistan (which, along with Jordan, has one of the highest recorded instances of "honor killings").[33] The Family Violence Prevention Project, on the other hand, reports that approximately 1,500 women are killed every year by their spouses or boy-friends in what are called "crimes of passion" in the United States, which has a population of 280 million (slightly more than three women are murdered by their boyfriends or husbands every day in the United States).[34] Despite these parallel statistics, discussions of "honor killings" are seldom analyzed within a comparative context. Instead, most discussions construct "honor killing" as symptomatic of "Islamic culture" (note the elision between re-ligion and culture in this formulation), while acts of man-on-woman ho-micide in the United States are presented as acts of either individualized pathology or excessive passion. In this logic, American men are represented as acting out of jealousy (a "natural" emotion) against their sexual rivals (albeit swept away by its force), while Muslim men are understood to be compelled by "their culture," irrationally and blindly acting out its misogy-nist customs and traditions. An individualized account of domestic violence in the West is secured, in other words, against a tautological account of "Islamic culture." Once this premise is conceded, then it follows that an appropriate strategy for combating this form of violence in the West is to transform individual behavior, whereas in Muslim societies one would need to reform, if not eradicate, "Islamic culture."[35] Such a polemical ac-count, in its drive to quantify sexism (West equals less; Islam equals more), fails to realize that both forms of violence are equally cultural as they are gendered, each depending upon distinct valuations of women's subordination, sexuality, kinship relations, and various forms of male violence. Any opposition to these different (if comparable) acts of male violence requires a precise and grounded understanding of the social relations and cultural grammar that give meaning and substance to such acts.

The point I am making here is rather simple and straightforward: no discursive object occupies a simple relation to the reality it purportedly denotes. Rather, representations of facts, objects, and events are profoundly mediated by the fields of power in which they circulate and through which they acquire their precise shape and form. Consequently, contemporary concern for Muslim women is paradoxically linked with and deeply informed by the civilizational discourse through which the encounter between Euro-America and Islam is being framed right now. Feminist contributions to the vilification of Islam do no service either to Muslim women or to the cause of gender justice. Instead they reinscribe the cultural and civilizational divide that has become the bedrock not only of neoconservative politics but of liberal politics as well in this tragic moment in history.

The pernicious nature of "culture and religion" as an explanatory paradigm for misogynist and sexist practices has been criticized and exposed by a variety of postcolonial feminists, and its reemergence in the current moment of civilizational war between "Islam and the West" alerts us that its utility is far from exhausted. The labor that the trope of "honor killing" has been made to perform in the post-9/11 imaginary might be grasped through a brief examination of the dramatic rise and fall of Norma Khouri—a self-described native of Jordan—who penned one of the more extravagant accounts published recently on the topic, provocatively titled *Forbidden Love: A Harrowing Story of Love and Revenge in Jordan*.[36] Widely described as a "tale of grief, passion, and rage," the book is an eyewitness account of a friend's murder by her kin for being romantically involved with a Christian man and of the author's own persecution under the putative "brutal desert code of behavior" (Mydans). Soon after its publication, the book became a nonfiction bestseller in a number of countries, including Australia, where the author was given asylum from "gender persecution."[37] Khouri's escalating stardom, however, came to a dramatic halt when an investigative reporter revealed that she had fabricated various parts of her story, including her claim that she had lived in Jordan and experienced the violence she described in her book and public appearances so movingly.[38] Notably, long before these revelations became public, the National Commission for Women in Jordan (one of the leading organizations involved in fighting the practice of "honor killing") had warned Khouri's publishers, Random House and Simon and Schuster, that her book had more than seventy factual errors, warnings the publishers refused to investigate, choosing to "stand by their author" (Kremmer). Following concerns about the lack of oversight in vetting publications on the topic of Islam, the publishing director of Harper Collins acknowledged that standards were indeed lax, given the "global post-September 11 demand for non-fiction, particularly books which perpetuate negative stereotypes about Islamic men" (Legge).[39] Not surprisingly, like other authors of this genre of nonfiction, it was reported that Khouri had also been a beneficiary of considerable diplomatic and political support from the highest offices of the Bush administration. Vice-President Richard Cheney's daughter Elizabeth Cheney, for example, had endorsed and supported the publication of *Forbidden Love* in her capacity as deputy assistant secretary of state in charge of the Middle East Partnership Initiative, a $100 million fund that promotes political and educational reforms in the region.[40] There were also reports that Cheney himself had written a letter of recommendation to the Australian government to support Khouri's application for a resident visa.[41]

Despite the amassing of social facts about Khouri's imposture, a consensus soon emerged among the commentators that the true power of her book lay not in its personal or individual narrative but in the larger truth it captured about Islam's unparalleled record of the subjugation of women. The factuality of Khouri's account came increasingly to be seen as incidental to the larger reality that the book documents, a reality whose truth the Western world already knows. This is similar to the favorable reaction Hirsi Ali continues to elicit despite the discovery that she, too, lied about her personal suffering at the hands of Islamic customs. The regnant assumption undergirding such a consensus is that insomuch as Islam's victims are not individuals but entire collectivities, its essential brutality cannot be falsified because it transcends the (merely) empirical register.[42] In scouring the public debate surrounding this publishing scandal, I was struck by the lack of analysis about the wider political and cultural role texts like Khouri's have come to play for the Euro-American audience and their feeding of the insatiable desire for ever more harrowing tales of Islam's atrocities.

Given Khouri's success, it is important to point out that her book, and others like hers, are not simply expressions of the reigning consensus about

Islam's mistreatment of women but also a crucial means of producing this consensus in a post-9/11 world. This consensus about Islam's unparalleled misogyny—its inherent fundamentalism—is secured through an equally reductionist representation of "the West" as the space of ever-increasing possibilities and liberation for women. It is hard to escape the conclusion echoed by Wendy Brown, in her recent book on the liberal discourse of tolerance, that "we *need* fundamentalism, indeed, we project and produce it elsewhere, to represent ourselves as free" (*Regulating* 189). What would it mean to place accounts of "honor killings" against equally reprehensible incidents of "crimes of passion" to rethink constitutive assumptions about how male violence is ascribed distinct kinds of meanings, sustained and re-produced under different regimes of gender inequality? What sorts of femi-nist projects and alliances would be animated and strengthened through an engagement with the particularity of difference—rather than the superior-ity of difference? How might such an alliance yield a critical perspective on the current and past imperial ambitions of Euro-American power?

WOMEN, DEMOCRACY, AND FREEDOM

In these last two sections, I want to examine the work that the rhetoric of democracy and freedom has come to perform in the "war on terror," with particular attention to the secularity of this rhetoric and its constitutive as-sumptions. As is evident from even the most cursory reading of the media, progressive and conservative strategists agree these days that one of the most compelling strategies for eliminating Islamic fundamentalism consists in empowering Muslim women by educating them and giving them access to economic resources and political representation. The logic underlying this project is rather simple. In the words of the *New York Times* reporter Barbara Crossette: "When women's influence increases . . . it strengthens the moderate center, bolstering economic stability and democratic order" (4). The conventional wisdom seems to be that insomuch as feminism is "the opposite of fundamentalism,"[43] and fundamentalists are supposed to hate democracy, it follows that empowering women will further the cause of feminism, which in turn will help eliminate Islamic fundamentalism.

Apart from the more complicated fact that a number of Islamist move-ments—those pejoratively referred to as fundamentalist in the literature I cite here—seek to broaden the scope of political debate in the Muslim world rather than narrow it,[44] I want to question the facile equation made between democracy and women's socioeconomic status, the idea that promoting the latter will automatically lead to the former. This equation is easily put to the test if we look at the conditions under which women lived in Iraq prior to the first U.S. war on Iraq in 1990. Despite the fact that Iraq was not a democracy under Saddam Hussein, Iraqi women enjoyed one of the highest rates of literacy in the third world and were widely represented in various professions, including the army and public office. At the height of Iraq's economic boom, Saddam Hussein implemented a series of policies to attract women to the workforce by providing them incentives such as generous maternity leaves, equal pay and benefits, and free higher education.[45] In this important sense, Iraq was no different than a number of socialist countries (such as Cuba, the former Soviet Union, and Eastern Europe), where the lack of liberal democracy did not translate into the marginalization of women from the socioeconomic and political life of these countries.

Iraqi women's condition declined after the Iran-Iraq war (1980–88), but suffered the most serious setback after the first Gulf War (1990–91) and the subsequent economic sanctions imposed by the United States in cooperation with the United Nations and its European allies. Female literacy dropped sharply after the Gulf War, and Iraqi women's access to education, transportation, and employment became increasingly difficult. The current U.S. occupation of Iraq is the most recent chapter in twelve years of debilitating sanctions that directly contributed to the most dramatic decline in Iraqi women's living conditions. Needless to say, in the current situation of violence, chaos, and economic stasis, women (along with children, the elderly, and the disabled) are the most vulnerable victims of this disorder, and they are not likely to experience even a modicum of social order in the foreseeable future. Not only has Iraqi women's dramatic loss of "life and liberty" failed to arouse the same furor among most Euro-Americans as have individualized accounts of women's suffering under Islam's tutelage but a number of political pundits now suggest that perhaps the promotion of electoral democracy in the Middle East is not a good idea after all since it might bring Islamist political parties to power (as indeed was the case in the 2005 elections held in Palestine and Egypt).[46] Apart from the fact that these commentators find Islamist ascendance to political power inimical to American strategic interests, the fate of women under Islamic regimes is often marshaled as the ultimate reason for thwarting Islamist success at the polls. Note here once again the neat equivalence drawn between Euro-

American strategic interests and women's well-being, between democracy (narrowly defined in electoral terms) and women's status.

One heart-wrenching appeal for instituting democracy by legislating women's freedom was made by Barbara Ehrenreich in an op-ed piece written for the *New York Times* in the lead-up to the 2004 American elections. In this piece, Ehrenreich held up Carmen bin Laden's memoir *Inside the Kingdom* as the manifesto that all Democrats should embrace in their policy toward the Muslim world. As I mentioned earlier, *Inside the Kingdom* is Carmen bin Laden's account of her luxurious life both in Switzerland, where she was raised and currently resides, and in Saudi Arabia, where she lived as the sole wife of one of the rich scions of the bin Laden family for several years. Apart from the few titillating details Carmen bin Laden throws in about the fanatical behavior of her better-known brother-in-law Osama, much of the book lists the claustrophobic character of her life in Saudi Arabia, one punctuated by extended luxurious vacations in Europe, palatial houses with an army of servants, and lavish parties. Carmen, much like the authors I mentioned earlier, brims with her adulation for the West, its lifestyle, and its "opportunities."[47] Carmen's zeal for a Western lifestyle is matched only by her sneering and derogatory portrayal of Saudi women. She describes these women as bovine creatures who have gaudy tastes, lack bourgeois housekeeping skills (they buy gold furniture and decorate their houses with plastic flowers), and are wily with men. At one point she says,

> I was living in a society where women were nothing and *wanted to be nothing.* They didn't seem to seek the changes that I was expecting and longing for, and I felt frustrated, surrounded by women who didn't have the will or courage to resist. They had intelligence and energy . . . but they expressed it only in religion. They lived, but only for their faith; their personalities were completely annihilated. (105; emphasis added)[48]

For bin Laden, these women she could not stand for their religiosity and passivity were doomed to a herd mentality by the straitjacket of their cultural traditions: "You never develop as an individual in the Middle East. People may manage to escape their tradition for a short while, but those rules catch up to them" (16).

It is this account that inspired Barbara Ehrenreich's plea to the Democratic Party presidential candidate John Kerry to make gender parity a cornerstone of his foreign policy in the Middle East, because the real enemy, she opined, is not terrorism, but an "extremist Islamic insurgency whose appeal lies in its claim to represent the Muslim masses against a bullying superpower." Ehrenreich goes on to argue, "But as Carmen bin Laden urgently reminds us in *Inside the Kingdom,* one glaring moral flaw in this insurgency, quite apart from its methods, is that it aims to push one-half of those masses down to a status only slightly above that of domestic animals. While Osama was getting pumped up for jihad, Carmen was getting up her nerve to walk across the street in a residential neighborhood in Jeddah— fully veiled but unescorted by a male, something that is illegal for a woman in Saudi Arabia" (19). There are two misconceptions worthy of attention here. One, not only is the "Islamic insurgency" quite distinct from the Saudi regime but the Saudi monarchs, in collusion with the United States government, strongly oppose most popular Islamist political parties in the Middle East (including the Muslim Brotherhood in Egypt, Hamas in Palestine, and Hezbollah in Lebanon). Two, Ehrenreich reiterates a common but erroneous assumption that Islamic movements are a patriarchal plot whose primary aim is to rein in women's modern freedoms. As a number of studies have shown in the last fifteen years, however, Islamic movements have strong support among women, who are the backbone of the welfare work undertaken by these movements.[49] Far from curtailing their freedoms, these movements are the vehicles for women's participation in the sociopolitical life of their societies.

Not only does Ehrenreich misrecognize the source of women's oppression in Muslim societies by positing "Islamic insurgency" as the culprit, but in doing so she ignores the more systematic and pervasive causes of women's oppression in different parts of the Muslim world (such as poverty and war in Afghanistan, the cultural and political tyranny of the U.S.-backed Saudi monarchy in Saudi Arabia, and the political and economic breakdown in Iraq engendered by the U.S. invasion). A second flaw in Ehrenreich's argument is that it fails to account for the complicated social shifts, challenges, and political transformations produced by Islamic movements that do not fit the simplistic logic of patriarchal subordination and authoritarian politics. It is precisely such misrecognition that enables the imperialistic turn that Ehrenreich's argument then takes: having reduced the "Islamic insurgency" to a patriarchal plot, she goes on to insist that the best way to combat this misbegotten movement is for the U.S. government to empower Muslim women, offering increased support for their education (provided it is secular), giving asylum to women fleeing "gender totalitari-

anism," and restoring U.S. aid for the United Nations family planning program. She qualifies her recommendations by saying,

> I am not expecting these measures alone to incite a feminist insur-
> gency within the Islamist one. Carmen bin Laden found her rich Saudi
> sisters-in-law sunk in bovine passivity, and some of the more spirited
> young women in the Muslim world have been adopting the headscarf
> as a gesture of defiance toward American imperialism. We're going
> to need a through [sic] foreign policy makeover—from Afghanistan to
> Israel—before we have the credibility to stand up for anyone's human
> rights. You can't play the gender card with dirty hands. (19)

In conclusion she states, "If you want to beat Osama, you've got to start
by listening to Carmen." In this oversimplified logic—religion is to men
as freedom is to women, patriarchy is to men as economic change is to
women—there is a failure to understand Muslim women's support for Islamic movements as anything other than false consciousness that can be
overcome only through a secular education.

The fact that Carmen bin Laden's model of white elite bourgeois femininity is the symbol of this vision of "democracy" should alert us to its imperialist underpinnings. Callous and unrelenting in the modes of sociability
and subjectivities it seeks to remake, this vision ridicules and scorns women
whose desires and goals do not fit the telos of a liberal lifestyle. The veil, in
Ehrenreich's argument, particularly when worn willingly, is nothing but a
sign of the misguided judgment practiced by women besotted with the false
promises of a hopelessly patriarchal insurgency. It is precisely because Ehrenreich is so sure that this insurgency is not in the best interests of women
that she is led to conclude that it is up to the United States (better led by the
Democrats than Republicans) to free these enslaved souls. As I have written elsewhere, the violence of such a prescriptive vision lies in its inability
to apprehend, much less appreciate, lifestyles, projects, and forms of social
and political enfranchisement that depart from its rather narrow and parochial understanding of women's freedom.[50] The fact that orthodox Islamic
mores (such as donning the veil or the pursuit of piety) and Islamic political
action might enable forms of human flourishing remains incomprehensible
to feminists like Ehrenreich, certain as they are that their way of life offers
the best model for social and political realization for much of humanity.[51]

This missionary zeal to remake "cultures and civilizations" has strong
resonances with colonial projects of the nineteenth century and the early

twentieth, when European powers, also outraged by what they took to be Islam's degradation of women, undertook cultural and educational reform to civilize the local population. British regulation and policing of practices of widow sacrifice (*sati*) in India and feminine genital cutting in Sudan, symbolic of the colonized cultures' barbaric treatment of its women, seldom benefited those whom they were supposed to save. As Mani has noted, indigenous women were neither the objects nor the subjects of these reforms; rather, they were the ground on which European and national battles were fought for competing visions of empire and modernity.[52] It seems as if feminists like Ehrenreich and the audience to whom they speak have learned little from this history; or perhaps the impulse to reform is so well entrenched within certain forms of feminism that its realization requires the project of destruction and remaking no matter what its human and cultural cost.

SECULARISM AND EMPIRE

Calls for secularizing and liberalizing Islam so that Muslims may be taught to live a more enlightened existence are issued from a variety of quarters these days, left and right alike. These calls strike a chord with secular feminists (from a variety of political perspectives), who have long been convinced that religion is a source of women's oppression. While critical of neoconservative militaristic belligerence, many liberal feminists support a broad-based strategy of slow *progressive* transformation, one in which, as Katha Pollitt puts it, "organized religion [is made to] wither away or at any rate modulate away from dogma and authority and reaction toward a kind of vague, kindly, nondenominational spiritual uplift whose politics if it had any, would be liberal" (ix). This seemingly benign vision encodes a secular conception of religiosity in which religion is treated as a private system of beliefs in a set of propositional statements to which an individual gives assent. Secularism, often reduced to its doctrinal principle (the separation of religion and state), operates here as a sociocultural project, authorizing a privatized form of religious subjectivity that owes its allegiance to the sovereign state (rather than traditional religious authority). Importantly, the autonomous individual is the protagonist animating this secular liberal model of religiosity, a self-choosing subject who might appreciate the spiritual truths religious traditions symbolize but is enlightened enough to understand that these truths command no epistemological or political force in this world. These aspects of secular culture, now often noted under the rubric of secularity, are propagated not only through the agency of the state but through a variety of social actors and organizations that might well be critical of various policies and prerogatives of the state.[53]

This secular conception of religiosity (echoed in Katha Pollitt's quote above) embeds a number of presuppositions about autonomy and freedom that resonate with liberal feminist thought. The most obvious is the powerful trope of the autonomous individual—capable of enacting her own desires free from the force of transcendental will, tradition, or custom—that continues to animate many strains of feminism despite trenchant philosophical and anthropological critiques of such a limited conception of the subject.[54] A second assumption central to this secularized conception of religiosity is the understanding that a religion's phenomenal forms—its liturgies, rituals, and scriptures—are inessential to the universal truth it symbolizes. The precise form scripture and ritualized practices take, in other words, is regarded as inconsequential to the spirituality (immaterial and transcendental) for which they are made to stand in.

This secularized conception of ritual behavior makes it difficult for most secular feminists to entertain the claim made by many Muslim women that the veil is a doctrinal command. Women who contend that the veil is part of a religious duty, a divine edict, or a form of ethical practice are usually judged to be victims of false consciousness, mired in a traditionalism that leads them to mistakenly internalize the opinions of misogynist jurists whose pronouncements they should resist.[55] The veil—reduced either to its symbolic significance (a symbol of Muslim identity or women's oppression) or its functional utility (the veil protects women from sexual harassment)— is seldom entertained as an expression of and a means to a Muslim woman's submission to God's will, despite repeated evidence that for many veiled women this understanding is central.[56] To take such a claim seriously would require stepping out of the simple opposition liberalism constructs between freedom and submission, and instead exploring the forms of submission internal to a particular construction of freedom and the system of gender inequality in which such a construction resides. Sadly, this is not the direction in which Euro-American public debate is headed (evident in the French ban on the veil and the attempts in other countries to follow suit). Instead, contemporary calls for reforming Islam are built upon a narrow vision of a secularized conception of religiosity that mobilizes many of the liberal assumptions about what it means to be human in this world.

The problem of this prescriptive vision of secularized religiosity lies in its singularity and certitude that brooks no argument and makes no adjustments to different ways of living religiously and politically. It is the telos of a liberal democratic Protestant society—whose ethos is condensed in the cosmopolitan sensibilities and pleasures of its enlightened citizenry—that is posited as the Mecca toward which all Muslims should conscientiously head. Apart from the infeasibility and singularity of this vision, what strikes me as imperialistic is the chain of equivalences upon which such a vision rests. It is not simply Islamic militants who are the object of this unrelenting prescription but all those Muslims who follow what are considered to be nonliberal, orthodox, and conservative interpretations of Islam, key among them the wearing of the veil, the strict adherence to rituals of Islamic observance, the avoidance of the free mixing of the sexes, and the adjudication of public and political issues through religious argumentation. Inasmuch as the appellation of fundamentalism has now come to enfold within itself not simply Islamic militants but also those who embrace this range of practices, calls for the liberalization of Islam are aimed at the transformation of these Muslims, making their lifestyles provisional if not extinct through a process of gradual but incessant reform.

As I have shown elsewhere, the prescriptive force of this liberal project is not simply rhetorical ("Secularism"). It enjoys the support of the U.S. State Department, which recently allocated over $1.3 billion under an initiative titled "Muslim World Outreach" to transform the hearts and minds of Muslims through a range of theological, cultural, and pedagogical programs. Part of a broader strategy of the White House National Security Council, this initiative is engaged in training Islamic preachers, establishing Islamic schools that propagate liberal interpretations of Islam, reforming public school curriculums, and media production (which includes establishing radio and satellite television stations, producing and distributing Islamic talk shows, and generally shaping the content of public religious debate within the existing media in Muslim countries). What is notable about this broad-based multipronged strategy is that it is not the militants but ordinary "traditional" Muslims who are the targets of this reform in that they are seen as woefully lacking in the kind of secular sensibility required of modern subjects.[57] This project bears obvious similarities to the State Department's cold war strategy with one exception: the current campaign has an overt theological agenda that abrogates the same secular liberal principle—the right to religion and freedom of conscience—that the U.S. is supposed to be fostering among Muslims through this campaign.[58]

Furthermore, it is not clear to me that inculcating a liberal religious sensibility among Muslims is necessarily going to decrease militant attacks on the United States or other Western European powers. This is not because all Muslims are violent, but because the grievances they hold against the West have more to do with geopolitical inequalities of power and privilege. Even Osama bin Laden was clear in his message at the time of the World Trade Center attacks: he wanted American troops out of Saudi Arabia, a just solution to the Palestinian-Israeli conflict, and an end to Euro-American domination of Muslim resources and lands. His ends, if not his means, speak to a wide range of Arabs and Muslims who are currently witnessing one of the most unabashedly imperial projects undertaken in modern history, a project that, as a number of observers have pointed out, has done more to fuel the militant cause than to eliminate it.[59]

The Muslim World Outreach program seeks to build alliances and networks with what it calls "moderate" Muslim scholars who promote a liberal interpretation of Islam and who largely echo the programmatic vision championed by the U.S. State Department through this initiative. The fact that calls for liberalizing Islam are now increasingly made by a range of prominent Muslim intellectuals—such as Khaled Abul Fadl, Nasr Hamed Abu Zeid, Abdolkarim Soroush, Hasan Hanafi—is testimony to the hegemony that liberalism commands as a political ideal for many contemporary Muslims, a hegemony that reflects, I would submit, the enormous disparity in power between Euro-American and Muslim countries today. In their reflections, it is Islam that bears the burden of proving its compatibility with liberal ideals, and the line of question is almost never reversed. They do not ask, for example, what it would mean to take the orthodox practices of Islam, embraced by many in the Muslim world right now, and rethink some of the secular liberal values that are so readily upheld today—such as freedom of choice, autonomy, and indifference to religious forms of belonging. What would such a dialogue look like? How would such a conversation change our world-making projects?

As a number of critics of liberalism have pointed out, it is a characteristic of liberal thought—which, we must remind ourselves, cuts across conservative and radical projects—to assimilate unfamiliar forms of life within its own projection into the future, a future that is defined by the unfolding of the liberal vision itself. All life forms that do not accord with this futurity are to be subsumed within a teleological process of improvement and are destined to become either extinct or provisional. This attitude toward difference not only seems to animate calls for Islamic reformation but is also operative in contemporary strands of feminism—particularly in its certainty that women's sensibilities and attachments, those that seem so paradoxically inimical to what are taken to be women's own interests, *must* be refashioned for their own well-being. It is this arrogant certitude that I want to question here: Does the confidence of our political vision as feminists ever run up against the responsibility that we incur for the destruction of life forms so that "unenlightened" women may be taught to live more freely? Do we fully comprehend the forms of life that we want so passionately to remake so that Muslim women and men may live a more enlightened existence? Can we entertain the possibility that practices like the veil might perform something in the world other than the oppression and/or freedom of women? Have we lost the capacity to be able to hear the voices of Muslim women that do not come packaged in the form of Ayaan Hirsi Ali, Azar Nafisi, and Irshad Manji? Would an intimate knowledge of life worlds that are distinct from, and perhaps even opposed to, our cosmopolitan lifestyles ever lead us to question the certainty with which we prescribe what is good for all of humanity? At a time when feminist and democratic politics run the danger of being reduced to a rhetorical display of the placard of Islam's abuses, these questions offer the slim hope that perhaps a dialogue across political and religious differences—even incommensurable ones—can yield a vision of coexistence that does not require making certain life worlds extinct or provisional. It requires us to entertain the possibility, perhaps too much to ask in the current imperial climate, that one does not always know *what* one opposes and that a political vision at times has to admit its own finitude in order to even comprehend what it has sought to oppose.

NOTES

This essay would have been impossible to write without the assiduous research assistance of Noah Salomon, Michael Allan, and Stacey May. I am thankful not only for their help in locating the materials but also for keeping me abreast of the enormous popularity this genre of literature enjoys in various public forums. My thanks to Jane Collier, Charles Hirschkind, and Joan Scott for their critical comments, and to Mayanthi Fernando for introducing me to the French examples in this genre. I presented this essay at the Center for Middle East Studies at the University of California, Berkeley, and to the faculty resident group at the University of California Humanities Research Institute in spring 2006. I am grateful to the audiences at both these forums for their suggestions and comments.

1. A small sample of this vast scholarship includes Alloula, *The Colonial Harem;* Ahmed, *Women and Gender in Islam;* Lazreg, *The Eloquence of Silence;* Mani, *Contentious Traditions;* and Spivak, *In Other Worlds.*

2. This is not to deny that there are traditions of feminist thought that have been critical of the imperial impulse internal to liberalism. My own engagement here is in fact enabled by and deeply indebted to this tradition. I use the term "liberal feminism" in this essay to designate those currents within feminism where the connections between a certain analysis of gender inequality and the politics of empire are most dense and pervasive. For a further exposition of this critique of liberal feminism, see Mahmood, *Politics of Piety,* esp. ch. 1.

3. On Azar Nafisi, see, for example, Atwood; and Sontag at http://www .randomhouse.com/acmart/catalog/; on Carmen bin Laden, see Ehrenreich. Irshad Manji and Hirsi Ali have been hosted, among others, by a number of women's and gender studies programs across American campuses. See, for example, http://www.roosevelt.edu/misj/pdfs/Irshad.pdf (visited 9 March 2007) and http:// www.wmst.unt.edu/article.htm (visited 9 March 2007).

4. See, for example, the contributions of a number of academic and nonacademic feminists—such as Janet Afary, Seyla Benhabib, Barbara Ehrenreich, Valentine Moghadam, Martha Nussbaum, and Katha Pollitt—to *Nothing Sacred,* edited by Betsy Reed.

5. Manji is currently a visiting fellow at Yale University with the International Security Studies program.

6. In addition to the books I mention, there are countless others either already published or in press. New memoirs, snatched up by well-established publishing houses, are given early publicity by carefully placed prepublication reviews such as Joseph Berger's "Muslim Woman's Critique of Custom."

7. Amara is the cofounder of a feminist organization with the same title as the book, whose ostensible goal is to fight conservative social and religious mores affecting Muslim women who live in the poor suburbs of France. Critics of this organization claim that it has done more damage than good to the Muslim women it purports to support by taking attention away from the socioeconomic and political conditions that are responsible for the violence in poor French neighborhoods, and instead blaming it on an essentialized notion of Islam and Islamic culture. *Ni putes ni soumises* has found many supporters among the dominant white population and the French government, these critics point out, precisely because the organization confirms their prejudices, absolving the larger French

society of the role it has played in the ghettoization of the Muslim community in France.

8. Djavann, for example, declared that the act of veiling was akin to rape and made the dubious claim that only women who had chosen to discard the veil had the right to speak about the issue.

9. Leila's *Mariée de force,* originally published by OH! Editions in 2004, was published by a more prestigious house called "J'ai Lu" in 2005.

10. Given this resonance between anti-Semitic tropes and Islamophobia, it is ironic that it is European Muslims who are now held responsible for a "new anti-Semitism"—a move that not only exonerates contemporary French society but also European history for having invented and perfected the practice.

11. See Kuper; and Hirsi Ali 152–53.

12. Hirsi Ali gained further notoriety for her collaboration on a short film by Theo van Gogh entitled *Submission,* for which he was brutally murdered by a Dutch man of Moroccan origin. The film portrays the ritual torture of a Muslim woman by the men of her family, an act supposedly condoned by the Quranic verses that cascade across her nude and abused body. For an incisive analysis of this film and Ayaan Hirsi Ali's position within Dutch politics, see Moors.

13. For a critical review of *The Caged Virgin,* see Alam.

14. For a review of Hirsi Ali's new book *Infidel,* see "Dark Secrets."

15. These authors are able to take these liberties because they claim to "speak from within." Hirsi Ali echoes the French Iranian dissident Djavann I mentioned earlier when she says, "You are shocked to hear me say these things, but like the majority of the native Dutch population, you overlook something: you forget where I am from. *I used to be a Muslim; I know what I am talking about"* (qtd. in Lalami; emphasis added).

16. For a more recent expression of her uncritical support for Israeli atrocities committed against the Palestinians, see Manji, "How I Learned."

17. Middle East Media Research Institute (MEMRI) is a nonprofit organization founded by an Israeli military intelligence officer with the express purpose of making their translations of select Arab media available to the U.S. Congress and American academics and media outlets. MEMRI consistently promotes a selectively hateful picture of Arabs and Muslims, lacks critical reporting on Israel, and unabashedly champions the Likudite agenda. Not only has MEMRI promoted Manji's writings but the vast majority of sources in Manji's book come from MEMRI. On this, see Lalami.

18. Daniel Pipes is the founder of the notorious website Campus Watch, which posted dossiers of academics critical of Israel in order to intimidate them into silence. After much criticism, the dossiers have been withdrawn, but the website maintains a "blacklist" and continues to encourage students to "tattle" on critics of Israel and ostracize them for their views. For one example, see the website at

UCLA, http://www.bruinalumni.com/aboutuclaprofs.html, which incriminates professors for their criticism of Israeli policy. For a shrewd analysis of the impact of the coordinated efforts of the Israeli lobby on American foreign policy and domestic political culture, see Mearsheimer and Walt.

19. See http://www.muslim-refusenik.com/aboutirshad.htm.

20. For example, Manji describes the Reconquista, with all of its ethnic cleansing, as a product of internecine struggles between Muslim groups (*Trouble with Islam*, 56–57). Similarly, she portrays the Israeli-Palestinian conflict as an outcome of Palestinian intransigence and Israeli generosity (70–93).

21. Andrew Sullivan's uncritical support for Manji is not entirely surprising: both have made their name by playing on their gay identity while at the same time embracing conservative political positions. Sullivan's admiration for Manji's feminist proclivities sits at odds with his own opposition to abortion, a position he claims is consistent with his Roman Catholic faith.

22. For the most comprehensive treatment of Nafisi's text as part of the growing genre of what many call the "new Orientalist literature," see Keshavarz. Other key critical works are cited later in this essay.

23. It is widely acknowledged that President Khatami won the 1997 elections largely because of women's votes.

24. On this point, see Najmabadi, "Feminism."

25. Some of these people include clerical luminaries such as Shariat-Madari, Mahmoud, Taleqani, Abdollah Nouri, and Hossein Ali Montazeri. For an account of the dissent from within, see Abdo and Lyons.

26. In his astute reading of the conditions of production and reception surrounding Delacroix's famous painting, Todd Porterfield writes: "While passing for scientific, Delacroix's painting elicited a long-standing refrain about the harem. It evoked both desire for the women and repulsion at the Orient's inferior social and political systems . . . [E]ven if Delacroix had attempted to paint a sympathetic picture of an Oriental subject by, for instance, insisting on the women's cleanliness, it would not have mattered to this public. The critic's previously informed knowledge about the Orient stepped in to insure the invocation of the Orientalist discourse" (63).

27. See Ghoreishi. This is a statistic provided by the Naval Postgraduate School's monthly journal *Strategic Insights*.

28. Janet Larson attributes this development to a state policy that has promulgated "[increased] access to health care and family planning, a dramatic rise in female literacy, mandatory premarital contraceptive counseling for couples, men's participation in family planning programs—[with] strong support from religious leaders." On this issue, see also Hoodfar and Assadpour.

29. See Seymour Hersh, "Annals of National Security: The Iran Plans" and "Annals of National Security: Watching Lebanon."

30. Susan Sontag, for example, offers the following praise for Nafisi: "I was enthralled and moved by Azar Nafisi's account of how she defied, and helped others to defy, radical Islam's war against women. Her memoir contains important and properly complex reflections about the ravages of theocracy, about thoughtfulness, and about the ordeals of freedom—as well as a stirring account of the pleasures and deepening of consciousness that result from an encounter with great literature and with an inspired teacher." See the Random House website: http://www.randomhouse.com/acmart/catalog/ (visited 4 Sept. 2006).

31. See Ahmed; Gole; Lazreg; Mani; and Northrup.

32. See Hirschkind and Mahmood.

33. Statistics vary depending on the news source. For a couple of different estimates, see the 2005 report issued by the Human Rights Commission of Pakistan at http://www.hrcp-web.org/women/ (visited 9 March 2007); and the Amnesty International Report issued in September 1999 at http://web.amnesty.org/library/ (visited 9 March 2007).

34. See the Family Violence Prevention Project website at http://endabuse.org/resources/facts.

35. The reigning presumption seems to be that the West has individualized and privatized culture so that when and if it is practiced, it is an expression of free choice. Muslims, in contrast, are subjects of their culture as a collectivity, lacking the values of autonomy and freedom that would enable them to choose rationally from their cultural practices. As Wendy Brown points out, culture and religion in this form of reasoning are understood to "perpetuate inequality by formally limiting women's autonomy, while the constraints on choice in a liberal capitalist order . . . are either not cultural or not significant" (*Regulating* 195).

36. Soon after its publication by Random House in 2002, the memoir became a bestseller in Australia and was republished by Simon and Schuster in the United States under the title *Honor Lost: Love and Death in Modern Day Jordan.*

37. Soon after its initial publication, the book sold over a quarter of a million copies in fifteen countries, generating close to a million dollars in royalties and invigorating campaigns to fight honor killings in Jordan and beyond. There was hardly a newspaper from across the three continents that did not cover the pathos of Khouri's plight: from the *New York Times* to the *Sunday Herald,* the *Guardian,* the *Jerusalem Post,* and a wide array of Australian newspapers. Khouri became a celebrity overnight, often appearing in high-profile media events, writers' festivals, women's rights forums, colleges, and high schools. Random House often added an electric charge to her public appearances by providing prominently displayed security guards ostensibly to protect her from Muslim rage and violence.

38. In July 2004 an investigative reporter discovered not only that Khouri had not visited Jordan since the age of three, living all of her life in southwest Chicago until her immigration to Australia shortly before the publication of her book, but

that she knew little or no Arabic, had been on the run from the Federal Bureau of Investigation for alleged fraud, and had basically spun a false tale about her ordeals in Jordan. See Walker and Thomas.

39. Despite statements such as these, many prominent publishing houses continue to capitalize on the market, and there is no dearth of poorly written (and often uninvestigated) accounts of Muslim women's subjugation living in "Islamic cultures."

40. The Australian government approved Khouri's application for a "Distinguished Talent Visa," which allowed her to remain in Australia along with her husband and two children (Koch and Whittaker).

41. At a time when the Bush administration has increasingly made it difficult for Muslims to procure visiting or immigration visas to the United States, it is all the more striking that Khouri and her husband won the Cheney family's support despite the fact that they had been under FBI investigation at the time on charges of real-estate fraud in the United States. For many Muslims, this sends a clear message: if you espouse the right rhetoric, you will be handsomely rewarded by the Euro-American establishment.

42. A well-placed Australian academic, for example, wrote that Khouri's redemption lay in the fact that she might have been personally transformed by her fraudulent performance because the truth of the cause she enacted was ultimately larger than, and transcendent of, the agency of her own imposture. See McCalman.

43. This formulation, while widely echoed in popular feminist writings, is from Katha Pollitt's introduction to the edited volume *Nothing Sacred* (xiv).

44. The Islamist movement is comprised of a number of different strands, including the much publicized but relatively small militant strand as well as grassroots political parties whose aim is to broaden the scope of electoral democracy through civic activism and public participation. The efforts of these parties are often thwarted by authoritarian Middle Eastern governments—as was the case in the 2005 Egyptian elections but also earlier in Algeria, Tunisia, Turkey, and Morocco. The broadest current within the Islamist movement, however, is what I loosely call the piety movement (in some places it is referred to as the *da'wa* movement), which consists of a network of charitable nonprofit organizations that provide welfare services to the poor (often through mosques) such as health care, education, etc. A second aim of this vast array of organizations and groups is to make ordinary Muslims more devout in their daily conduct. These various tendencies within the Islamist movement differ not only in the kind of critique they offer of Western hegemony and postcolonial states but also in the social and political imaginaries they endorse and enable. On this point, see Mahmood, *Politics of Piety*.

45. See Chew; Bahdi.

46. See Feldman; Friedman.

47. At one point in her autobiography, when a Safeway first opens in Jeddah, Carmen cannot contain her enthusiasm and writes: "Now every modern product could be bought—and it was. We filled basket after basket with Jell-O and Campbell's soup, Swiss cheese and chocolate. Bread from the bakery still came peppered with weevils—I insisted my cook learn to bake bread—but *now* we had pineapple chunks and real milk. *They tasted of progress*" (95; emphasis added).

48. Here, I am reminded of the condescension with which Nafisi at one point in *Reading Lolita in Tehran* describes her female students, whose lack of freedom she clearly mourns. She writes, "Throughout, from start to finish, I observe that they have no clear image of themselves; they can only see and shape themselves through other people's eyes—ironically the very people they despise" (38).

49. See, for example, Abdo; Deeb; and Mahmood, *Politics of Piety*.

50. See *Politics of Piety*, esp. ch. 1 and the epilogue.

51. For views similar to Ehrenreich's but written by academic feminists, see Nussbaum, "Sex and Social Justice"; and Okin.

52. See also Boddy.

53. For recent scholarly work on the understanding of secularism not so much as an abandonment of religion but as its reformulation along certain lines, see Asad, *Formations;* and Mahmood, "Secularism."

54. This critique is well known and I do not want to rehearse it here. See, for example, Butler, *Bodies,* as well as ch. 1 of Mahmood, *Politics of Piety,* for a summary of these arguments.

55. Nawal al-Saadawi, a prominent secular Egyptian feminist, expressed this view on observing a sign displayed by French Muslim women protesting the recent ban on the veil: "The veil is a doctrine not a symbol." Saadawi found this slogan to be an expression of the false consciousness of the protesting Muslim women, a sign of their naive complicity with the capitalist plot to keep the Muslim world from coming to a "true political consciousness." Once again, any concern with religious doctrine cannot but be a ruse for material power in this kind of an argument.

56. In addition to my own work, see Fernando; and Scott, *Politics.*

57. For an extensive elaboration of the threats traditional Muslims pose to U.S. strategic interests and the "Western lifestyle," see Benard.

58. There are many ironies in this, but one that merits some reflection is how this policy of promoting liberal religiosity in the Middle East sits in tension with the Bush White House's active promotion of a particular form of evangelical Christianity at home. As I have argued in "Secularism," these seemingly opposite tendencies need to be analyzed as part of what constitutes secularism today— particularly the understanding that secularism is not simply an evacuation of religion from politics but its reorchestration.

59. For a review of Osama bin Laden's speeches and political goals, see Glass.

TRANSFEMINISM AND THE
FUTURE OF GENDER

Gayle Salamon

What is the relationship between women's studies, feminism, and the study of transgenderism and other nonnormative genders? In asking after the place—or lack of place—of transgender studies within the rubric of women's studies, I want to suggest that feminism, particularly but not exclusively in its institutionalized form, has not been able to keep pace with nonnormative genders as they are thought, embodied, and lived. Recent contestations about the term *transgender* echo some of the same concerns about referentiality and identity that have surfaced with the circulation of the terms *queer* and *woman* within feminist discourses.

If it is to reemerge as a vital discipline, women's studies must become more responsive to emerging genders. Genders beyond the binary of male and female are neither fictive nor futural but are embodied and lived. Women's studies has not yet taken account of this and is thus unable to assess the present state of gender as it is lived or to imagine many of its possible futures. It is equally true that transgender studies needs feminism. Trans studies in its current, nascent state is often dominated by a liberal individualist notion of subjectivity, in which a postgender subject possesses absolute agency and is able to craft hir gender with perfect felicity. Without the systemic understanding that women's studies provides of the structures of gender—and the relations of power that underlie those structures—trans studies is unable to understand gender as a historical category and is powerless to account for how the present state of gender emerged. This is especially necessary when discussing violence against transpeople, which cannot be made sense of using an entirely individual and voluntaristic theory of gender.

In the spirit of these larger concerns, I would like to consider two sets of photographs that particularize and complicate the relation between trans identity and feminism, in both its institutionalized and popular forms. One of these sets gives us an image and a narrative of trans subjectivity offered in conformity with the popular view that transgender populations and lesbian and feminist populations—and by extension, transgender issues and concerns of lesbians and feminists—are not only different but mutually exclusive. The public view of trans and lesbian feminist communities as divided, and transfolks themselves as the agents of this division, has a mutually reinforcing relationship with the way that transgenderism does or does not merit attention in the academy. Encounters between trans and feminism are increasingly happening outside of the academy, where the public voice of feminism is seen as a direct product of institutionalized women's studies programs. Trans studies does not as yet have anything like a stable footprint within the academy. The amount of academic work on trans issues is increasing, but institutionally speaking, "Transgender Studies" is not quite yet a legible category.[1] This may be due to its defiance of categories more broadly, though it would hardly be singular in this respect, since the same might be said of several different kinds of "area" studies. Or it might be because there is still little consensus about the place of the study of gender within the university and still less agreement about the place of sexuality; transgenderism seems to imply that both of these things are at issue, and in provocative ways. Some of the work on trans studies being produced today emerges out of the social sciences—anthropology and sociology, for example. But much of the current work on trans issues is emerging from the humanities, and surprisingly little of this work is housed in women's studies departments. In some ways, this would seem to be a "natural" alliance: women's studies would seem to offer a rich array of tools, already in place within an institutional setting, to examine gender—its production, perpetuation, and transgression—and the ways embodiment, identity, and social structures are shaped by gender productions. Women's studies has also offered a place in the academy where discussion of bodies and difference, and an interrogation of the way power figures and disfigures bodies differently, can take place.

However, trans teaching and scholarship have not always received a warm welcome within the domain of women's studies. One might read this absence as a temporal fact, evidence only of the pace of institutional change, and conclude that inclusion at the level of both scholarship and curriculum is surely forthcoming. This view would suggest that transgenderism is merely the latest in a long line of identities whose existence has posed a challenge to women's studies and its own various moments of presumptive universalism and that women's studies as a discipline will reckon with the identities and concerns of transpeople, just as it has with the work of women of color, lesbians, sex radicals, and queers. Leaving aside the question of whether or not this work or these other marginal identities have actually been successfully integrated into women's studies or have found their own unassimilated home there, there are reasons to believe that a developmental model of the growth of women's studies can neither predict the shape of women's studies departments in the future nor describe the trajectory of trans studies within the academy.

There is a different way to understand the reluctance of women's studies to respond to trans studies. In some ways, trans studies is singular in the difficulty it presents to such a program, a difficulty that becomes manifest if, instead of understanding trans studies to be offering yet another subject position to be subsumed under the category of "woman," we understand the task of trans studies to be the breaking apart of this category, particularly if that breaking requires a new articulation of the relation between sex and gender, male and female. Indeed, the specificity of trans as a kind of subjectivity uniquely suited to pose a challenge to fixed taxonomies of gender meets resistance in the specificity of women's studies as a discipline whose very essence depends upon the fixedness of gender. The category of "woman," even if it is understood to be intersectional and historically contingent, must offer a certain persistence and coherence if it is to be not only the object of study but the foundation of a discipline, and a subject formation that describes a position of referential resistance might not be easily incorporated into such a schema. Such a subject would prove useful, however, to the extent that that subject embodied and literalized a position perpetually *outside* of the referential system of gender. I would argue that the trans subject has been just such a subject for women's studies, necessarily proximate but unassimilable, able to enact and secure gender as a binary system only to the extent that sie is exiled from that system. The transgendered subject is the constitutive outside of binary gender.

Wendy Brown points out that the definitional instability that attends all disciplines is especially acute in women's studies and that its institutional specificity inheres in the fact that its task is not quite to provide particular tools or methodologies—impossible given its interdisciplinary foundings and scope—but to function as a discipline on the basis of its description of a particular kind of subject: women. This leads to one of the "very real conundrums currently faced by those of us in women's studies." Brown continues:

> Women's studies as a contemporary institution, however, may be politically and theoretically incoherent, as well as tacitly conservative; incoherent because by definition it circumscribes uncircumscribable "women" as an object of study, and conservative because it must resist all objections to such circumscription if it is to sustain that object of study as its raison d'être. Hence the persistent theory wars, race wars, and sex wars notoriously ravaging women's studies in the 80s. ("Impossibility" 21)

Brown offers a context for current crises in women's studies by suggesting that those crises may themselves be necessary for the perpetuation of the field itself. She points out that while women's studies demonstrates an ever-expanding attention to different adjectival permutations of its subject, its perpetuation as a discipline depends on an ever-tightening focus on that subject, which leads to an unsustainable paradox:

> There is something about women's studies, though, and perhaps about any field organized by social identity rather than by genre of inquiry, that is especially vulnerable to losing its raison d'être when the coherence or boundedness of its object of study is challenged. Thus, paradoxically, sustaining gender as a critical self-reflexive category rather than a normative or nominal one, and sustaining women's studies as an intellectually radical site rather than a regulatory one—in short, refusing to allow gender and women's studies to be disciplined—are concerns and refusals at odds with affirming women's studies *as* a coherent field of study. (23–24)

If there are no methodologies here, only subjects, then the only way to expand the reach of a discipline is to increase the range of subjects, an expansion that often happens in an additive way. There are thus two models of additive subjectivity at work in mainstream women's studies: first, an addition of unrecognized (for they could hardly be said to be "new") subject positions to a universal that had not previously included them (women of color are also women, lesbian women are also women, disabled women are also women), and second, the admission that those other aspects of subjectivity are also vital to personhood.[2] Brown argues that this additive model of subjectivity championed by women's studies in its attempts to reckon with difference is insufficient in three ways. First, it operates under the mistaken assumption that power functions primarily as a force of subjugation, ignoring the productive capacities of power, the fact that it does not just oppress subjects but fundamentally makes them. Furthermore, power cannot be understood to operate the same way in making race, or class, or sexuality; different kinds of power, operating according to different norms and having different aims, are operative in each instance. Finally, a subject conceived as "intersectional," that is, with cleanly joined layers or partitions of identity demarcated along separate axes of interpellation, bears little relation to any kind of lived subjectivity:

> As so many feminist, postcolonial, queer, and critical race theorists have noted in recent years, it is impossible to extract the race from gender, or the gender from sexuality, or the masculinity from colonialism. To treat various modalities of subject formation as additive in any of the ways suggested by the terms above is to elide the way subjects are brought into being through subjectifying discourses, a production that is historically complex, contingent, and occurs through formation that do not honor analytically distinct identity categories. (24)

If it is true that mainstream women's studies has a historical and sustained commitment to an additive model of identity, and also true that the discipline has an equally entrenched belief that identity must be a matter of privileging "experience" as an inevitably gendered cornerstone of feminist epistemology, then women's studies offers a description of subjectivity that would seem particularly poorly suited to understanding trans subjects.[3]

If there is a certain ossification of identity necessary to the continuation of women's studies as a discipline, might there still be some less circumscribed home for trans work within the academy? And is there a way trans studies might negotiate some of the more vexing difficulties of women's studies, such as the cultivation of a space that can bear a certain degree of gender nominalism, without lapsing into normativity?

QUEER

Riki Wilchins has suggested that "trans identity is not a natural fact. Rather it is a political category we are forced to occupy when we do certain things with our bodies" (25). This insight offers trans identity something akin to an act but also something that is not reducible to a question of choice. More-over, it might suggest that transgender studies is more closely aligned with lesbian and gay studies than women's studies, despite its being an identity based on gender rather than on sexuality. However, some of the same diffi-culties that attend the confluence of trans studies and women's studies also mark the relation between trans studies and gay and lesbian studies. Susan Stryker makes a similar point to Brown's in discussing the current state of trans studies in relation to lesbian and gay studies and politics and describes the hope she sustained in the mid-1990s that queer theory might offer a radically progressive, even revolutionary, model for understanding gender and sexuality within academia. Stryker's current sense is that this hope was never quite realized:

> While queer studies remains the most hospitable place to undertake transgender work, all too often *queer* remains a code word for "gay" or "lesbian," and all too often transgender phenomena are misappre-hended through a lens that privileges sexual orientation and sexual identity as the primary means of differing from heteronormativity. Most disturbingly, "transgender" increasingly functions as the site in which to contain all gender trouble, thereby helping secure both ho-mosexuality and heterosexuality as stable and normative categories of personhood. This has damaging, isolative political corollaries. It is the same developmental logic that transformed an antiassimilation-ist "queer" politics into a more palatable LGBT civil rights movement, with T reduced to merely another (easily detached) genre of sexual identity rather than perceived, like race or class, as something that cuts across existing sexualities, revealing in often unexpected ways the means through which all identities achieve their specificities. (214)

Just as the term *gender* often functions as a descriptor that promises to unsettle some of the difficulties with "sex" (determinist, binary, natural, etc.) but means only and exactly "sex," Stryker understands *queer* to now function as a term whose lack of referentiality is no longer the mark of an anti-identitarian politics, no longer the name for a deviation from a norm that might regulate either gender *or* sexuality, but as a code for "lesbian or gay." There is similarity, then, between Stryker's and Brown's critiques of additive identity politics, though it is interesting to note that Stryker finds some cause for hope in using "gender" as a vector that might "cut across existing sexualities."

Not all proponents of trans studies would agree with this characterization of the object or aim of trans studies as the radical disruption of familiar modes of gender and subject production, and there has been a fair amount of criticism from those who understand this way of perceiving (or, indeed, *doing*) trans studies to be a violent denial of transgendered subjectivity.[4] Figured thus, trans studies would seem to be in rather close accord with other challenges to the stability of the subject, namely postmodernism and its iteration within sexuality studies, and queer theory. Indeed, there are some trans theorists who understand postmodernism to be uniquely useful to trans studies. Stephen Whittle suggests that it is precisely the postmodern decentering of the subject and its insistence on "a multiplicity of voices" that has allowed the voices of transpeople to enter discourses on gender. In her text "The Empire Strikes Back," which has been foundational for trans studies, Sandy Stone agrees with the necessity of "heteroglossic" accounts of gender and offers the still more radical position that transpeople utterly destroy the reliance on "experience" and the nomenclatures and identity categories that it ostensibly confers—categories crucial for feminism and institutionalized women's studies.

Those categories are changing, and this is true within the gender binary as well as outside it. For example: for at least two decades, there has been much discussion and hand wringing about the decline in the number of young women who will not call themselves feminists. I do not know if it is going unnoticed or simply unremarked upon, but there has been another generational shift slightly to the side of this one, in the register of gendered self-description: a majority of the women who take my classes do not identify as women. That is, among the more or less feminine, more or less normatively gendered women whom I have had as students in women's studies classes, I would venture that over half of them do not call themselves "women," nor do they describe each other by that term. They use the word *female* instead. It goes beyond the scope of this essay to examine why that might be the case, but many interesting and important questions might be asked here: Is it possible that the legacy of institutionalized women's studies has been to decrease the number of female subjects willing to, in the words of Denise Riley, *be* that name? Is it an instance of liberation to refuse "woman" or a sign of something less celebratory? Is there something about the seeming indisputability of the category of "female" that is more comfortable or manageable than the category of "woman"? If "woman" is understood to be a cultural achievement, does this enhance the possibility of its failure, and does that risk of failure evoke a disidentification? The fact that many women enrolled in women's studies classes do not identify as such seems to me to suggest that, both inside the binary and outside of it, women's studies has not yet met even the low bar of descriptive positivism in terms of either sex or gender.

LGB-FAKE-T

The strongest affiliation of trans studies is with lesbian and gay studies. This connection is sometimes made under the sign of coalition, of similar terms and struggles, but it can also be symptomatic of a certain confusion about what transgenderism is and what its relation to gay or lesbian identity might be. The trans writer Dean Spade has coined the acronym "LGB-fake-T," in reference to the ways trans is often assumed under the aegis of lesbian and gay studies without any attention to its difference and specificity. This conflation is sometimes made because of the suspicion that gender *means* sexuality, that gender here is merely a cover story for not only sex but sexuality as well. Sometimes gender comes to stand in for sexuality, and sometimes sexuality is actually standing in for gender. The recent marriage debates, for example, have been framed by the press and lesbian and gay advocates alike as a *gay* issue rather than a *gender* issue, though sexual conduct is only implicitly rather than explicitly addressed, as it was in *Bowers v. Hardwick* or *Lawrence v. Texas*. One could just as easily imagine that the marriage debate might have coalesced around issues of gender and gender freedom; it certainly seems true that it has done so for the religious right's opposition to gay marriage. Their slogans are, of course, infused with a loathing of queer sexuality and the "abomination" of sodomy, though the ubiquitous slogan "marriage is between a man and a woman" imagines itself to be a corrective to improper *gendering* as much as to wayward sexuality. Similarly, what are primarily *gender* issues are misread as *gay* issues. Recent newspaper headlines reporting on trans issues reflect this conflation: "Transsexual Ousted from Shelter Shower for Sexual Orientation" (Hampton) and "Nuances of Gay Identities Reflected in New Language: 'Homosexual' Is Passé in a 'Boi's' Life" (Marech). That last title enunciates anxiety, or perhaps scorn, that "homosexual" as a signifier is being thrown over in favor of this newfangled term "boi," momentarily forgetting the fact that "homosexual" never *was* a signifier of gender in the way that "boi" is and that the "nuance" of the identity reflected by this word is precisely not *gay*, but a nuance of gender. Further, the anxiety that the bois are about to overthrow the homosexuals might be assuaged with the observation that, for all we know, this boi might indeed be a homosexual boy who likes other bois. We err when we assume that these descriptors must be mutually exclusive by rendering the boi presumptively heterosexual and by rendering the homosexual presumptively gender normative.

The transwoman referred to in the headline cited above was assaulted and dragged out of a public restroom not because of her sexual orientation but because of her gender presentation. There was no sexual activity in that restroom; the prohibited "activity" was the presentation of her gender. Like most people who harass or assault transpeople in public restrooms, including the police, the occupants of this women's restroom decided that this person was not sufficiently feminine to lay claim to that space, and the disproportionate response of the attack points to one of the more pernicious assumptions of these conflations: that the presentation of gender transgression both conceals and reveals something about sexual transgression, a something that is perceived to be threatening. The intersection between transgression and violence here is both sobering and widespread, both frequently remarked upon and also covered over. The film version of *The Celluloid Closet*, for example, concludes its argument that lesbian and gay people have long been the subjects of onscreen violence with a montage of scenes from Hollywood cinema in which gay and lesbian characters meet with violence or death. Though it claims to be cycling through representations of homophobic violence in cinema, a closer look reveals that many of these characters are trans, and the punishments enacted and repeated onscreen are visited on characters who are transgressing gender norms rather than sexual ones.

Parsing sex from sexuality in this way is obviously a fraught enterprise, and I do not want to exaggerate the gulf between them. Gender and sexuality are inevitably, if unpredictably, bound. But this does not mean that they are the same thing, and the assertion of their fungibility can have quite dire consequences for transpeople. One of these conflations is now vexing discussions about transpeople in the popular press. A 2006 article in the *New York Times* (Vitello), one in a series on FTM transmen that the *Times* ran intermittently for several years, begins by offering a conflation of gender and sexuality but ends up postulating not a collapse of trans and lesbian communities, but an antagonism between the two. The relation between these communities is decried as an all-out war, a "conflict" that "has raged at some women's colleges." The parties to this war, the article asserts, are intractably divided. The article briefly mentions the Michigan Womyn's Music Festival, probably the most visible site of conflict between trans and feminism. Lisa Vogel, the owner of the festival, bars all transpeople (both MTFS and FTMS) from the women's-only space, while transpeople and their (mostly) dyke and genderqueer supporters oppose the ban, arguing not against separatist space, but insisting that transwomen *are* women. One former producer of the festival is cited as saying, "By turning yourselves into men, don't you realize you're going over to the other side?"

Stryker's observation that all gender trouble has now become consolidated under the sign of trans and that members of the gay and lesbian community, through that containment, are able to represent themselves to the public as ever more similar to heterosexuals and thus more safe is exemplified in the premises and conclusions of the *Times* article. There is an incendiary rhetoric mobilized whereby the discrimination and violence that transpeople face are asserted as emanating from lesbians, an aggression figured as the defensive response of a community whose existence is threatened by the encroachment of trans. The article opens with a quote from one of the lesbian characters on Showtime's lesbian soap opera *The L Word*—she is dismayed that another character on the show has come out as trans, is adopting the name Max, and is about to start taking testosterone. She responds to the news with sadness: "It just saddens me to see so many of our strong butch women giving up their womanhood to be a man." The article reports that a furor erupted on lesbian blogs after Max's transition, citing one blogger who called for the murder of the character by "testosterone overdose." That the suggested virtual murder of a fictive transman at the hands of lesbians opens the *Times* story is chilling. It soon becomes clear that the story is not about transmen at all, but is instead a story about the response of angry lesbians to the peril that transmen represent to their communities. But the anger and specter of violence behind it are offered with a kind of preemptive logic; it is implied that the lesbian anger that leads to online murderousness is in some way justified, a community-wide strategy of self-defense in response to the threat that transmen pose to the categories of woman, lesbian, and butch.

This representation at first begs to be dismissed as merely a recycling of the most threadbare of clichés: the angry, man-hating lesbian. I would like to suggest two things, however, that point toward something more disturbing at work. Lurking behind the rage at transmen and the rhetoric of war and self-defense that peppers the article is the suspicion that transpeople are danger-ous, and dangerous in a way that violates women in particular. This suspicion becomes transmogrified into fantasies of trans predation, where transpeople are compared to rapists or claimed to embody a threat, sometimes particular and sometimes vague and unspecified, to non–trans women.

Questions of violence and violations have circulated in sometimes tell-ing ways in popular coverage of transgenderism for many years.[5] Indeed, violence is offered as an essential feature of trans identity. The *Times* article contends that the FTM trans movement "has gained momentum only in the last 10 years, in part because of increasingly sophisticated surgical options, the availability of the Internet's instant support network, and the emotions raised by the 1999 movie *Boys Don't Cry,* based on the true story of the murder of Brandon Teena, a young Nebraska woman who chose to live as a man." One could dispute this claim with relative ease: FTM transgen-derism has, of course, been an important issue inside and outside lesbian communities even before the *Times* started covering it. But what is being of-fered with this chronology is an origin story of sorts, and for the *Times,* the birth of transgenderism can be dated with some precision to a particularly performative speech act. In 1994, Kate Bornstein wrote an opinion piece for the *Times* called "Her Son/Daughter," in which she referred to the "trans-gender movement." The editors balked at this phrase, telling Kate that if they printed the phrase "transgender movement," it meant that there *was* such a thing.[6] It is certainly true that transmen have received increased me-dia attention in the past few years. But the most disturbing thing about the *Times's* chronology is that it locates the birth of the movement at the moment of a transman's death and the "emotions raised" by that death. Thus the origin story of the transgender movement is crafted as a reverse Stonewall, where the founding moment of violence does not rally the com-munity and the public against discrimination and harassment, but instead marks the first instance in a chain of endlessly repeated stagings of that death. Stonewall as a founding myth gains its power from the claim that the queers and queens fought back. Citing *Boys Don't Cry* as a founding myth would seem to insist the fatal opposite,[7] that Brandon could not fight back then, that those like Brandon cannot fight back now—and it implies that those on the other side of the barriers, so to speak, are lesbians.

There is a second kind of violence here, in addition to the preemptive violence against transmen who supposedly represent a threat to lesbianism. This second violence is a disfiguration of the category of butch, which undergoes a kind of disciplinary feminizing in order to make it conceptually distinct from transgenderism. Butches who choose to transition, for example, are described as "giving up their womanhood." The claim that butches have an unambiguous and possessive relationship to their "womanhood" is necessitated by the claim that they are different from transfolks. Since a butch and a transman might look alike in terms of gender, having equally masculine gender presentations, then that "attachment to womanhood," vaguely defined and not necessarily accompanied by bodily femininity, would be the only thing that might distinguish them. The category mistake here insists that butches are resolutely women in order to outline the parameters of butch identity in contrast to transmen. To wit: transmen loathe their breasts, but butches do not. Transmen attack and reject their bodies, but butches celebrate theirs. Transmen want to pass as men in public, while butches want to be recognized as women. Transmen think of themselves in masculine terms and prefer masculine pronouns, while butches reject masculine pronouns and male roles and ego ideals. Transmen want male privilege, but butches reject male privilege. Transmen hate themselves, butches honor themselves. If this seems to be a portrait of butchness that is both highly motivated and staggeringly inaccurate, it is no coincidence. This line of protest is identical to the "feminist" reaction against butch/femme identities and sex roles all too familiar from decades past. The argument is exactly the same, save only that transmen are now cast in the role of the villain previously played by butches.

This is itself staging the death of the butch precisely to save her from the contaminatingly dysphoric masculinity of the transman. Before laying the blame for the death of butchness at the doorstep of transguys, it seems important to pause and recall that hand wringing about the death of "real" butchness, mourning the end of its era, or grieving over the loss of butches has been a constant accompaniment to butchness itself. Butchness as a style of queer masculinity is in part constructed by the model of a nostalgic where-have-they-all-gone scarcity.

The *New York Times* article criticizes transition in precisely this mode and effects a denigration of transmen through the valorization of butchness. Butchness is held up as a desirable ideal in opposition to trans, whereas previously, before the current trans debates, it was butchness and butches themselves who were castigated for these same reasons, for being too close to an unacceptable limit of masculinity or maleness. It appears that the line has moved, that transmen are now the new limit case of masculinity as opposed to butches, who are now held up as a lesbian ideal. This tendency has been noted and criticized extensively in trans theory, perhaps most notably by Judith Halberstam. Halberstam notes that this assigning of gender transgression to trans bodies and the marking (or unmarking) of all other bodies as normative happen in trans theory and transphobic theory alike; and she wants, along with Stryker, to complicate "models that assign gender deviance only to transsexual bodies and gender normativity to all other bodies" (153).

The sort of rhetoric Halberstam identifies has the effect of constructing the lesbian community as more palatable to heterosexuals, as Gayle Rubin points out in "Thinking Sex," and it is particularly apparent in popular discourse. First, it distances lesbians, who are then presumptively gender normative, from transgendered people. (One might think of Ellen Degeneres's or Rosie O'Donnell's disdain for transfolk, a disdain that functioned as the gesture that allowed their uncloseting.) Second, it suggests that if gender-normative lesbians are just as uncomfortable with the strange universe of gender change as heterosexuals are, then the readers of the *New York Times* need not linger too long in considering their own homophobia or transphobia.

The violence in circulation in discussions of transition, even in those feminist responses that attempt to be awake to it, continues to happen in several different registers. Transition is framed as if it is akin to a death or as if the post-transition subject will, with hir emergence, enact the death of the pretransition subject. Transition is further figured as murderous in discussions of the procedures of FTM transition, which are sometimes described as self-mutilation or, more hyperbolically, "violence against women." But there is something about these discussions of "self-mutilation" that very quickly end with the knife pointed the other way. Bernice Hausman has suggested that the bodily interventions of transition are violence toward the self and that this violence toward the self is evidence of the incompatibility of trans theory and feminism because "feminists precisely understand their gender investments by attacking the social system, and not their own bodies, as the origin of the problem of dysphoric sexed embodiment" (9). The lesbian writer Alix Dobkin, who frequently refers to FTMS as "mutilated women," ended one of her pieces against transgenderism with the sentence "Let's put away the knives," making clear that somehow lesbians rather than transmen are now the target of that violence.

Lesbianism in these exchanges becomes refashioned in conformity with the shape of heteronormative relations. Where transgenderism is about *breaking up the family,* lesbianism is about family. Where transgenderism is about *exile from community,* lesbianism is about community—virtual (viewers of *The L Word*), online (bloggers), educational (women's colleges), and political (women's spaces). Where transgenderism is about *danger* (to self from transition or to others through the *invasion* of women's space), lesbianism is about safety (domesticity, separatism). Note that there is scarcely any mention of the trans communities that these men join if and when they leave the lesbian community. The space outside the lesbian community is figured as a space of utter isolation and disconnection. The *New York Times* article moves through a number of options, starting from the blogosphere murder and moving to the less fatal but perhaps no less definitive solution of exile. A quotation from a graduate of Mills College (read: professionally trained feminist) frames the rhetorical question this way: "When do we kick you out? When you change your name to Bob? When you start taking hormones? When you grow a mustache? When you have a double mastectomy?" According to this logic, lesbian communities can and must reject transpeople; it is not a matter of *if* transmen will be exiled from lesbian communities. It is only a matter of *when* and *how.*

WAVE OF MUTILATION?

The *New York Times* article by Paul Vitello is accompanied by two pictures of Shane Caya, a transman who is discussed in the article. The first is a shot of Shane, his ex-partner Natasha, and their three-year-old child. All three are smiling as Shane lifts the young child into the air. The second depicts Shane from the waist up, without a shirt on. He sports a head of short, salt-and-pepper hair, an upper arm covered with tattoos, and a muscular, well-sculpted male chest. The caption on the photo reads: *Shane Caya displays his mastectomy scars.* The caption shocks not because of its tone—fairly matter of fact, really—but because of the mismatch between what it reports and what the reader first sees, which is simply a male body. No matter how normal looking Shane's chest is, what it shows, according to the caption, is not his masculinity, but a violence done to femininity in order to achieve that masculinity. The caption sees missing breasts rather than a male chest, and we are asked to read his body for evidence, to search the photograph for the scars that trace the lower contour of Shane's pectorals—the "tell" that would give the lie to that maleness. This is, by now, a familiar mode in photographs that accompany media coverage of transfolks. A photograph of a "normal-looking" transperson will be shown next to a caption or sidebar that announces either hir trans status or surgical status, functioning as the "reveal" that offers the transperson's portrait as a game of spot-the-missing-gender. In this case, the second photograph is positioned beneath the first, as if it were negating or undermining the picture of familial happiness above it. There is a triple shaming in this portrayal, for Shane is both recalled into femininity with the invocation of his former breasts and named as the agent of his own castration. The photographic strategy of framing transition as that which ends familial happiness is also enacted at the level of narrative: Shane and his partner break up, we are told, because of his transition. These sorts of photographic strategies serve, finally, to rearticulate the *difference* of transpeople, their irreducible dissimilarity from both the lesbians they are understood to have been and the men they are now wanting to become. The article seems to take some pains to reassure us that even if transsexuals walk among us, we will always be able to pick them out. This rhetoric of difference mimes another kind of war, in which cultural anxiety about difference is mobilized to fuel a war on terror in which we are told always to be alert because potential terrorists could be hidden among us. In each kind of war, danger is embodied as difference masquerading as sameness, precisely the affront that the lesbians in the article locate in the bodies of transmen. And in each kind of war, preemptive violence is offered as the only weapon effective against such an enemy.

Insisting that this is a picture of Shane's *scars* rather than Shane's *pecs* offers his chest as "the horror of nothing to see." This last, of course, was Freud's assessment of the child's apprehension of female genitals, which comparison with the penis renders not just nothing but a horrible nothing. Indeed, much of the anxiety and anger in discussions both popular and academic about FTM transition centers around the loss of the breasts from top surgery, so much so that the focus on breasts and their fate during transition is becoming an analog to the centrality of the penis in popular discussions about transwomen. The preoccupation with transmen's bodies extends beyond the physical presence of the scars resulting from top surgery to the question of what it is, exactly, that those scars signify. The excessive concern for the breasts, and the desire to "save" them or to save the "young women" who are considering top surgery from "mutilating" their breasts and themselves in this way, understand transition to be a transaction whereby the transman purchases the nonmaterial privileges of the phallus at the price of the material flesh of the breasts. Thus, an ostensibly feminist concern offers a disingenuous grieving for the removed breasts as a symbol of the transman's relinquished femininity, though I would venture that those breasts were rarely affirmed or avowed as such when they were still a part of that transman's body.

If public fascination with transpeople often becomes consolidated into a fixation with "the" surgery, which in MTFS is misunderstood to be castration, the focus in people's discussions of FTMs becomes top surgery, again misunderstood as a kind of castration, or reverse castration. The breasts become the absolute signifiers of femininity, offering a positive confirmation of sex, even when clothed or covered, in a way that the female genitalia do not. The fixation on the breast is displayed in the *Times* article, which has nearly nothing to say about bottom surgery, making only one mention of an "ersatz penis." And while this might have the refreshing effect of not reducing gender and sexuality to genital morphology, so often the case when transexuality appears in the popular press, that fascination is not banished, but rather finds itself attached to a new part. In commenting about people's fascination with her penis and "the" surgery, Wilchins offers, in a remark that characteristically insists on both her trans specificity *and* her feminism: "Transexual women are unerringly described as 'cutting off their dicks.' No one ever formulates this act as gaining a cunt—not even lesbians, feminists, or transgender women" (193).

THE MAKING OF A MAN

I would like by way of comparison with the *Times* photographs to turn to a series of photographs taken by Jana Marcus and displayed in a show called

"Transfigurations: The Making of a Man." The insistence on "making" here resonates with the language of "becoming" that Judith Butler sees as the legacy of a certain strain in feminism that is now being carried on by trans theorists: "In some ways, it is Kate Bornstein who is now carrying the legacy of Simone de Beauvoir: if one is not born a woman, but rather becomes one, then becoming is the vehicle for gender itself" (*Undoing* 65). I want to suggest that these photographs portray their transitioning subject quite differently from the *Times* photographs, thereby offering us a quite different narrative about the making of gender.

The series consists of three black-and-white photographs of a young transman named Aidan. The first photograph shows Aidan seated, looking relaxed and somewhat pensive. His arms are folded loosely over his chest. He is wearing a t-shirt that says, in letters that are only partially discernible, "AMBIGUOUS." The second photograph shows a shirtless Aidan with a bound chest. In the third, Aidan is unwrapping the gauze and gazing down at his chest and the results of a very recent top surgery inscribed there. These and the photo from the *Times* both show shirtless transmen, but their content, framing, and stance toward both their subjects and their viewers are quite different.

The Aidan series is striking for a number of reasons, but particularly interesting is the way it portrays and literalizes gender as a matter of the relation between inside and out, between self and viewer, between the visible and the invisible. The triptych of Aidan's chest—clothed, bound, naked—offers a progression from total concealment to naked revelation. This contrast between outside and inside is ubiquitous in transwriting, where inside stands for a certain immaterial truth of gender, and outside for a false and unwanted fleshly covering. From Jay Prosser's *Second Skins* to Jamison Green's *Becoming a Visible Man*, transition has been described as a process of transforming the body so that its visible signifiers of gender come into accord with the subject's internal invisible sense of gender. In this model particularly, and in the lives of transpeople in general, transition is not a sudden leap across a precipice into a wholly unknown gender; to insist that Aidan was resolutely female prior to surgery would seem inaccurate at best and interpretively violent at worst. External bodily change here becomes the sign of internal continuity and persistence.

In the case of this image, the photograph shows Aidan without a shirt, chest bound. His arms are lifted above his head, his head is turned slightly to the left, his eyes are closed. The binding produces an almost perfectly flat contour, as the curve of both breasts is compressed by the binding. But we are able to *see through* this binding, which is made of Saran Wrap or a similar material. The effect is the presentation of a bodily modification that can only do its work as a *gender* modification when covered or concealed, a covering or concealing that is nevertheless made almost magically transparent to the viewer. The photograph thus offers a remarkable reversal of relations of inside and out, which become entwined; Aidan's internal self-image of the chest as a flat, masculine plane becomes externalized and enabled through the binding that itself disappears, leaving only its effects behind. We are offered a certain identification with Aidan in this act of looking, an identification that is perhaps intensified with the quotation that accompanies the photograph, in which he describes the pain of binding and the bodily dilemma with which he feels faced:

> Depending on what I'm wearing I can look like a guy. I wear big clothes to cover my body, but I don't feel very confident. If I'm wearing a jacket it covers my chest and I tend to pass more, but in the summer I wear t-shirts and need to bind my breasts. In order to look flat-chested the binding can be fairly painful and intense. People use ace bandages, saran wrap, or anything that will hold you in tight. If I bind too tight I can't breathe. Now I wear a sports bra cause I'm just not willing to be in pain anymore. I've been struggling with this for a number of years and now it's just getting worse. I just want to be comfortable in my body. Soon I'll have chest surgery.

The taxonomies that we saw earlier would have transmen and butches as separate kinds of beings, with the former fleeing the body and the latter at home in it. The above description, though, might describe a butch or a transman with equal ease

After surgery, Aidan has this to say about his new chest:

> I'm sure surgery was right for me. I wanted to take my transition one step at a time. . . . Chest surgery had become an immediate need for me because the breast thing was just getting worse and worse. I felt like if the only thing I did was chest surgery, I would feel a lot better about myself. I would be able to wear shirts that fit and look the way I want to. My chest is very concave where my breasts used to be, but I love that it's flat. I have to wait a couple months to lift weights, so my chest won't look the way I want it to for a long time. But, my physical

transition has started and soon I'll take testosterone. Yesterday it was windy outside and my shirt pressed firmly against my chest and for the first time I wasn't conscious of my breasts . . . it felt amazing!

The last photograph is indeed one in which *Aidan shows his mastectomy scars*. But that description seems more apt here than in the *Times* photograph, and its effect is exactly the reverse. Aidan faces the camera squarely, again shirtless, again shown from the waist up, but whereas in the first photograph his eyes met ours, and in the second his eyes were closed and his head averted, in the third he looks down at his chest. His hands open up a large piece of cloth that circles his chest, though the material this time is opaque, perhaps made of gauze, and seems to reference both binder and bandage. He gazes down at his chest and the quite prominent postsurgical scars there, still new and healing. Whereas in the previous photograph, the camera was given a view of Aidan's chest, from which he averted his eyes, in this final photograph the camera, Aidan, and the viewer are all focused on the new topography of his chest. We are invited to look *with* him rather than *at* him.

Aidan does not yet report that he is utterly at home in his chest or in the rest of his body. He indicates that he sees his new chest as the beginning of male embodiment—"my physical transition has started . . . my chest won't look the way I want it to for a long time"—and that top surgery is the start of this process, rather than its culmination. Again, transition is shown as a *process* of embodiment, a continual becoming, rather than one act that begins and ends with a surgical procedure. And this structure of being and becoming exceeds a simple dichotomy of inside and outside. Aidan reports the exhilaration of being outside after surgery, feeling his shirt pressed flat against his chest by the wind and not having to feel conscious about his breasts. It is significant that this is not a purely internal consciousness of self. His uncomfortable awareness and disavowal of his breasts grows stronger over time as a result of failing to pass, as other people, perhaps reading him as gender ambiguous, examine the chest of a presurgery Aidan and read the breasts visible beneath the shirt as confirmation of his femaleness. This external misrecognition leads to an extreme feeling of consciousness of that particular part and a self-consciousness about its presentation that becomes impossible to separate from Aidan's consciousness of himself. Thus his internal sense of discomfort with his external appearance may not be a simple misalignment or mismatch between inside and outside at all, but an internal sense of dysphoria that becomes amplified as it circuits from his body to the gaze of an external world brutally hostile to gender ambiguity, to become internalized and incorporated as a part of his gendered sense of self.

The trans position is often described by lesbian-feminist critics as a capitulation to gender normativity that is both an abandonment and a selling out of lesbian sisterhood. The critique would have us understand that there is, in the abandonment of the ostensible solidarity of the position of "woman," a profoundly unethical relation to one's lesbian "sisters." But it seems crucial to consider what ethical stance is taken when someone insists that the only position for a transman that is not a betrayal of lesbianism or feminism is to bear his pain and his discomfort rather than considering having his breasts removed. If his passing is understood as some sort of betrayal, what is it, precisely, that has been betrayed? What is our response if failure to pass endangers him or makes him the target of violence? What would it mean to insist that a transman must not modify his body in order to bear the visible marker of a "womanhood" with which he has no possessive relation? If, for example, Aidan's desire to feel comfortable in his own body is objected to on the grounds of lesbian solidarity, should we not ask why it is Aidan's body in particular that must be mobilized for this goal, why the bodies of the gender transgressive among us are forced to differentially bear the weight and responsibility of solidarity? Might it be that the lesbian desire for masculinity—a sexual longing for masculinity embodied in someone who is not male—can still incite crisis in the lesbian community?[8] And is lesbian reassurance that this desire does not make them straight, and their need to be reassured about their own *lesbianism,* purchased at the price of the safety and bodily habitability of butches, transmen, or masculine women? Crushing disfigurations result when we insist that the other deserves my respect only to the extent that she is *the same as I am.*

I would like to conclude by considering Lily Rodriguez's photograph *Mud* (2005) as a different kind of representation of trans bodies and subjectivities. *Mud* breaks with the still, composed framing of portraiture in several ways. Most obviously, there are two subjects in the frame instead of one, suggesting that we are already in the territory of relation, difference, and engagement with the other, rather than contained within the more monadic confines of solitary identity represented by the conventions of portraiture. Indeed, spectatorship is at issue in the photograph, but this spectatorship is more obliquely presented than a locked gaze between a

Mud, © 2005 Lily Rodriguez

sitting subject and an unseen camera. Within the frame of the photograph, a pair of dimly discernible shoes stand in the background, indicating that relations here are not simply dyadic but at least triangular. In this scene, spectatorship is bound with identification is bound with desire, and some "I" is probably looking on, to borrow from Freud. The horizontally splayed tangle of the bodies of these two people that refuses to be quite captured temporally (the figures are blurred with movement) or spatially (the stretch of each of their bodies exceeds the frame). The photograph is centered on the point of contact between their two bodies, and they are engaged in a struggle that reads as agonistic, playful, and erotic in equal parts. It is not easy to discern whether the figures are pushing each other away, drawing each other near, or attempting both at the same time. We witness an engagement of masculinity with masculinity, which nevertheless refuses to reduce them to sameness. One of these figures bears a scar on hir bare chest; the chest of the other figure is bound by a sports bra. A bodily difference, to be sure, but what kind of knowing do we believe to be delivered by that difference? Does it announce a difference of gender identity? Of sexual identity? Of class? Of access to surgery? Of age? Of politics? I would suggest that we cannot possibly know the answer and that this undecidability with regard to what conclusions we can and cannot, should and should not, draw from the bodily markers of masculinity can help open up a space where we might ethically engage otherness without the fear of mutual annihilation. Feminists have learned—and championed—these distinctions in the realms of race, class, sexuality, ability. Why, then, does this resistance stubbornly and surprisingly remain in the realm of gender?

NOTES

1. *The Transgender Studies Reader,* edited by Susan Stryker and Stephen Whittle, is an important milestone in this regard.

2. These models are, of course, not monolithic; there are alternative ways to organize the study of women, a fact perhaps reflected in the recent prevalence of departments and programs calling themselves "Gender and Women's Studies."

3. Joan Scott's critique of experience as a foundational category has been the most important challenge to this kind of epistemology ("Evidence").

4. See Namaste; and Prosser.

5. Kate Bornstein, lecture, University of California, Berkeley, 27 April 2000.

6. See David Valentine's "The Calculus of Pain," in which he asks how violence against transgendered people might be discussed or represented without making the term itself synonymous with violence and death.

7. For a discussion of the "border wars" both within and outside queer communities, particularly in the wake of Brandon Teena's death, see Halberstam; and Hale.

8. For one example of this position, as well as a deft explication of lesbian ambivalence about the desire for masculinity, see Findlay.

Part III. **EDGING IN**

DISCIPLINE AND VANISH:

FEMINISM, THE RESISTANCE TO THEORY,

AND THE POLITICS OF CULTURAL STUDIES

Ellen Rooney

Cultural studies is not one thing; it has never been one thing.
—Stuart Hall, "Emergence"

1990

In November 1988, the National Association of Scholars held a conference in New York City. Three hundred academics attended, including such well-known media figures as John Silber, then president of Boston University, later a candidate for governor of Massachusetts, and Jeane J. Kirkpatrick, a political scientist, formerly of the United Nations. The assembled scholars were exhorted "to redeem American higher education from intellectual and moral servitude to forces having little to do with the life of the mind or the transmission of knowledge." These usurping forces, composed of academic "radicals" engaged in "oppression studies," apparently threatened the objective pursuit of knowledge with politics. Feminists figured prominently in the convention's apocalyptic narratives of giddily declining standards, "radical egalitarianism," and "chilling" demands for political correctness. At the same time, the purveyors of radical scholarship were paradoxically described as frail and timid. As one speaker put it: "The barbarians are among us. We need to fight them a good long time. Show them you are not afraid[;] they crumble" (Berger, "Scholars" 22). "Say to the feminists, 'What do you mean by separate courses? You have no methodology.' When you lose, make them state their agenda to the world.

They haven't got the guts to state it, and you'll beat them that way" (Mooney 11). This imagery conflates an urgent call to arms with the contemptuous and imperial assurance that the "barbarians" lack the courage to put up much of a fight; it suggests that the campus radical is more fearsome as a lurid spectacle than she proves to be in an honest confrontation.[1]

A few weeks after this rousing affair, in December 1988, I delivered the following essay as a talk in an MLA program that might be characterized as the NAS's worst nightmare come true. The session was one of five organized by Nancy Armstrong and Richard Ohmann for the Division on Sociological Approaches to Literature. Over the course of three days, four workshops titled "Third World and Multicultural Studies," "The Politics of Cultural Studies," "Practicum: Making a Cultural Studies Program," and "Feminism and Cultural Studies," and a general forum all addressed the question "What Should Cultural Studies Be?"[2] The politics, internal and external, of this question was a topic raised in every session. The coordinated series of panels could easily be interpreted as a response to the onslaughts of right-wing critics of the university like William Bennett or the National Association of Scholars. The Chronicle of Higher Education, for example, reported the MLA sessions under the headline: "In Face of Growing Success and Conservatives' Attacks, Cultural-Studies Scholars Ponder Future Directions." Yet this angle of the story can be overstated; thus far, at least, cultural studies has not allowed reactionary ideologues to set the terms of its debates. This has been especially true with regard to the category of the "political." Neoconservatives demand that the allegedly recent politicization of the university be reversed; cultural studies has generally been committed to a heterogeneous and inclusive account of the political and suspicious of efforts to "return" politics to its "proper" venue. And yet, as the U.S. cultural studies movement has expanded (mounting more panels and bigger conferences), the question of politics, specifically, the question of what counts as political, has reemerged. As Meaghan Morris suggests in "Politics Now (Anxieties of a Petty-Bourgeois Intellectual)," this question often revolves around the relation (or the difference) between, on the one hand, "aesthetic gestures, textual 'subversions,'" [and, on the other,] "political actions." Morris cautions that "in a mass-media society with mass-media cultures and mass-media politics, the relationship between signifying (rather than 'aesthetic') gestures and political ones may not be so clear cut" (185). In practice, the "political" anxiety attacks of cultural studies scholars seem both warranted and gestural. Strangely, the rhetoric of clarifying limits echoes the redemptive language of neoconservative polemic, though of course the cultural studies scholar intends politics rather than intellectual objectivity to be the object of her or his saving grace; the intertwined imagery of denunciation and dismissiveness also *reappears in exhortations to attend to real political acts, not mere texts. At the same time, the politics of cultural studies remains problematic.*

My essay intervenes in this discussion to propose the feminist model of a politics of knowledge production as a possible strategy for cultural studies. I have retained the polemic of my oral presentation in the present text. This seemed especially important as I reworked the talk and discovered (yet again) the problem of the pronoun. In New Orleans in 1988, it seemed fairly clear who "we" were; in 1990, in differences: A Journal of Feminist Cultural Studies, *the "we" has shifted and reemerges as one of the stakes in the construction of cultural studies within the university.*

MY ARGUMENT BEGINS by articulating feminism as a network of feminist practices. I want to approach the politics of cultural studies through an analysis of the relation between cultural studies, on the one hand, and women's studies, feminist theory, and the women's liberation movement, on the other. The asymmetry of this formulation, in which cultural studies is opposed to women's studies *and* to feminist theory *and* to the women's movement, is an allegory of my argument.[3] The historical and institutional situation of cultural studies in the United States does not yet allow us to name any particular political movement (outside the university) as "properly" affiliated with cultural studies. This fact makes the second term of the feminist configuration—that is, theory—a crucial weapon for cultural studies as it tries to stake out its political position(s), both within the academy and elsewhere. In my analysis, the question of the politics of cultural studies in the United States is inseparable from the question of the theory of cultural studies, where theory is understood primarily as the *practice* of interrogating the production of knowledge. Stuart Hall has suggested that cultural studies can only resist "the remorseless march of the division of knowledge and the gap between theory and practice" by "developing a practice in its own right, a practice to bring together theory and practice." Suggesting that the politics of cultural studies can never be reduced to a "populist intellectual project," Hall argues that "the vocation of intellectuals is not simply to turn up at the right demonstrations at the right moment, but also to alienate that advantage which they have had out of the system, to take the whole system of knowledge itself and, in Benjamin's sense, attempt to put it at the service of some other project" ("Emergence" 18). This alienation of advantage requires a theoretical and political reading that forces the system of knowledge out of its "proper," disciplinary context. As a politics of knowledge production, cultural studies can have far-reaching and radical effects; a theoretical practice that interrogates the disciplinary production of systems of knowledge can ground its progress. On the other hand, if cultural studies collaborates in the resistance to theory, it will quickly be assimilated to the disciplinary structure of the university, which is to say, it will trade its political effects for a proper place among the disciplines.

If we examine cultural studies in light of the example of feminism's triple practice as women's studies, feminist theory, and the women's liberation movement, three topics emerge immediately for consideration. First, the politics of women's studies, especially in relation to students, who constitute one of the most important constituencies scholars and critics address and who may act in the university either as agents of recuperation or of radical critique. Second, the effort to theorize the object of cultural studies, that is, the struggle among practitioners to answer the question put by Richard Johnson: "What is cultural studies anyway?" And finally, the *form* of the dangers the university's disciplinary logic presents to any oppositional discourse at work within its precincts: what kind of deformations will cultural studies as theory and practice undergo if it succumbs either to the temptations or the bullying of disciplinarity?

The specter that haunts my analysis is the possibility that the institutional emergence of cultural studies in the United States will lead to its rapid recuperation by the disciplines as a reactionary discourse.[4] I intend the word *reactionary* in as literal a sense as possible: the cunning of ideology all but assures that the university will respond to the challenges presented by cultural studies by promoting its own version thereof. This kind of reaction-formation would reinforce the very disciplinary effects that cultural studies even now disrupts. The ideology of free and objective inquiry, of knowledge beyond power, which structures the liberal university and conceals many of its social and political functions, demands that cultural studies be assimilated to a disciplinary logic. To anticipate myself for a moment, I want to suggest that cultural studies molded into a disciplinary format would lead, at a minimum, to the following unhappy results: first, our students (and eventually our faculties) would never need to confront the fundamentally political significance of their own intellectual labor, thus deadening the acute awareness of the politics of knowledge that now characterizes cultural studies; second, our object of study would be redefined as a historical-geopolitical period or as a unit of area studies and thus naturalized as the proper content of a disciplinary domain; finally, cultural studies would abandon its position as a critical reading of the traditional disciplines and of the disciplinary as such (Green 84; Hall, "Cultural" and "Emergence"; Johnson 38–43) and take up its own authoritative niche among the disciplines.

My anticipation of disaster gains urgency from an analogy with the history of American studies. Despite the leftist strains in its past and the important work of many individual scholars (like Janice Radway, Michael Denning, and Mary Jo Buhle), American studies too frequently participates in the resistance to progressive work in the humanities. There are exceptions to this tendency, but the rule holds well enough to make us pause over this institutional history. As a field, American studies has no particular political constituency or valence. Indeed, the disciplinary character of American studies, its institutional status as a discipline, is indistinguishable from that of other disciplinary formations, like English, philosophy, or romance languages.[5] My point here is not to accuse the late, great forefathers of American studies—much less its current practitioners—of some failure of political insight or will, but to disclose the ruses of disciplinary recuperation as they have played themselves out in the history of American studies' life in the university.[6] At the moment, the disciplinary structure of American studies is such that it is *as difficult* to undertake critical work there as it is in any of the traditional disciplines. This is at least partly due to the fact that American studies has been established as a "period," a well-mapped geopolitical and historical domain in which objects of inquiry appear as givens; to be sure, these objects are investigated from various perspectives and even occasionally "redefined," but they are freighted with the full authority of the disciplinary object. In other words, the problematic of American studies has been naturalized and thus has disappeared as an object of contestation or inquiry (see Althusser). We must confront the possibility that cultural studies could repeat the institutional trajectory of American studies.

Institutional context and the history of the disciplines are everything to the analysis I propose. As Stuart Hall suggests, cultural studies is "an adaptation to its terrain . . . a conjunctural practice" ("Emergence" 11). The prominence I want to assign to theoretical practice is a response to conditions in the U.S. academy. The importance of this caveat cannot be exaggerated. In no sense do I mean to suggest that theory with a capital "T" serves, by virtue of its apparent self-reflexivity, as an infallible prophylactic against recuperation or as the guarantee of an essentially radical practice in any field. (Countless examples, many from my own "home" discipline of English, demonstrate the politically conservative or negligible effects of theoretically sophisticated work.) I do not propose that theory-as-self-consciousness will set us free; on the contrary, theoretical practice seems important to me primarily insofar as it discloses degrees of unfreedom, irreducible limits and exclusions, the often harsh terrain. As Bruce Robbins has persuasively argued, theory is neither "a determinate set of philosophical positions" nor an "authoritarian ruler" that seeks to dominate practice from without. Rather, theory is itself a practice within a particular "*historical conjuncture*," that is, an "event," and Robbins insists that we should define it "in terms of [the] historical moment" (4, 5–6).

> The public insufficiencies and internal contradictions of the New Criticism, the urgencies of the Vietnam War and the feminist and civil rights movements, changing ethnic and gender proportions of students and teachers along with the pressure for capitalist vocational-izing of the universities, movements of national liberation abroad energizing Lévi-Strauss' critique of Eurocentrism and literary criticism's slow surrender to a global, anthropological view of culture—all were clearly part of the conjuncture, and if it is difficult to assign a specific weight to any one element, to accumulate them is to feel their collective force. Consent to speak around theory's new series of propositions (though not necessarily to assent to them) had emergent social power behind it. (6)

The question of theory is a question of what we can do now, given where we are in the history of the United States and of the U.S. academy, and in the history of cultural studies as an intellectual practice and as a field of work within the university. For the foreseeable future, I believe that a theoretical practice that concentrates on exposing the enabling assumptions and the stakes of intellectual projects is essential to grounding the progressive politics of cultural studies. We require, as Adrienne Rich argues, a theory and a "politics of location." Given its present location in the U.S. academy, cultural studies must foreground the conflict of (its) theoretical problematics—within the "field" of cultural studies and between cultural studies and the disciplines it challenges. This *strategy* enables what Gayatri Spivak has called a persistent critique of the disciplinary production of knowledge all around cultural studies, as well as within its boundaries, a critique that can never elude the question of politics ("In a Word" 126).[7]

To speak very generally, those scholars and critics pursuing cultural studies are united by the desire that their students (and their colleagues, for that matter) see culture not as a "canon" or a "tradition," but as the embodiment and site of antagonistic relations of domination and subordination, that is, as a productive network of power relations. In principle and in practice, it matters relatively little whether students come to this critical position by earning a degree in a cultural studies program or on some disciplinary site. Indeed, many of those who currently practice cultural studies are extremely wary of disciplinarization: "Cultural studies must be interdisciplinary (and sometimes antidisciplinary) in its tendency" (Johnson 42). At the same time, programs are being established willy-nilly (Ohmann "Thoughts"), and they may be less vulnerable to recuperation if we are prepared to recognize and resist the specific forms of disciplinary recuperation.

Cultural studies in the United States has a political problem insofar as its relationship to a specifically political struggle outside the university is *at best* contested. Practically speaking, women's studies has an enormous advantage over both cultural studies and American studies: its students are often a politically conscious constituency before they enter the field, that is, before they are subjected to the relatively loose "disciplinary" practices of women's studies. (African American studies has a similar advantage in some settings.) I realize that in many colleges and universities only a significant minority of the students in women's studies courses are also part of the women's movement. But feminist students have a disproportionate weight within the field and within their programs. Frequently, they parallel their work in women's studies with some form of political work, where the political includes cultural activity under the rubric of feminism. The oppositional politics of women's studies is forged as much by these students as it is by the women (and men) teaching in the programs and writing essays and books "in" women's studies. This practical advantage has theoretical consequences in the form of students' awareness that their political work is intimately linked to their intellectual projects; indeed, this tie to so-called "real world" politics suggests the ideological interestedness of women's studies, reminding everyone that this "field" is not ideologically neutral, but merely disciplinary.

The simple fact that its youngest scholars are often also activists of some kind does not ensure that women's studies will play a disruptive political role within the university. (There are, of course, dramatic limits to the current politics of women's studies in many places; the feminism of many women's studies' faculties guarantees no particular politics.)[8] Indeed, it runs counter to my entire polemic to suggest that the politics of women's studies is simply parasitic upon the so-called real world politics of women's liberation. Nevertheless, I want to stress the theoretical importance of the political activities of women's studies' students outside the university, without idealizing them. This emphasis is not meant to imply that some students (or faculties) have "authentic" politics that "naturally" express themselves, while others need prosthetic devices; nor do I mean to suggest that any programmatic link between cultural studies as a (political) activity within the university and some particular practice (of cultural politics) outside the university is impossible in the United States. My point is simply that its current absence robs cultural studies of one strategy of resistance to disciplinarization and alerts us to the possibility that cultural studies may be peculiarly vulnerable to political neutralization *within the university.*

I place such a strong emphasis on the positioning of students not simply because the existence of programs assumes the existence of students but because they can so easily be invoked as an alibi for the university's demands (generally presented by a curriculum committee of some kind) for "discipline." It is frequently in their name (though often not through their efforts) that disciplinary standards are established, codified, and printed up in course catalogs as requirements. And as this scenario suggests, the critique of the production of disciplinary knowledge is *institutionally specific to the university.* As Gayatri Spivak continually argues, this critique is always a "made" thing ("In a Word"), requiring painstaking construction and reconstruction, "with no end in sight" ("Political" 218).

In other words, a critique of the politics of knowledge production is never merely a side-effect of political activity outside the university. The feminist students who choose to major in women's studies *construct* their choice as a political one. I believe this is always true (though I write that phrase with a certain dread). This sense of the politics of the field itself prepares them to work against the disciplines, as feminist theory demands. The creation of women's studies programs entails a specifically feminist critique of the disciplines. This critique is predominantly anti-essentialist and attacks the common-sense view of disciplinary discourse as at least potentially objective in its representation of the real.[9] These interventions insist that the university organizes knowledge politically and that the disciplines themselves are political at every level. Feminist theory in the academy is constituted by the discovery that a politicized, theoretical intervention within the disciplines is unavoidable. There follows a rejection both of the figure of the neutral, transparent investigator—the subject of disciplinary knowledge— and of the disciplinary myth of the given object of knowledge, innocently discovered in the world. As Jane Gallop suggests, "One of the goals of what we so ambiguously call women's studies [might] be to call into question the oppressive effects of an epistemology based on the principle of a clear and nonambiguous distinction between subject and object of knowledge" (15–16).[10] "Men's studies modified" (Spender) means a recognition of the interested nature of all knowledge, of every construction of an object, and of every inquiring subject's position.

Cultural studies seeks to participate in a similar critique, to "alienate" the system of knowledge, as Hall puts it ("Emergence" 18). But while women's studies joins its intradisciplinary critique to a project of feminist theory building that interpellates its subjects as "feminist," it is not at all clear yet what (or who) the "subject" of cultural studies will be. At a minimum, cultural studies must pursue an antidisciplinary practice defined by the repeated, indeed, endless rejection of the logic of the disciplines and of the universal subject of disciplinary inquiry (Johnson 42; Spivak, "Political" and "Can the Subaltern"; Rooney, "What"). Without such a consistent effort to politicize the subject of inquiry, the insinuating subject of disciplinary knowledge will inevitably reemerge. As Michael Green argues, "The relation of cultural studies to the other disciplines is . . . one of critique: of their historical construction, of their claims, of their omissions, and particularly of the forms of their separation. At the same time, a critical relationship to the disciplines is also a critical stance to their forms of knowledge production—to the prevalent social relations of research, the labour process of higher education" (84). This antidisciplinary practice begins by rejecting the universal subject of disciplinary knowledge; it produces new relations to knowledge and new subjects.

The plural is essential and may remain so indefinitely. The politics of the students initially attracted to cultural studies are obviously heterogeneous, and I use that term not entirely in its honorific sense. (I am thinking here of vague feelings of discontent and resentment that may have so little political focus as to approach the genuinely apolitical.) This amorphous situation

cannot be remedied by assigning a particular politico-theoretical model—
on the order of the Jameson of *The Political Unconscious,* for example, or
the "Birmingham School"[11]—and demanding that students adopt it, even
assuming such a thing were possible. The problem cannot, in other words,
be solved by giving students a theory of culture and assuring them that *its*
politics are *the* politics of cultural studies. Whatever the limits of political
heterogeneity, I do not see any possibility of elaborating a "line," a unified
theory, or even a political center to orient the whole of the enormous and
diverse project of cultural studies. Indeed, in the U.S. context, such a unify-
ing project would very likely contribute to the process of disciplinarization
that I have been at such pains to oppose. In contrast, to place the political
conflict among theoretical problematics at the center of cultural studies
programs would be to enable students (and scholars) to confront their own
intellectual projects as political from the ground up: choices about subject
matter, methodology, and theory cannot be made according to any set of
invariant principles but are always an effect of the project one privileges
and seeks to pursue. The student of cultural studies is a cultural worker.
Within the university, her or his politics must *begin* with that positionality.
In the U.S. academy, a specific form of consciously theoretical discourse
is essential to pursuing this point, precisely because it directly contradicts
the positivist emphasis of what Margaret Ferguson has called the "hidden
curriculum" of the university (219). I must repeat that this is not because
theoretical self-consciousness is innately subversive. Rather, cultural studies discloses theoretical choices as political choices. The visceral antipathy
that certain self-nominated defenders of tradition have for theory becomes
more explicable in this view. The student-scholar of cultural studies should
work from the beginning with what Althusser calls a "guilty" sense of the
political effects of her theoretical and practical choices, beginning with the
choice of cultural studies itself (14). This can only happen if students and
critics have the theoretical tools to see their own work simultaneously as a
tactic of resistance *and* an exercise of power, a process of exposing the concealed investments of disciplinary systems and deliberately reorganizing
the pursuit of knowledge as such.

   As a discipline, American studies has lost this political sense of position.
Despite the efforts of many, many individual practitioners, in most universities, a student's choice of the field of American studies is neither politically nor
theoretically discomfiting.[12] Uneasiness is a sign that the myth of the neutral
division of reality into appropriate disciplines is under pressure; those fields

most vehemently attacked at a National Association of Scholars convention are those cultural studies should emulate. While a women's studies major or graduate program can never escape its resonance as a political choice, and will thus always be available for attack, there is no political weight whatsoever to the choice of American studies as a discipline. It remains to be seen if cultural studies will be constituted as just another major.

"Just another major" is institutional shorthand for disciplinarization, the effort to obscure the position and thus the political investment of the inquirer and to naturalize the object of inquiry. An antidisciplinary practice (such as women's studies) cannot be disciplined if it insists that the object of knowledge, the content that defines the discipline as such, is always a political fiction and a political choice, never a given. Women's studies struggles constantly to maintain these insights, to avoid "reverting to the very terms of opposition which feminist theory has sought to undo" (Kamuf 42),[13] and there is certainly nothing new in arguing that cultural studies ought to be self-conscious about its production of objects. But an emphasis on this *process* itself as an aspect of critical practice needs to be central to our curricula. One disturbing trend in cultural studies is a tendency to discipline programs as the study either of a geohistorical period, such as "culture under capital," or of media practices within the culture industry, such as "Hollywood," "rock and roll," and "sport." At my own institution, one of the sites for cultural studies work is the program Modern Literature and Society, which effectively excludes cultural materialist work that situates itself before the French Revolution. In a recent report on "CS in the U.S.," Richard Ohmann, who has long been an advocate for cultural studies, as well as one of the most cunning and lucid of countercritics on the left, traces the genesis of cultural studies to the efforts by intellectuals to understand the "massive cultural transformations" of consumer society, especially the "role of mass culture in shaping consciousness"; in the course of this analysis, the term *mass culture* appears in four consecutive sentences, most interestingly in the phrase "mass cultural studies in the U.S."[14] Although nothing could be further from his intention, to reduce cultural studies to the study of mass culture (that is, to a period) is to invite a disciplinary fix that will ultimately displace the politics that Ohmann hopes to foreground. Disciplinary logic presses cultural studies to define its object in just such positivist terms, terms that conceal the contingency of the gesture of definition itself and, with it, its political effects. Women's studies has never permitted itself to be delimited in these terms, and as a consequence, it is continually (and sometimes bitterly) retheorizing its project. On the other hand, American studies is defined precisely as a historical and geographical period study.

If cultural studies becomes a new "period," it will inevitably become a natural object for disinterested inquiry, a discipline. The irony is that this process is encouraged by some cultural studies scholars. Not surprisingly, the drive to fix a subject/object for cultural studies is often accompanied by vehement resistance to the "textualization" of culture, which is then associated with theory (or "bad" theory). The respectful hearing accorded recent suggestions that the so-called theoretical era is coming to a close is also related to disdain for "the ideology of the text," and this disdain, too, tends to pride itself on political tough-mindedness. This resistance to textuality is announced as an effort to maintain a proper space for political action "outside the text,"[15] but its actual effect is to depoliticize the very signifying practices that enable us to engage in any kind of politically motivated intellectual work whatsoever. In the name of politics, politically useful strategies are dismissed. The coincidence of this backlash with growing institutional support for programs in cultural studies suggests that the dominant discourses of the university have perhaps found a way to have their cultural studies and not have it too. The NAS view of politics as something external to intellectual work itself can slip in unmarked.

Margaret Ferguson reminds us of an old women's studies adage when she argues that radical work in the academy requires that "changes in the *content* of the curriculum . . . be correlated with changes in the *forms* of instruction" (219). When cultural studies burdens all of its students with the political effects of their intellectual work; when it owns political and intellectual responsibility for the construction of its objects; when it clings to its antidisciplinary polemic and refuses to cultivate its own garden to the neglect of neighboring fields—then, in this specific and temporarily privileged form as a critique of the disciplinary organization of knowledge, cultural studies *will be* a radical transformation of the forms of instruction, a direct threat to the entire "hidden curriculum" of the disciplines.

NOTES

I am grateful to Richard Ohmann and Nancy Armstrong for including me in the MLA panel; to Elizabeth Weed, Neil Lazarus, and Khachig Tololyan for their helpful comments on the text; and to the Center for the Humanities at Oregon State University for a fellowship that enabled me to pursue these questions.

1. In "Conservative," Mooney reports one conferee's conclusion: "They're small in numbers, but so are termites" (11). She also notes the discrepancy between the willingness of "many conferees [to] describ[e] themselves as conservative—intellectually, politically, or both," and the official line, which fabulates a silent (and unrepresented) majority: "We don't intend to be a bunch of right wing scholars pushing for our own beliefs. I think we represent a much larger group out there" (11).

2. The forum, presided over by Ohmann and including presentations by Gayatri Spivak, Janice Radway, Catherine Gallagher, and Richard Johnson, was itself entitled "What Should Cultural Studies Be?" echoing the title of Johnson's essay, "What Is Cultural Studies Anyway?"

3. I use the word *opposed* only in the sense of "in contrast to." Obviously, women's studies, feminist theory, and the women's liberation movement are not "opposed" to cultural studies in the sense of being antithetical or in opposition to them. *differences* itself testifies to the existence of "feminist cultural studies," as do works like *Women Take Issue* (Women's Studies Group, eds.); hooks's *Yearning*; Sheridan's *Grafts*; and essays like Hall's "Cultural" and Johnson's "What Is Cultural Studies?"

4. I am specifically concerned here with the dilemmas of cultural studies within the academy; the institutional pressures brought to bear by the peculiar practices and ideologies of the university differ significantly from those that shape cultural workers on other sites, including cultural studies scholars who are not affiliated with universities.

5. This is not to say it is static or even stable; but in this age of the "crisis" of the humanities, critical interrogation has engulfed every discipline. American studies is often housed in programs and centers rather than in departments, but this is changing slowly, and twenty-year-old programs can behave very much like departments. In "Interdisciplinarity," Shumway analyzes the uneven process of disciplinarization. He notes that a commitment to interdisciplinary work does not necessarily forestall the development of disciplinary structures and effects; he also observes that "American Studies had never given up th[e] ideal [of interdisciplinarity], and it had never recognized its own disciplinary nature" (20).

6. I am sympathetic to the view that American studies, as a discourse that seemed unavoidably to reflect (and celebrate) American ideology at large, was particularly vulnerable to reactionary recuperation, but I cannot enter too deeply into that argument here. I will argue only that today American studies scholars must struggle *against the grain* of the discipline just as scholars in the so-called traditional disciplines do. The relative rates of success are extremely variable and often depend on "external" forces. Denning makes a very helpful distinction in his reading of "American Studies as a Substitute Marxism." He contrasts "American cultural studies" pursued under the sign of American studies with "marxist work

in social or labor history . . . sociology or economics" that deals with the United States (373); the former seems to him to be the site of an "exceptional" resistance to marxism and British cultural studies. For some recent discussions of the ideology of American studies, see Giroux; Denning; Shumway; Wise.

7. See Spivak, "Political," for a discussion of the upward mobility and material rewards that may attend a career as a feminist scholar in the "first world."

8. My inclination to worry about this particular matter is part of my own intellectual and political history as a feminist. As a Wesleyan undergraduate on the committee investigating/agitating for the creation of a women's studies program, I was the doubter, anxious to craft a proposal that placed as much power as possible in the hands of students, "us" at that point. I did not care very much about being able to major in women's studies. I cared about being a feminist and about making that as easy and as radical a practice as possible within the confines of the university, where ease and radical intervention seemed opposed. To make a course of study easy, or rather, how easy to make it—specifically, how easy to make it to major in cultural studies—is for me a crucial question.

9. I do not use the term *anti-essentialist* as code for *poststructuralist*. The enormous and growing bibliography of the theory and practice of women's studies in a wide range of institutions reveals varied and complex relations to theory and to the problem of the disciplines. While the word *anti-essentialism* is certainly not universally privileged in these analyses, the emphasis is always on a critique of the production of knowledge itself, not simply on the marginalization or trivialization of women as objects of study. This is true even in those texts that ultimately do call for an effort to think feminist scholarship in disciplinary terms: women's studies "as a discipline" is always a counterdiscipline. An extremely abbreviated list of texts touching on this topic includes Bowles; DuBois et al.; Farnham; Hull, Bell, Scott, and Smith; Minnich, O'Barr, and Rosenfeld; Mohanty; Spender; Treichler, Kramarae, and Stafford.

10. See also Bell and Rosenhan.

11. Stuart Hall has recently protested the tendency to position the Birmingham Centre as the origin of or an authority on cultural studies: "There is no such thing as the Birmingham school. To hear 'the Birmingham School' evoked is, for me, to confront a model of alienation in which something one took part in producing returns to greet one as thing, in all its inevitable facticity" ("Emergence" 11). Johnson also insists that "the research and writing [at Birmingham] has been political, but not in any immediate pragmatic sense. Cultural studies is not a research programme for any particular party or tendency. Still less does it subordinate intellectual energies to any established doctrines" (42).

12. This may not have always been the case. Insofar as American studies represented an alternative to the traditional belles-lettristic view of literature, which privileged English over American texts and elite culture over popular, and pro-

posed to transgress the boundaries separating history from literary studies, it did disrupt business as usual in those disciplines.

13. See Derrida.

14. See Ohmann, *English in America* and *Politics of Letters*, for discussions of topics ranging from "English 101 and the Military Industrial Complex" to canon formation, teaching mass culture, and "The Function of English at the Present Time."

15. The tendency to see cultural studies as a period can easily develop out of a position that discounts theory as ahistorical and lacking in specificity or that opposes "concrete," "particular" projects to abstraction; these moves are often correlated with a deep suspicion of categories like "textuality." Among contemporary cultural critics tending to this line are Edward Said, Fredric Jameson, and Terry Eagleton. See Rooney, "Going"; Shumway, "Transforming"; Robbins.

WHITHER BLACK WOMEN'S
STUDIES: INTERVIEW
Beverly Guy-Sheftall with

Evelynn M. Hammonds

In the midst of much debate within African American communities about the relevance of women's studies and the very definition and meanings of feminism, Beverly Guy-Sheftall has been unequivocal in her assertion that "feminism" is not a foreign concept imposed from outside black communities. In her work she has documented the presence of a continuous feminist intellectual tradition among African American women since the early nineteenth century. She has eschewed labels such as "womanist" and "Afrofemcentrist" for the term "feminist." For her, "feminist" "capture(s) the emancipatory vision and acts of resistance among a diverse group of African American women who attempt in their writings [and practices] to articulate their understanding of the complex nature of black womanhood, the interlocking nature of the oppressions black women suffer, and the necessity of sustained struggle in their quest for self-definition, the liberation of black people, and gender equality" (xiv).

As a consultant to women's studies programs around the United States, she is intimately aware of the institutional, pedagogical, and methodological problems faced by these programs in the current political climate.

When this interview was first published in 1997, Evelynn M. Hammonds was Associate Professor of the History of Science at MIT. A graduate of Spelman College, she was coorganizer of the 1994 national conference "Black Women in the Academy: Defending Our Name, 1894–1994."

This interview was conducted on December 24, 1997.

EH: I want to start with a set of questions about women's studies programs. Among the goals that informed the founding of women's studies programs was the integration of women into the existing curriculum. Whether that meant changing the disciplines, rethinking theoretical and analytic approaches, or adding new knowledge about women to ongoing research and teaching projects, the point was to have women included in every branch of knowledge. Has that been accomplished at historically black colleges? Are they operating on a different time line at these institutions? Are there specific and different issues that women's studies has to address on these campuses versus predominantly white ones? How would you characterize the mission of women's studies at a black women's college? What are the barriers you've encountered in establishing your program? What are your successes?

BG-S: The first thing that I would say is that Spelman has been fairly unique in the commitment that it's made to the establishment of the Women's Studies Program. It is still the case that we are the only historically black college with an undergraduate women's studies program. Atlanta University has a doctorate in African women's studies, but since its merger with Clark College it has kept the doctoral program without an undergraduate option. There are some historically black colleges with a smattering of women's studies courses here and there, but I don't think that there are any that have either a women's studies minor or major, which we at Spelman just passed in the fall of last year. It is still the case that women's studies with respect to coherent programs are just not cropping up at historically black colleges, despite thirty years of agitation on the part of women's studies folk, and I think that there are a number of reasons for that. One, there is a paucity of interdisciplinary programs in general in these colleges, even, for example, with respect to African American studies. And there is still the assumption that women's studies is not critical to the education of students at historically black colleges. It is also the case that there just hasn't been a critical mass of faculty willing to struggle over a number of years to get a program going without adequate resources. Overall these efforts are really struggling. The advantages that we have had at Spelman are first, administrative support, and second, external funding.

EH: Do you think that there has been an integration of knowledge about women into the traditional disciplines at historically black colleges?

BG-S: Not to any substantial extent. I'm making this assertion on the basis of my knowledge about curricula from examining catalogs but also from anecdotal reports from faculty at historically black colleges. I have a number of contacts, including the people I met recently when I cotaught a comparative women's studies seminar at NYU with Professor Chandra Mohanty (of Hamilton College). Many faculty from historically black colleges were in that seminar and most of them acknowledged the absence of women's studies either as separate courses or in terms of mainstreamed courses. There are some pockets at particular places. For example, at Howard University in the history department you certainly have a women's studies presence and maybe to some extent in English, but I would say that probably it is still the case in 1997 that women's studies has not been mainstreamed into traditional disciplines in any significant way.

EH: How would you characterize the mission of women's studies at a black women's college?

BG-S: At a black women's college as opposed to a historically black college in general?

EH: Well, both.

BG-S: I believe that any undergraduate college in 1997, including historically black colleges, ought to have reflected in their curriculum important new scholarship on women that's been emerging in the last thirty years, particularly as it relates to women of African descent, women of color, and women in the diaspora (the Americas, the Caribbean, and Europe). This should be done at the most fundamental level in order to have students understand the entire range of human experience. I would also add that this is critical, perhaps even more critical, at historically black colleges because there's been such a preoccupation with race and not sufficient attention paid to gender. The addition of women's studies in these colleges would be correcting an imbalance in the way that we transform curricula with respect to race at majority institutions. Dealing with race *and* gender issues at historically black colleges is extremely important.

EH: Can you say something about the specific barriers that you encountered at Spelman in establishing the program and also from your experience in the NYU seminar this past summer?

BG-S: The first barrier was the assumption that because we were and are a women's college, that we were already by definition doing this work— which of course would be incorrect. The second barrier, and this would have been clearer in 1981 more than fifteen years ago, was the tremendous discomfort about an explicitly feminist curriculum at historically black colleges. The assumption was that feminism was not relevant to black folk. There was also some resistance to what was perceived to be a radical political feminist agenda which was perceived to have nothing to do with traditional disciplinary scholarship. The assumption also was that women's studies would cripple black students by not providing them a traditional, acceptable education and that somehow we were disadvantaging them. In other words, I think there was even greater sensitivity at historically black colleges about providing students with something that was perceived to be "off color."

As a result, far too few black students have been exposed to women's studies courses. The situation has changed somewhat over the years; however, the fact that women's studies in general has paid inadequate attention to issues of race and class has also limited the participation of black students. In addition, in many women's studies courses, white students express hostility in discussions about race and class in ways that black students find unsettling.

EH: How would you characterize your successes then?

BG-S: We were able to overcome these barriers because we had a friendly administration that recognized the importance of women's studies, particularly after President Johnetta Cole arrived in 1987. In addition, we always had supportive provosts, both in Donald Stewart's administration and in Cole's with Barbara Carter, Ruth Simmons, and Glenda Price. So we didn't have administrative resistance, which is not the case in many historically black colleges, where the leadership has been predominantly male. The other advantage we had from the very beginning was external funding, much of which came from the Ford Foundation, which meant that we had sufficient external financial support to really do the kind of faculty development on campus that I think was necessary for the curricular transformation. Finally, over time we began to get a critical mass of faculty and students who were very interested in women's studies courses as well.

EH: There's been this fairly extensive critique about identity politics both within and outside of the academy. The argument is that programs like women's studies have institutionalized political agendas, which you referred to when you were talking about some of the barriers at historically black colleges. It has been suggested that this political agenda perpetuated rather than ended discriminatory treatment of women because the programs are often cast as victim studies. Is this a problem for black women's studies? Or is the problem somewhat different in that women's studies is perceived to be aligned with feminism and feminism is perceived as "white?" As a result is the question of identity politics posed in terms of "feminism" vs. "nation/black community"—expressed in neonationalist rhetoric which argues that black women don't need to study/research or critically interrogate their position as women separate from the concerns of the "race"?

BG-S: I think that people who identify with black women's studies are aware of, and in opposition to, the victim studies orientation of traditional Western feminist approaches to understanding women's experience. Black women's studies, almost from its inception, wanted to theorize about the oppression of women of African descent but also wanted very much to talk about the ways that black women resisted. Black women's studies consciously and very explicitly wanted *not* to construct a discourse that primarily emphasized black women's victimhood. At the same time though, black women's studies' advocates were up against the notion that black women were in fact not oppressed and had not been victimized. So we had to find a balance between the two premises because within African American communities there's the notion that black women have not been victimized at all, particularly vis-à-vis black men. This was the difficult balance that black women's studies had to negotiate. I think we have done a pretty good job of both emphasizing the multiple oppressions that black women face, but also we have emphasized the issue of resistance and the need to interrogate the different ways black women experience patriarchy.

EH: What about the question of feminism?

BG-S: I think that black women's studies has as one of its main contributions its reconceptualization of feminism. It has not rejected feminism, but we have said that it needed to be expanded, broadened, and made more sensitive to the issues of race and to global questions with respect to constructions of womanhood outside the United States, around the world. I think black women's studies really reinvigorated and reconceptualized feminism in such a way so that now it is not a narrow, culturally specific manifestation of one group of women's experiences.

EH: I agree that black women's studies has been successful in pluralizing women's experiences, but do you still see a tension in talking about the need to critically interrogate the position of black women vis-à-vis the concerns of "the race" especially when it has been said, pejoratively perhaps, that "the race" is really a code for the concerns of black men?

BG-S: I agree with your assessment of this persistent dilemma, which may also explain why it is that you don't have adequate women's studies curricula at historically black colleges. Or in publications that black people produce. I still think that there's the assumption that teaching African American studies means primarily dealing with racial questions.

EH: Yes, so do you think that identity politics and the whole question of difference as it's characterized in women's studies programs in predominantly white institutions—is the same kind of problem that women's studies faces in the historically black college context?

BG-S: I don't think so. I think that one of the problems that women's studies faces at white colleges is an inability to deal with difference, and here I'm talking primarily about white faculty and white students. There's still tremendous reluctance on the part of women students of color, particularly African American women, to come into women's studies at white institutions, to literally bring their bodies to the court. That is not the same problem that you have at historically black colleges. In other words, we get students into women's studies courses at Spelman because they are not assuming that when they enter the courses they're going to be about white women or taught only by white faculty. The problem that we have at Spelman is that there are many students who are uncomfortable or hostile to feminism. They think our courses are about feminism, which they find uncomfortable because they see it as something that is going to make it difficult for them to have relationships with men.

EH: What about the difference in terms of other women of color or the difference of sexuality or sexual preference?

BG-S: With respect to those questions, black women's studies is still dealing with a number of problems. In my experience in teaching women's studies at Spelman, the questions of sexuality are probably the most contested and result in the most tension and the most difficulty in the classroom. I think that's because there's so little in the curriculum otherwise that helps students to understand sexuality beyond what they already know. They've had very little discourse which helps them to analyze sexuality in an intellectual and analytical manner, so they're just coming at it with their personal belief systems, like most college students, with their personal values that haven't been subjected to any rigorous analysis. So this remains a big problem. With respect to other women of color, there is a lack of information or misinformation about other peoples of color, particularly in the United States. We have to spend a lot of time discussing the fact that black people are not the only group of people who have had difficulties with race in this country or the world.

EH: Now it's often talked about that women's studies in the United States has been successfully institutionalized, although everything you have just said about what has happened in historically black colleges suggests that is not the case in all institutions. Institutionalization of women's studies, as you've pointed out, is at a very different point in historically black colleges. Given that there are your program and others, including the one at Howard, how are they perceived from abroad? I ask this because I think that American women's studies is perceived to be very well established, very well funded, very well supported. Do you think your program and Howard's are seen in this way? For example, I remember when a student of Philomena Essed's came over from Holland to do interviews for her dissertation on black feminism. When she visited me and Fran White at Hampshire College, she said she was looking for the black feminist institute. She believed from reading a number of anthologies and other books on black women's studies that have been widely translated that it must have had an institutional location here in the States. Fran and I laughed somewhat ruefully, but that exchange along with many others gave me the impression that there's this idea that black women's studies is as well established in the United States as women's studies more generally.

BG-S: Let me say two things quickly. First of all, I think that even the question about the institutionalization of white women's studies is a complicated one. I think that in some ways, despite the fact that there are over six hundred women's studies programs in the U.S. academy, women's studies is still institutionally fragile, in the sense that most women's studies programs are without their own faculty lines and have inadequate budgets and very little control over their curricula because they depend on departmental courses or joint appointments. There've also been in recent years a tremendous backlash and some tightening of resources, so that, though women's studies is visible and has had a tremendous impact, it may not be the case that it is institutionally strong in the sense that we think about traditional departmental studies. It is still the case that even if they are fragile, black women's studies probably has almost no institutional strength.

EH: Yours is still a program—not a department?

BG-S: Yes, it's still a program. Ours functions more like a department, but the program is how it is instituted. Structurally, it is not quite as fragile for the reasons I discussed earlier. However, I think that could quickly change.

It helps that our women's studies program is in an institutional home (the Women's Center) where it functions more like a department, though it's still problematic because we don't have any faculty lines. My faculty line is still in the English department. There are no prominent black women's studies programs in the United States. And I think it's also fair to say that most well-established African American studies programs do not have even what I would call a serious black women's studies concentration.

You might assume that since the institutionalization of black women's studies has not happened within women's studies it is happening within African American studies. Yet this is not the case. As you know, before Elsa Barkley Brown left the University of Michigan, she and other faculty there were working on a gender concentration within African American studies. If they had succeeded, this would have been tantamount to mounting a black women's studies component within that program. Currently, there are no major African American studies programs with a focus on gender. On the other hand, another potential site for the institutionalization of black women's studies is within women's studies programs with a significant number of black women faculty. The University of Maryland's women's studies program, because of the presence of so many black women faculty, certainly has this potential. If black women's studies has a future, in terms of institutionalization, I think it is in those women's studies programs like Maryland's because the difficulties in developing autonomous black women's studies programs are so severe.

EH: I want to take that up in a second, but what about the question of perceptions from abroad?

BG-S: Oh, I think that you're right. The assumption about the strength of black women's studies has no relationship to the reality. But you can also understand why there would be that perception because of the huge popularity of black women writers (mostly novelists) outside the United States—which prompts people to think that there's a cultural context that produces those writings, but it's not in women's studies or the academy by and large. The reception of these books also speaks to the popularity of black feminism outside the United States, which supports the assumption that it is institutionalized within the American academy—which it's not.

EH: Does the popularity of black feminist writings make a demand on black women's studies programmatically to try to address questions about women of color in the diaspora? In other words, when you engage in conversations with other women of color from around the world, as you do when you participate in Andrée McLaughlin's International Cross-Cultural Black Women's Studies Institute, do you have to represent black women's studies as being engaged programmatically with the broader concerns of women in the diaspora?

BG-S: Absolutely. Black women's studies can't be narrowly focused on the United States.

EH: I would argue that's somewhat different from white women's studies. It is not always forced to have that engagement.

BG-S: Right. I think that black women's studies is much more inherently, or at least potentially, global because it is interested in black women's experiences all over the world. As early as 1981, with the publication of Filomena Steady's edited volume *The Black Woman Cross-Culturally,* black women's studies has tried to address the experiences of women on the African continent and in the diaspora, especially in the Caribbean.

EH: Let's return to the question of integrating women's studies into the curriculum more broadly. There's a lot of debate going on right now about whether or not women's studies programs should change their names to feminist studies or gender studies . . . and people are talking about the advantages and disadvantages of such a change. You were just speaking about the integration of black women's studies into African American studies. Would an emphasis on gender rather than women make that integration more possible?

BG-S: I'm one of the people who believe that women's studies ought to keep the name women's studies. I think the whole debate about gender studies is mostly a political one, and I also see a problem with the name feminist studies. If we change to feminist studies, we will face more problems among persons of color.

EH: Well, a change to feminist studies also narrows women's studies.

BG-S: It also narrows it. That's right. I think that women's studies is sufficiently generic and also keeps in the forefront that it emerged from a political movement that began twenty or thirty years ago that's still in progress.

EH: What about gender studies?

BG-S: First of all, I think that women's studies is inherently gender studies. Women's studies claims that it uses gender as a major category of analysis—so therefore to me it's already gender studies. Now that women's studies is moving more toward interrogating constructions of masculinity, I don't think we have to change the name for gender to remain a primary focus. I believe women's studies has already been primarily interested in gender—which has been the major critique by women of color. It hasn't been sufficiently concerned about issues of race and class. I don't think the problem is gender.

EH: I also wanted you to think about this question in light of the position taken by Mamphela Ramphele in her essay "Whither Feminism?" [initially given as a response on a panel at the "Transitions, Translations, Environments: Feminisms in International Politics" conference held at the Institute for Advanced Study and Rutgers in 1995]. In the essay, Ramphele argues, quite persuasively I thought, that feminists need to outline a new vision of gender equity and to directly confront the oppression of men by patriarchy. I thought she specifically put this challenge to African American feminists to address and produce a theory of power.

BG-S: I found her essay problematic, or maybe I could agree with her if she's mostly thinking about the South African context. I think it would be very difficult for me to argue that patriarchy has had as detrimental an impact upon men as it has had on women, which I think she basically says. I could agree, and I think she is probably one of the people who noted early on, that racism has had a very profound impact on white people in ways that we don't think that much about. (James Baldwin also made this point, much earlier.) I don't think, however, that it means racism has had the same impact or as devastating an impact as it has had on black people. And I think that she actually says that.

EH: Well, I agree with you, but I also think that in the positive reading of it from my perspective, it's her insistence that we need to think about the next step. I think she was speaking specifically to the South African context: now that they're in the place of making a new society, they've got to think about gender equity in a new way and therefore take into account the oppression of black African men by white men.

BG-S: What she does not mention in that essay is the oppression of black South African women by black South African men. I think that's the part that was missing. Her premise can be tested in the African American case, but African American feminists have also argued that black men have been complicit in the oppression of black women, and I don't see that in her equation. She also doesn't address the serious problem of violence against black women in South Africa by black men. That is one of the ways the patriarchy has also impacted South African men.

EH: Yet, you don't think she goes far enough in her analysis.

BG-S: No. I agree with her—that it certainly is the case that women of African descent are as concerned about black men as they are about themselves.

EH: Her point raised for me the ongoing difficulties that black feminists have had in confronting patriarchal attitudes within black communities. I think of the problems we encountered in the group of black feminists, largely academics, when we were drafting a black feminist response to the Million Man March. Or earlier when we responded to the Anita Hill/Clarence Thomas hearings. We had real problems trying to talk about male power. And maybe we don't want to go so far as to call it patriarchy, but I felt there was an urgent need to figure out some way to theorize the power that men of color have over women of color. In other words, don't we as black feminists have to find a way to theorize race and gender at the same time?

BG-S: I absolutely agree with that. One of the comments Ramphele makes is that black women want to understand the behavior of black men. I think that this should be a focus of black women's studies, to really look at issues of black masculinity. When we talk about black men, we usually discuss how they have been disempowered racially, but we don't talk about their gender. We race black men, but we don't gender them. This is a critical issue that black feminist scholarship has to address.

EH: In a sense what you're saying is that black women's studies has fallen into the same trap that women's studies has more broadly, in conflating gender with women and thus failing to adequately theorize race *and* gender. As a result, you are arguing that the issue of black male power has to be considered under the rubric of black masculinity.

BG-S: Right. I put it under black masculinity and patriarchy. Which I think, speaking about the future, should be a key area within African American studies as well, which it currently is not.

EH: But hopefully the integration of gender into African American studies might bring that conversation into being. What other issues do you most worry about in terms of the future of women's studies?

BG-S: I continue to worry about the inability of women's studies to deal—in appropriate ways—with issues of race and difference, particularly difference in a cross-cultural context. I don't think women's studies does a good job of addressing women's issues outside the West. Those issues are not always related to race. It could be religion; it could be all kinds of issues, though race continues to be a problem. Also, the persistent white face of women's studies in the United States continues to be a problem. There just are not enough faculty of color within women's studies. The problem is equally dismal within African American studies. The hostility to feminism and to black feminism in black studies is as strong as it was ten years ago, I suspect—with a few exceptions in places where black women and a few black men in black studies are actually self-identified as people who use feminist frameworks. I continue to worry about the hostility to black feminism within African American studies and the continued domination of that field by men hostile to feminism.

EH: What about affirmative action rollbacks?

BG-S: This is going to be devastating with respect to black students' access to white institutions. Think about the situation in Texas, where the affirmative action guidelines in place at the University of Texas have been overturned by recent court orders. Also, the latest data from California show a decline in admissions of students of color as a result of affirmative action rollbacks. The other thing is that the assault on affirmative action also confirms for many black people that race is still the primary problem that black people face, which provokes even more resistance to foregrounding gender.

EH: You hear black people arguing that race is still primary because white conservatives are not going after programs to prevent gender discrimination.

BG-S: And they also see white women as successful.

EH: Yes, but I think that perception only highlights the way in which gender is misunderstood, if not ignored, by some black people. Affirmative efforts to end gender discrimination are seen as only benefiting white women, not black women or women of color. This is precisely why, as you've already suggested, it is critical for black women's studies to engage the intersection of gender and race.

Finally, what do you dream about for black women's studies? You know you have to end up with a comment about your vision for the future of black women's studies.

BG-S: The thing that still keeps me committed to this is that I am absolutely certain that women's studies has the capability of transforming black students so that they can develop a radically different lens by which to view the world, one that allows for a more complicated, more nuanced, and more ambiguous view that ultimately would support a deeper intellectual curiosity. Women's studies can force these students to question their values and the ways in which they have been socialized, which I think would produce students who are more critical, more willing to engage in activist projects that would propel them out of the classroom and that would push them out of their "comfort zone" to engage a broader range of questions instead of having a narrow focus on race.

My visionary statement is that women's studies can radicalize students of color and help them see the world in very different ways than they saw the world before they entered a women's studies class. Especially around issues of sexuality. I taught one of the first women's studies courses in the English department at Spelman in the mid-seventies. I've been doing this for over twenty-five years, and I am as excited about the women's studies classroom as when I began.

SUCCESS AND ITS FAILURES

Biddy Martin

If women's studies has reached a point of stasis on some campuses, it is due in no small measure to its success. Women's studies has succeeded in defining and delimiting objects of knowledge, authorizing new critical practices, significantly affecting scholarship in a number of disciplines, defining important political issues, and establishing itself as a legitimate academic and administrative unit on hundreds of college and university campuses. With these kinds of successes come problems. Having delimited a proper object and carved out particular domains, having generated and disseminated specific analytic practices, having developed consensus about at least some key political problems, and having been institutionalized on equal footing with other academic and administrative units, women's studies has lost much of its critical and intellectual vigor.[1] Women's studies has now settled in. It has and is a location, and the business it conducts could not be more usual. Many of the terms of political analysis and debate, some key critical procedures, and our modes of interacting with one another across disciplines have become so entrenched as to be stultifying; however conventionalized they have become, they are often protected from challenge and change by the piety with which they are repeatedly invoked and the familiarity they have come to enjoy.

In an intellectual and educational environment, endless repetitions of the already known eventually begin to fall on deaf ears. Many feminist scholars find their departmental homes more capacious and invigorating than women's studies. Of course, in some of those departments, women's studies scholarship deserves credit for having reanimated the discipline. In some domains, the conceptual tools developed in interdisciplinary feminist exchange have been refined by subjection to larger disciplinary debates and methodological rigor. However, many of the "refinements" could now stand to be challenged from outside the comfort of disciplinary homes. Unfortunately, women's studies is in no position to lead such a challenge because women's studies itself has succumbed to the insularity and then to the wars of the disciplines. To be exciting again, women's studies would have to assume leadership in making major transformations of university curricula and interdisciplinary scholarship and learning. At the moment some women's studies scholarship and some programmatic structures stand in the way of such transformations.

To anticipate the direction of my argument, our discussions of women's studies need to be set in the context of larger discussions about the organization of knowledge and of learning in universities and efforts to change the forms of disciplinary and intradisciplinary balkanization that constrain our intellectual vision and prevent us from providing students a more integrated education. As Nelly Furman argues in an essay on French studies, many disciplines continue to organize knowledge in the ways it was institutionalized in the nineteenth century, according to a sequential, cumulative logic, as though knowledge building and learning were not also analogic, diachronic, and dialogic. Furman makes two crucial suggestions for reorganizing French studies that apply as well to some other disciplinary formations. She recommends that literature and cultural studies departments cease relying on exclusively sequential, chronological, cumulative models in which acquisition of knowledge begins with the beginning and moves forward through time, and shift instead to problem-based learning that entails identifying salient lines of inquiry, or what she calls "virtual sites," and teaching students how to analyze backward from and across those specific sites. In my view, there is no need to oppose sequential, chronological knowledge to the analogic or diachronic. Problem-based interdisciplinary inquiry is essential, however, and there is no reason to believe that the knowledge it produces is less sound than more traditional disciplinary approaches. Disciplinary knowledge and in-depth knowledge of the history of specific problems or methods do not become unimportant, but intradisciplinary debate would play a less dominant role in setting our questions than it currently does. Assuming an administrative job in the College of Arts and Sciences at Cornell University has put me in a position to see the extraordinary redundancies of scholarly interests among the faculty and in curricula across the disciplines. It has also increased my frustration about how little interaction there is across traditional lines despite the apparent changes in university curricula over the past several decades. I will return later to these often only apparent changes.

WOMEN'S STUDIES HAS BEEN PLAGUED from the outset by the exclusions its self-definition entails. We have become habituated to a language that associates such exclusions with the sexual, racial, ethnic, and, to a lesser extent, class differences that are obfuscated by uncritical invocations of an internally consistent category of "woman." We have at our disposal enormously sophisticated theoretical and critical analyses of the exclusionary work that identity categories do.[2] Still, what we enact in our intellectual and institutional interactions with one another admits of little nuance. Righteousness accrues to positions with apparent claims to marginality, while the privilege of unknowing continues to protect those who choose single-mindedly to pursue only their own career successes. Still others use guilt to absolve themselves of the responsibility to engage one another or themselves in ways that would change hopelessly rigid suppositions and rhetorical habits.

Crisscrossing and exacerbating the often routinized ways of representing race, class, sex, and transnationalism are forms of difference that have received very little discussion. These are differences in institutional and professional status, for example, that are inevitable once significant numbers of women gain a foothold in their universities and their disciplines and once feminist scholarship has professional cachet. In the days when "love of women" and women's studies resonated with each other, we seemed capable of eroticizing individual women's strengths, authority, even power, and of enjoying seduction without abandoning claims to justice. (Some people still can.) In these sparer days, when institutional transferences and their accompanying eroticisms have given way to a much more insistent vigilance about abuse (or to equally or even more problematic claims to have transgressed puritanical claims to injury for the good of all), a more exclusively negative competitiveness reigns. I realize, of course, that these "days of old" are mythical, but they help highlight the bind for feminist intellectuals in an environment that requires, or perhaps it would be more honest to say allows, us finally to distinguish ourselves, but only if distinctions do not introduce differences that we find difficult to square with our political biases against institutional authority and its assessments of merit. The mixed messages we get and pass on to each other about distinctions in merit, status, visibility, and influence need to be fully acknowledged and then abandoned in favor of serious discussions about how to introduce into the institution greater differentiation in views of and rewards for different strengths and functions. As long as the current system of rewards and privileges dominates, certain talents and commitments will continue to be undervalued and the present system of values will continue to have gendered implications. We tell ourselves that resentment and relentless competitiveness can be blamed on the scarcity and unfair distribution of rewards and recognition, and this defense can never fail since it always contains truth. But there are also other sources of negativity such as the mistrust we seem at times to think we owe ourselves as oppositional intellectuals of the possibility of even minimally legitimate forms of authority and distinction, a cynical mistrust that can excuse us from acknowledging how, as educators, we inevitably exercise both. Oppositional stances can sometimes become rigid defenses against political participation. Though I think these issues warrant a great deal more discussion and action, I am not going to assume responsibility for engaging them here.

I want to focus on how and why knowledge and learning need to be more significantly reorganized, not only in women's studies but in the university as a whole. As I suggested above, women's studies' scholarship and curricula have come over time to replicate rather than challenge entrenched wars between the disciplines, with the consequence that neither feminist scholarship nor women's studies programs are in a particularly good position to take the lead in completing transformations they helped begin. Because assumptions about what it means to "study women" have constrained feminist scholarship across a range of disciplines, many feminists and queer theorists have long advocated a shift from the identity politics that inhere in women's studies to the apparently more expansive terms of gender and sexuality studies. I have supported that shift, but for some time I have also been teaching, speaking, and writing about the excesses of "social constructionism" and the repetitive and predictable analyses of gender that constructionist languages have inspired. Here I want to suggest that gender studies does not necessarily hold out the promise it has been assigned. Gender, too, may have outlived its usefulness, requiring of us more substantive forms of reflection and change if interdisciplinary feminist studies are to contribute again to the changes that are occurring and need to occur in our modes of thinking and writing in higher education. Every field in which feminist analysis has had a significant impact has a similar story. Putting "women" at the center of inquiry initially opened canonical works to questions about their often troubling images and, later, added writing by women to curricula and to the canon. The centering of woman and of feminist concerns also exposed the "sexist" premises at the heart of a range of traditional and oppositional approaches, putting their adequacy into question and generating exciting revisions and transformations of marxist, neomarxist, and liberal theories of (in my field of German studies) socioeconomic and cultural relations. Formalist, structuralist, and marxist approaches to literary texts were appropriated, negated, and reformulated. The influences of "French feminist" theory introduced new terms and practices from deconstruction and psychoanalysis and expanded the scope of inquiry to phallocentric and repressed workings of "the feminine." But the exclusive focus on "women" and "the feminine" also constrained feminist work. Significant developments in the field with no immediately apparent relationship to "women" or gender received little attention from feminist scholars, with the result that both feminist criticism and larger theoretical debates have been impoverished by ignorance of each other.

At the same time, the shift from the study of women to analyses of gender and sexuality has opened up new fields of interest and made feminist work central to the emerging field of cultural studies. But the alliance of gender studies with cultural studies has also had leveling effects. Cultural studies' projects on gender and sexuality have produced innovative syntheses of different disciplinary methods and objects but are organized by a split that has come to seem one of the most symptomatic and disabling—the split between theories of culture and its construction of gender, on the one hand, and developments in the biological sciences, on the other. Some cultural studies work on gender defines its critical agenda precisely by way of the exclusion of science, and of biology in particular. As a result, gender studies is caught between traditional ways of organizing knowledge (humanities and social sciences versus the so-called hard sciences) and more innovative modes of interdisciplinary inquiry that cross these lines.

My concern about the radical critique of science in the humanities and some social sciences has intensified over the past three years for several reasons. First, collaborative work with a child psychologist on theories of clinical intervention and play has forced me to question a tendency in the humanities to adopt what we take to be properly Freudian, Lacanian, and to a lesser extent Kleinian theory and then to produce dogma, dismissing out of hand revisionist psychoanalytic or alternative psychological approaches to psychic life, psychopathology, and clinical intervention—not necessarily or even primarily on the basis of our knowledge of those alternatives and certainly not on the basis of clinical or research experience in psychology, but simply because we *know* there is nothing adequate to the task of explaining psychic life except specific psychoanalytic theories and their anti-essentialist forms. (For their part, social scientists dismiss not only psychoanalysis but increasingly all interpretive approaches to emotion, cognition, and behavior with horribly leveling consequences.) A second reason for my concern comes from contact with a neurobiologist with whom I shared administrative duties in the College of Arts and Sciences and whose interests overlapped significantly with my own. I also spent most of my administrative time chairing a task force charged with a structural review of the Division of Biological Sciences at Cornell and, hence, speaking with biologists about their work and the future of the biological sciences in general.

From neurobiologists I have learned that cognitive and neuroscientists work with model systems in their efforts to map neural networks, not with what they take to be one-to-one relations between observation and underlying facts about causation. Few of them harbor the illusion that the neural connections they can now activate or see authorize simple causal explanations. Even the most reductionist biologists, with their faith in the possibility that human cognition and emotion can be localized once and for all, acknowledge that they are a long way from being able to explain human emotions, cognition, or behavior with recourse to specific, putatively determinative parts of the brain or even with recourse to the pathways and networks they are increasingly able to map. A less reductionist interpretation would hold that the whole is always greater than the sum of its parts and that what emerges and manifests human consciousness, affect, and behavior will never finally be located, but will instead prove to be overdetermined and explicable only in the relative terms of "differentness" methods, that is, assessments about the differently weighted intensities of activation across or within networks.[3]

In the humanities, we have defended against the dominance of the sciences in the university and outside it by nominating ourselves critics of empiricism and anti-essentialist watchdogs. Radical challenges to objectivity, empiricism, and essentialism have had important consequences, but we have also permitted them to absolve us of the responsibility to recognize scientists' own antifoundationalisms or to acquaint ourselves with what is going on in science at all. The resistance among many feminist scholars to the notion that "biology" might play any role at all in the construction of subjectivity is indicative of a defensive rather than a genuinely curious and interrogative procedure. The social sciences seem split between the harder social sciences, with their claims to be scientific and hence outside the overly narrow parameters of (humanities) feminist inquiry, and the soft, interpretive social sciences that risk falling into the underfunded humanities. The only way to sustain the vital tension between the inferential and the empirically verifiable is to lower or make permeable the defensive boundaries, to cease and desist from the "wars of the faculties," to interrogate the interpretive for its explanatory adequacy, and to study the scientific for its embeddedness in the inferential, the interpretive. In order to reorganize education and scholarly exchange around problems so that we bring our different areas of expertise to bear on one another's assumptions, we have to become curious again, curious about what different disciplinary formations and knowledge can contribute to problems or questions that we share. Whether women's studies, as it is currently organized, can generate productive forms of curiosity and reorganization remains an open question. I will venture an answer at the end of this essay.

WE RESEARCH, WRITE, AND TEACH in an environment in which technology and information threaten, so we are told, to make literature and the book obsolete, in which resources for education continue to diminish, in which the imperative to prepare students for a rapidly changing job market makes the humanities an expensive and unduly time-consuming luxury in the eyes of many and, in the eyes of the far right, a decadent luxury represented by the "ne'er-do-wells" and advocates of cultural devolution. In such an environment, we cannot afford to be smug, complacent, or defensive. What options do we have? Let us consider two different approaches to changes in the educational environments in which we work.

In *The University in Ruins,* Bill Readings provides a historical and political analysis of the crisis in university education and our responses to it. According to Readings, we live and teach in a posthistorical, transnational era in which the traditional mission of the university has declined, even disappeared. The transmission of culture and the production of national citizens who share a general education have given way to "the pressures of the cash nexus." The university has changed from being "an ideological arm of the state" to "an autonomous, bureaucratic corporation whose internal regulation is entirely self-interested without regard to wider ideological imperatives" (40).

Readings emphasizes the pressures on universities to integrate fully into bureaucratic, administrative, information-based systems that demand efficiency in the transmission of information from one level of administration to another and also from teacher to student. Transparency is enjoined everywhere in the system and between systems, and decisions about inclusion and exclusion are made on the basis of the relative opacity / transparency of one system to another. Organizational and intellectual complexity are abandoned not for ideological reasons but because of the need for simple sequential processing. When it costs more for the [computer] system to create or accommodate nontransparencies or opacities, for example, decisions are negotiated at least in part around questions of cost. Evidence for Readings's point is provided every day in university planning and program reviews, where the infatuation with the measurable and with instruments for measurement have reached all-time highs. Perhaps the most pointed example of Readings's view is the emergence and growing popularity of distance learning and "Drive-Thru Universities" as substitutes for on-campus, classroom learning. At a recent presentation about the benefits of distance learning, I noted with some alarm that the decreased need for faculty and for classrooms was being sold to universities as one of the major advantages even of traditional liberal arts and research campuses. Rather than merely lamenting or worrying about such developments, humanities faculty need to think seriously about the technological and economic forces that drive them and respond with something other than refusal, dismissal, or invocations of tradition. Readings argues that we live in a "de-referentialized" university, one in which the discourse of excellence has replaced the discourse of culture and in which familiar ideological battles are replaced with struggles for administrative rationalization. *Excellence* is an empty term and for that very reason marks the moment when "nation-state is no longer the major site at which capital reproduces itself." What we teach or write now "matters less than having it taught excellently." "Excellence," writes Readings, "serves as a unit of currency within a closed field" and allows for the maximum of internal administration (13). The discourse of excellence, he concludes, draws only one boundary: the boundary that protects the unrestricted power of the bureaucracy (27). The university, in other words, is saturated with an antihumanism far more radical than any theory produced in the humanities.[4]

Readings maintains that the differentialized university produces more and more internal administration without reflecting on substantive questions of value. Indeed, program reviews, strategic planning, academic leadership workshops, and "Quality Improvement" initiatives do seem designed to bring deans and faculty into our proper roles as assessors, measurers, regulators, and promoters of efficiency, transparency, and excellence. But the fact that all this activity creates enormous inefficiency seems to have escaped Readings's and many university administrators' notice. According to Readings, "All the system requires is for activity to take place" because activity produces the appearance of accountability in the form of accounting (39). Activity generates visibilities, the visibility of excellence that attracts student tuition and outside funding, despite or because of the difficulty of ascertaining the bases for assessments of merit. In such a universe, there is always the threat that everything substantive will be dissolved in the "acid bath of specularity."[5] Readings insists, however, that there is also opportunity in this universe.

Readings evinces no nostalgia for the "referential" university in which a general education produced or reproduced national values and cultural norms. Nor does he yearn for the liberal individual freed from tradition, poised to pursue individual achievement and success. The tools of citizenship have been defined in the terms of limitless possibility, acquisition, and expansion for too long. Freedom from tradition *is* our cultural tradition or our favored legitimation strategy, undergirded nonetheless by fantasies of community predicated on various forms of exclusion.

What are our options, then, if we do not wish more frantically to do what can be measured more excellently, or do more excellently what can be measured? Readings argues that we have three possibilities: we can return to national culture; we can reinvent cultural identity in changing circumstances; and/or we can abandon the notion of redemptive education altogether and challenge the idea that the social mission of the university is linked to realizing a national or cultural identity, even a resistant or oppositional one (90). We can, he maintains, dedicate ourselves instead to the incompleteness of Thought and the interminability of pedagogy, opposing them to the imperative to produce an excellence that can be measured, easily administered, made transparent to consumers, and learned or acquired once and for all.

The return to national culture is not off the table, certainly not in the U.S. Congress or even in the NEH, but for our purposes it seems more important to dwell on the second of Readings's three possible strategies, "the reinvention of cultural identity for changing circumstances," because this is the project to which women's studies and feminist cultural studies have at least tacitly committed themselves. In Readings's view, this strategy is doomed to failure. Women's studies, even queer studies, can succeed in establishing themselves in the university; they can even become significant trends, because ideology has given way to administrative transparency, integrated (market) systems, and claims to "excellence." In an environment where a unified culture no longer matters, cultural studies and multiculturalism can become all the rage, but for Readings the claims to marginality and the appeals addressed to the center demonstrate a clear failure to see that there is no center, or at most, that it is empty. "Representation is no longer the battleground," Readings writes, and "if the ideological has become visible, it is because the high-stakes game has moved on to another table" (104). This is an important if controversial argument. "In general," he writes, "the effect of multiculturalism is necessarily to homogenize differences as equivalently deviant from a norm" (113).

So, the ideological has become visible, the marginal has achieved a measure of representational significance, and cultural politics appear salient at the very moment that the center of culture has been evacuated. We enter the fray, demanding representation when there is no Other to whom we might represent ourselves and no center to disrupt. Without adjudication or even prohibition at the hands of the traditional bearers and protectors of culture, our cries for a hearing will be neither suppressed nor heard since there is no place from which we could continue to be excluded. This is not to say that wrongs have been righted or problems solved, but only that our approaches to wrongs and to problems may require new strategies.

The evacuation of a center has generated a great deal of confusion in women's studies at Cornell, where much recent activity has been concentrated in "Gender and Global Change" and "Lesbian, Bisexual, Gay and Transgender Studies." Some faculty members have wondered out loud where women's studies stands or where it is in relation to what were once subgroups or offshoots of the program that now seem to have moved into the center. How should we interpret these questions? Is it possible that there are no "women" left, no unmarked or "normal" women to occupy the center of our programs or our analyses? This could be seen as a conceptual and political triumph, but many would argue that a number of significant problems that affect women as women have dropped out of serious deliberation and debate. It may also be the case that the most helpful analyses of women's situation and of gender as a construct are being generated within these only apparently specialized fields within women's studies. Or we could imagine with Readings that the demands of the competitive market system (of ideas) requires constant movements of specialization and unceasing presentations of "the new," with the result that domains located on the "cutting edge" merely obscure critical questions or issues that remain at the heart of things because they have gone out of intellectual fashion. All these interpretations have some merit, and I would add that entrenched analytic procedures characteristic of specific domains within women's studies and disciplinary standoffs contribute significantly to the fragmentation of enclaves. Only where scholarship and teaching are problem based and genuinely curious can fragmentation along disciplinary or theoretical lines be challenged. For now I fear that center-periphery arguments are bound to continue inside women's studies programs, and assaults from the outside on transnational and sexuality studies will exacerbate but not necessarily clarify the tensions.

Readings maintains that right-wing and conservative critics of the university and of the humanities are not distressed about the incursions into the canon or the curricula of marginal works and ideas, but are outraged, whether they know it or not, by the evacuation of any center or referent, or any coherent cultural capital available for unfair or fair distribution. He is only partially right in my view—insofar as our own persistent and insistent self-marginalization masks the absence of a center, and in masking it, keeps our attention focused on the wrong turf. As the political theorist Wendy Brown argues, the failure to understand how power works inevitably leads to ever more hyperbolic claims to injury on all sides and fewer efforts to negotiate social and political relations (States).[6] Our ideological struggles with and against one another, particularly in the context of identity politics and representation, can at times seem remarkably parochial given what appear to be larger forces at work in the university and in education as a whole.

Readings reserves a particularly strong set of criticisms for cultural studies work that appears less obviously politicized and more "scientific." About the more academic form of cultural studies, Readings asks us to notice:

1. "how little it needs to determine its object" (99), since it defines culture as signifying practice and explains nothing in terms of anything *in particular* (97);

2. how little it *can* determine an object or mission, since it has "committed to the generalized notion of signifying practice, to the argument that everything is culture [and] can only oppose *exclusions* from culture—which is to say, specifications of culture" (102);

3. how it has academicized culture, "taking culture as the object of the university's desire for knowledge, rather than the object the university produces" (99);

4. how it has misdiagnosed the situation, focusing on exclusions from culture for understanding "our abiding sense of non-participation *despite the fact that we are no longer excluded*" (103).

I have reproduced this critique because I, too, lament the relentless "becoming science" not only of the social sciences but also of the humanities and the abandonment of any commitment to sophisticated thinking about the gap between first-person and third-person knowledge. It seems important to link Readings's emphasis on the institutional will to transparency with what he calls the "academicizing" of culture in our calls for interdisciplinarity. For Readings, pressures to be interdisciplinary may serve only to turn more and more material into culture and thereby render it nonresistant to the leveling effects of a nonreferential excellence. And indeed, the question remains: in what spaces in the university or in its accounting logic is there room for complexity, depth, pleasure, or the intensities that cannot be made transparent—not even as transparent as desire can be made?

Martha Nussbaum's effort to make women's studies central to a new redemptive mission and a reinvented cultural identity does not answer these questions, but it does allow us to explore another approach to changes in the university. Nussbaum's project, *Cultivating Humanity,* defends curricular reform against right-wing attacks by reorienting liberal education toward the preparation of transnational citizens. Nussbaum's study casts itself as a response to the right wing's assaults on university curricula and research, and she defends curricular reform in terms that challenge conservatives' claims.

Nussbaum makes a strong case for what she calls Socratic education, by which she means reasoned debate, systematic questioning and self-questioning, and forms of achieved objectivity that "transcend the play of forces" (38). She is concerned to distinguish between a general preparation for citizenship and a specialized preparation for a career (294), and she makes a strong case for preparing students to deliberate and negotiate with curiosity, respect, knowledge, and reason. Her principles for Socratic education are designed to encourage critical thought without moral relativism and without intellectual elitism. She favors a curriculum that is problem oriented rather than department or discipline based, and she emphasizes the positive potential in new curricular areas that have generated the most criticism on the far right—African American studies, women's studies, sexuality studies, and transnational studies (to which she refers, symptomatically and problematically, as the study of "non-Western cultures").

Nussbaum could be said to agree with Readings's skepticism about equal representation, given her disdain for identity politics and for the institutionalization of academic projects organized around identity or reparation. In this rigorous and thoughtful study of difference, however, she sees signs of progress in the struggle against prejudice and bias, and she distinguishes between reasonable and unreasonable constructions of difference in each of the new curricular areas. For Nussbaum, each of the reform projects in American universities has not only produced new knowledge at the level of content but refinements of the techniques of reason themselves. Women's studies' emphasis on relational as opposed to absolute knowledge receives a great deal of attention. And Nussbaum spends somewhat more time distinguishing between viable and nonviable approaches in the fields of critical race studies and the study of sexuality than she does on their potential for redefining what critical and rigorous thought might mean. In all three cases, she stresses that new information or knowledge is crucial but that rigorous, critical thinking is even more essential if the university is to fulfill its purpose to help young people learn "how to situate their own tradition within a highly plural and interdependent world" (299).

Nussbaum's version of a curriculum that will cultivate humanity for a transnational world includes the integrated study of gender, sexuality, race and racism, and non-Western cultures. She insists that these projects be moved into the core of undergraduate studies and demands that we provide students not only with new in-depth knowledge but also with certain principles of critical reason and debate to ensure that the teaching of difference is ethical and transferable from one learning experience to another. Nussbaum enjoins us to provide students with a more integrated education rather than asking them to swallow whole the fragments that constitute our separate areas of research specialization. These, it seems to me, are all ethical injunctions worthy of our attention.

Nussbaum's support for making the study of non-Western cultures part of the core of an integrated, undergraduate curriculum and her insistence on modes of thinking about differences rather than on modes of appropriation provide an important intervention into the culture wars over curriculum. But she draws predictably rigid boundaries between reason and its others. Her axioms for the study of difference do not unsettle the assumption that Western culture can serve as ground and referent for reason, even if, as she argues, reason is not an exclusively Western possession. (She reserves her greatest contempt and criticism for those on any point of the political spectrum who claim or imply that logic and reason are specifically Western, phallogocentric, or colonial attributes.) About the claim that particular forms of reason are white, male, and Western, Nussbaum counters that "such criticisms [of logic] typically show ignorance of the logical traditions of non-Western cultures and a condescending attitude to the logical abilities of women and racial minorities" (38). While Nussbaum's warning against excessively rigid oppositions between phallogocentric and feminine— or Western and Africanist—modes of thinking have merit, she assumes too much authority for reason, for the possibility that with reason we can determine where the line between reason and unreason lies. Nussbaum rules trenchant critiques of logic out of bounds by accusing them all of being unreasonable. In the context of women's studies, Nussbaum credits feminist scholarship with having helped transform conceptions of reason through critical examination of received notions of autonomy. However, those feminist critiques of reason that make its rehabilitation more difficult (the work, for example, of Luce Irigaray on the relentlessly phallic construction of logic) do not make it into Nussbaum's discussion except as negative examples.

It is indicative of her implicit definition of reason that Nussbaum makes no mention of queer theory in her chapter on the study of sexuality. Nussbaum defends the centrality of sexuality to core undergraduate curricula by arguing: "Human sexuality is an important topic of scholarly inquiry, as it is an important aspect of life. . . . [I]ndeed, this is one of the most lively research areas in the current academy, in part because it is so unusual to find a central area that has not been thoroughly studied" (223). As she has in every other case, Nussbaum contends here as well that "any program in the study of sexuality is a failure if it remains isolated from the rest of the campus" or "when sexuality studies are dominated by literary theory or initiated entirely from within the Humanities" (248, 254). Nussbaum focuses a significant portion of her defense of the study of sexuality on history but also generates tools for the analysis of our culture's prejudices. What her definitions of value and reason exclude are the more radically critical dimensions of critical race, sexuality, and postcolonial studies, not to mention the insights of psychoanalysis about unconscious motivations or desires. While emphasizing the compatibility of social constructionism and "normative moral evaluation" (230), she stresses the dangers of post-modern critiques of normalization and fails, in my view, to do justice to the difficult relations between normalization and normativity. Not even sexuality interrupts Nussbaum's anxiety-free guidelines for enlightened transnational citizenry.

Nussbaum offers a normative definition of a cultivated transnational citizen, one free from hatred, prejudice, and irrationality, capable of empathic identification and reasoned debate. Given the nature of her project, its implicit and actual audience, and its visibility in public debate, Nussbaum's definitions can be considered expansive within certain obvious limits. Her call for empathy and reason suppresses the more stubborn and less pleasant aspects of our humanity. And she assumes, at least for the sake of argument, that the project of cultivating humanity will synchronize with the availability of time and resources and with the capabilities and desires of the human beings she wishes to cultivate. Her conception of an integrated education elevates philosophy to the master of all others, prohibiting thought that occurs outside the parameters of the good and the intelligible. Her proposals are important but depressingly tame and premised upon surprisingly traditional boundaries among disciplines, replicating the terms that have become familiar from recent "wars of the faculties" in just the ways Readings had predicted would govern the elevation of "reason" as the new referent. In Nussbaum's proposal, literary study is reduced to the status of handmaiden to a philosophical/historical study of the universal and the good, useful for expanding students' narrative imagination and their capacity for empathy. Literary theory, and its poststructuralist variants, are cast as the devil because of their assaults on truth, their putative lack of rigor, and what Nussbaum sees as their purposeful unintelligibility.

Yet Nussbaum gives little ground on the question of the availability of truth, refuting "the idea that we can have access to the way things are in the universe entirely independently of the workings of our minds." Citing advances in the philosophy of quantum mechanics and the philosophy of language, she argues: "Some philosophers hold, with Kant, that we can still defend a single conceptual scheme as the most adequate to reality; some hold that there is a small plurality of adequate schemes governed by stringent criteria of rightness; some adopt a still more elastic pluralism. . . . All with the exception of Rorty still think we can establish claims as true by arguments that rightly claim objectivity and freedom from bias" (39). For Nussbaum, challenges to realism and empiricism can be contained and cast as "new articulations of the goals of objectivity and truth" (40). But she forecloses possibilities for reinvigorating interdisciplinary inquiry by closing the gap between what we consider reasonable and what we fear as unreason.

Over and against this kind of education in national or transnational values, or even in the reasonable negotiation of those values, Readings suggests that we think in terms of "the University as a space for a structurally incomplete practice of thought" (19) and that we think community without recourse to notions of unity, consensus, or communication. It is useful to compare Readings and Nussbaum on these questions.

Readings suggests that we should resist the pressure toward transparency, mindless activity, and total integration into bureaucratic, administrative information systems, that we should resist the empty signifier of "excellence" and refuse to make "reason" the new referent. He embraces dereferentialization rather than indulging in nostalgia for a time when the university appeared to have a "general culture" to transmit or values to which it could refer. In the place of "excellence," Readings suggests substituting questions of value and promoting "reflection upon the intersection of community and communication that *culture* names" (123). Rather than "academicizing culture," Readings insists that we remain mindful of the fact that we produce the forms of community and communication that culture names, and he urges us to reflect upon them together.

Nussbaum, too, focuses concretely on classroom situations in which the putative object of study is produced even as it is discussed, where ethical interactions are as central to the work of the university as the content of any course. She continues to support a redemptive mission in the name of reason, and her text is replete with stories of contemporary heroes of education—primarily teacher-heroes, but also students. She urges us to resolve all internal conflict and negative affect through reason, a tool that begins to sound strangely outside us—in that transcendental realm where the individual is only an abstraction and bodies have been rendered fully virtual. Readings, on the other hand, urges us to abandon "the subject" and think of human beings in the terms of peripheral singularities, "aggregated in multiple demographic bands," in a pedagogical relation that is "dissymmetrical and endless." "The parties," he writes, "are caught in a dialogic web of obligations to thought. Thought appears as the voice of an Other that no third term, such as 'culture,' can resolve dialectically" (145), and we must answer to thought as to the Other, to an unknowable, unmasterable network of obligations. Citing the Italian philosopher Giorgio Agamben, Readings suggests that religion is "the discursive sphere in which the awareness of the possibility of an incalculable (and hence unpayable) debt has been preserved in modernity" (188). We do not know in advance the nature of our obligations to others, and the community in formation is always a community of heteronomy and dependence, not emancipation.

To argue that we cannot know in advance the nature of our obligations to one another is to challenge an identity politics that assumes that we already know our obligations to one another, that we know the lines along which they run and the nature of the debt we owe or the payment we deserve. To suggest that we reflect on the culture we are in the process of building, rather than simply turning culture into an apparently fully academic, inert object whose meanings and implications we are positioned to know, introduces a space of deferral into our work, a pause or a break that interrupts the smooth workings of the productivity machine. Reinventing women's studies in this vein would mean suspending, in that breach, what we think we know about our debt and developing a new attentiveness to the relations and the forms of community we enact. Holding open a space for not knowing would permit the study of gender, race, and sexuality to become an exploration again rather than a contestation over what is already known and already owed. For Readings, this requires the third term of "Thought" as an Other to which we have an unanswerable debt, a third term onto which the differences, equivalences, or debts we have distributed among us can be displaced and revisited. This is not a way to unknow what we already know—about forms of oppression, subordination, and discrimination. It is a way to suspend or defer what we know long enough to reflect on a responsibility to that which exceeds, though it ought not to exclude, actual others. The deferral cannot be left uninterrupted or unspaced by efforts at change, efforts based on a belief in what philosopher Gillian Rose calls "a good enough justice" in her critiques of postmodernism.

Nussbaum's university leaves too much intact, makes critical projects too safe, and subjects us all to Reason, to logical argumentation through which our proper positions can be established. Nussbaum's university still has a referent, a center, a redemptive mission, and leaves too little to chance, to play, to unreason, and to the possibility that the effects of the forces of transnationalism may not be so easily contained by reason or by liberal education. In Nussbaum's case, the gap between objective knowledge and subjective experience is filled with ignorance or bias that can be eliminated, since ignorance, for Nussbaum, appears not to be motivated in the strong sense. In Readings, the gap between objective knowledge and subjective experience cannot be closed, and the subject is dissolved in the play of forces out of which subjects and objects take form. However, it is difficult to see in Readings's postmodern language how that gap can be negotiated, what kinds of thought and interaction might go on in the here and now of our exchanges with one another. Nussbaum continues to promote interdisciplinary transparency to reason, while Readings advocates that we create opacities to administrative technologies.

To some degree, despite their very different political and intellectual foundations, both analyses risk too little. Both stay safely within the confines of discourses that have become conventionalized and predictable, Readings within the safety of impossibility and Nussbaum in the security of an easy resolution. In Love's Work: A Reckoning with Life, Gillian Rose argues against both the elevation of reason and its denigration. The "authority of reason," she writes, "is not the mirror of the dogma of superstition, but risk. Reason, the critical criterion, is forever without ground" (128). Rose likens the exercise of reason to children's aggressive play at the borders between fantasy and actuality and laments what she considers to be a simplistic tendency among postmodern thinkers to blame reason for violence. "The child who is locked away from aggressive experiment and play will be left terrified and paralysed by its emotions, unable to release or face them, for they may destroy the world and himself or herself. The censor," according to Rose, "aggravates the syndrome she seeks to alleviate; she seeks to rub out in others the border which has been effaced inside herself" (126). Neither Reason nor dissemination can save us from the difficult pleasures and violences of limits, encounters, and conflict.

To dismiss either Readings or Nussbaum or both for these reasons would replicate horrifyingly easy gestures. I am convinced that we need them both and that they inform each other in productive ways. Where Readings permits himself to get more and more abstract and to emphasize the impossible, Nussbaum reminds us that we have a responsibility to an at least medium-level specificity about what a liberal education in the humanities entails. Readings's commitment to Thought and resistance to consumerism open up the space in which possibilities for less easily imagined and less contained languages, ideas, and interactions might occur, prying us loose from now routinized investments and closures. Nussbaum takes the risk of formulating a positive project, one that responds to a market that demands to know what value the humanities still have, something many postmodern thinkers are loath to do. She assumes responsibility for defining a set of problems around which our students' education and, to some extent, our work ought to be focused. Unless we want to dismiss the need for humanities education entirely, I do not see how we can do without both Nussbaum's redemptive and Readings's disseminatory approaches.

Reinvigoration, however, requires that we do more, that we enter domains that have been excluded by the humanities in general and by our approaches to gender in particular. In the process of engaging what has been disavowed, refused, or ignored, we might unsettle what have become routine and thus impoverished practices. In addition to transforming critical practices, we need to educate ourselves about developments in technology, knowledge, and administrative systems in and outside the university, suspending or deferring questions about what they have to do with women or gender long enough to make our analyses of gender and sexuality new again and supple enough to help us intervene usefully in those developments.

IN THE SPACE REMAINING, I want to hint at one kind of interdisciplinary exploration that may have the potential to move theories of gender in a new direction. I begin again with my objections to forms of social constructionism that indulge a social determinism of psychic life and a psychic determinism of the body—to what Slavoj Žižek, drawing on Fredric Jameson, has characterized as constructionism's "vertiginous progression of universal virtualization" with the consequent loss "of our anchorage in the contracted physical body" (67–68). Žižek writes that "we can never cut the links with our real body and float freely in cyberspace; since, however, our bodily self-experience itself is always already 'virtual,' symbolically mediated, this body to which we are forced to return is not the constituted body of the full self-experience, of 'true reality,' but the formless remainder, the horror of the Real" (66–67). From what vantage point does Žižek think in the terms of a return? Where does he think we have been? What theoretical or metaphorical space does he create between the reductionist assumption of "the constituted body of the full self-experience," on the one hand, and "the formless remainder" or the "horror of the real" on the other? According to Žižek's Lacanian account, *the empty screen onto which we project fantasies,* the "big Other" of symbolic authority, provides the idealizing frame that guarantees internal (because apparently external) consistency and possibility, even as it renders unmediated self-relations and conflict-free intersubjective encounters unthinkable (77). To achieve consistency and coherence requires alienation, alienation from the "formless remainders which resist symbolic integration" (24) and from imaginary assumptions of full self-presence. Intersubjectivity, then, occurs in what Rose has called the "broken middle," the space of redoubled alienation and contingency where both consensus and contestation become far more complex than Nussbaum or Readings would have it. "Ugliness," writes Žižek, "stands for existence itself, for the resistance of reality, which never simply lends itself effortlessly to our molding." Ugliness is also "the site of unbearable, filthy, excessive pleasure—of *jouissance*" (24).

What permits us to approach the real or *jouissance,* the physical reminders of what is truly other in the Other and in ourselves? For Žižek, the psychoanalytic cure and its "traversal of fantasies" returns us from the misrecognitions of our desires to the (sublimated) drives. Presumably, awareness at an affective as well as a more cognitive level of the necessary alienation/separation from formless remainders that has made our own self-consistency possible, if constraining, permits us to integrate rather than *only* abject what is other in the Other. Or perhaps, in Žižek's universe, no more capacious bearings are possible:

> In order to render this notion [the *jouissance* of the Other] palpable, suffice it to imagine an intersubjective encounter: when do I effectively encounter the Other "beyond the wall of language," in the real

of his or her being? Not when I am able to describe her, not even when I learn her values, dreams and so on, but only when I encounter the Other in her moment of *jouissance*: when I discern in her a tiny detail—a compulsive gesture, an excessive facial expression, a tic— that signals the intensity of the real of *jouissance*. This encounter of the real is always traumatic, there is something at least minimally obscene about it, I cannot simply integrate it into my universe, there is always a gap separating me from it. (25)

Here, Žižek succeeds both in making palpable the difficulties of intersubjectivity and in elevating impossibility to an absolute. That we cannot completely integrate the *jouissance* of the other into our universes, that the encounter is "always traumatic" or "minimally obscene" does not entail that it be unalterably unbearable in its intensity or that forms of incomplete integration are not possible. But for Žižek, it is sexual difference that ultimately stands for the imposition of a limit, a limit that puts obstacles in the way of virtualization or desire even as it separates us from the unbearable real to which *jouissance* is bound.

For Judith Butler, on the other hand, our relation to "the contracted physical body" is determined neither by a primordial lack for which sexual difference stands nor by mediation by a necessary symbolic division of the sexes, but by the operation of the social and discursive fields that naturalize their exclusionary workings.[7] Butler argues for a less rigid closure and for more capacious configurations of the social and symbolic fields, *not* a return to the body, to formless remainders, or to the constraining and enabling screens of sexual division. She remains dedicated to the always unfinished, nonredemptive, difficult work of contestation, of politics. Butler has been charged, nonetheless, with deriving the body from the psyche and the psyche too directly from the sociosymbolic in her effort to refute arguments that sexual difference is a necessary and inevitable organizing principle that protects us from both social and biological determinism.

One of the challenges to Butler's efforts to expose the gendering at the heart of sex has been formulated by Pheng Cheah in his work on "mattering" (199). According to Cheah, Butler presupposes an ontological gap between language and the Real, a presupposition she needs in order to invest human bodies with agency, since agency, in anti-essentialist terms, is born of iteration. Cheah suggests that "Butler's account of productive historical forms and her theory of performative agency take the notion of phantasmatic identification . . . as the paradigm for oppression and subversion." He offers an explanation for the limits of this view:

> Generalized into a political theory, this notion of phantasmatic identification promises to democratize contestation through the interminable proliferation and destabilization of provisional cross-identifications. . . . The implausibility of identification as a paradigm of oppression is especially salient in scenarios of oppression where material marks are constituted through physical and not ideational ingestion. . . . The apparent plausibility of the identification paradigm is, in part, based on the tacit presupposition of an established culture of democratic contestation within the constitutional nation-state form. (120–21)

With his focus on "ingestion," Cheah points to something as literal as the availability and intake of food, which he characterizes as a dimension of the conditions of women transnationally that cannot be adequately explained with theories of noncoercive coercion or normalization, that is, with discursive theories of subject formation. Cheah distinguishes Butler's use of repetition and discursive constructions of bodily morphology from Derrida's thinking on dynamism and mattering, in particular, Derrida's focus on organization, on interimplication, and on immanent transcendental weaves:

> Derrida has always desisted from privileging language and instead generalizes the diacriticity of the linguistic sign into a mobile and web-like "structure" of differences and referral that is the condition of possibility of any self-identical unit or formation. . . . Rephrased from the side of individual bodies, spacing or différance designates the constitutive susceptibility of finite bodies to a process of othering from their self-identity. This process of othering inscribes or weaves those bodies into a larger network, a nontotalizable "structure," a moving base that sustains and relates every determinate object, entity, subject, or social formation. This structure is not a transcendent exteriority but a sensible transcendental weave (Derrida calls it "general textuality") where the ideal and the empirical, form and matter, are no longer separate levels that meet at various interfaces but infinitely interlaced. (133)

I have quoted Cheah at length because he uses Derrida against a linguistic determinism that would prevent us from thinking materiality in nonanthropocentric terms while at the same time working against an essentialist assumption about the dynamism of organic matter. Cheah uses Derrida to challenge assumptions about human morphology that ground or justify what he considers to be idealist theories of power. He aims to bring the Derridean trace into contact with theoretical concerns in domains outside literary and cultural studies, a growing theoretical and conceptual imperative and my primary interest here.

Yet another challenge to the conception of deconstruction as a linguistic determinism can be found in the systems-theoretical work of Niklas Luhmann, which has been called German studies' brand of deconstruction. In her introduction to the English translation of Luhmann's *Social Systems*, Eva Knodt writes:

> Genealogy and its contemporary post-structuralist variants perform the shift from a subject-centered to a linguistic frame of reference commonly associated with the "linguistic turn" and radicalize the subject-critical implications of this turn to the point where they run up against the limits of a language that reinstates the God-subject through the very act that proclaims its death. . . . Ironically, the pan-textualist assumptions underlying contemporary critical thought turned out to be one of the toughest obstacles to the formulation of consistently posthumanist positions . . . [T]he linguistic turn and its subsequent problematization never seriously challenged the disciplinary boundaries between the sciences and the humanities. (xxx–xxxi)

Knodt concludes her discussion of the limits of the linguistic turn in deconstruction with the warning that "exploration of the potential convergences between the 'two cultures' remain blocked as long as difference is modeled upon linguistic difference and linguistic self-referentiality is considered the paradigm for self-referentiality in general." She advocates shifting the "Kantian question of how a subject can have objective knowledge of reality" to the question "How is organized complexity possible?" (xvii). Neurocognitive scientists might ask how rhythms get generated out of potential chaos, for example, and how the proliferation and complexity of rhythms get bound, rendered systematic.

My purpose is not to argue for systems theory over deconstruction, but to think about what kinds of conceptual emphases might open our humanities projects onto "their potential convergences" with social sciences and sciences, the exclusion of which has been formative for constructionist projects. Let me stress again that interacting with the social and biological sciences requires that their practitioners reconfigure their presuppositions and analytic practices in ways that make space for and acknowledge the working of the inferential. Potential convergences and mutual reconfigurations are, for example, beautifully developed in Elizabeth Wilson's book on feminism and cognitive science, *Neural Geographies: Feminism and the Microstructure of Cognition*. Wilson puts connectionist theories of cognition, Freudian neurology, and Derridean conceptions of the trace to work on one another, demonstrating their interimplication and providing the immanent transcendental weave through which they take their distance from one another.

Wilson begins her book with a challenge to what she calls feminism's "naturalized anti-essentialism," and she sets out to "rethink our reflexive critical recoil from neurological theories of the psyche" (14). Taking psychology as her focus, Wilson argues that the psychology of women and, later, feminist theories of gender have been enormously constrained in large part because definitions of what it means to do feminist psychology have ruled so much of mainstream psychology irrelevant, reproducing age-old and disabling splits between putatively more objective knowledge and knowledge pertaining to women. She also contends that feminism's "own internal configurations" have excluded biology and that the exclusion of biology is what "render[s] theories of gender intelligible in our current political context" (52). As Cheah does in his work on "mattering," Wilson challenges the premises in gender theory and in social constructionism more generally that "sex and biology naturally incite the need for critical supplementation" and that "biology requires modification and supplementation in order to be analytically viable" (54).

Wilson does not make the mistake of countering such assumptions about supplementation with a return to "the Real" or to a body as full presence. She works instead to put the essentialist tendencies in neurology into question even as she forces gender theory, including feminist appropriations of psychoanalytic theory, out of its now unearned dependence on the negation of the biological sciences—unearned because theories of gender and anti-essentialist rewriting of psychoanalysis so consistently fail to acknowledge "the possibility that biology is always already rewriting itself according to a morphological complexity of difference . . . that biology's outside is already within, its interiority already scattered" (63).

Wilson uses Derrida to expose the "constitutive equivocation over interpretation" in cognitive science, and specifically, in the connectionist theories that lend themselves in any case to comparisons with deconstruction. Wilson acknowledges that she is not the first scholar to bring deconstruction and connectionist psychology into contact with each other; her goal is to show that "biology can be rearticulated as a site of play" once neurological, biochemical, or genetic discourses are refused their tendency to "constitute the biological as fixed, locatable, and originary" (95–96).

The neurological trace becomes the key to restoring mobility and force to analyses in which organic localization has been made the key to causality. Distinguishing connectionist network models from computer or information-processing models, on the one hand, and essentialist neurological models, on the other, Wilson explains that "connectionist models are composed of a web of interconnections between units or between groups of units rather than being arranged in simple linear systems." "Cognitive processing," she continues, "is assumed to be distributed and parallel rather than sequential and linear" (159), and "knowledge is implicit, stored in the connections rather than the units . . . [that is,] stored in the spatial and temporal differences between connection weights" (160). It is worth quoting at some length Wilson's efforts to emphasize "force" over topography:

> Rather than a presence-structure, which processes present and locatable traces, the connectionist network is a trace-structure, wherein the familiar and fixed space of cognition is realized through the mediation of location and mobility, place and force. This refiguring of the cognitive trace and architecture inevitably forces a refiguration of cognition itself. Put technically, it is unclear whether cognitive processing in a connectionist system should be construed as a spatial-structural transformation (the propagation of activation through the network, from input to output, and the correlative back-propagation of feedback) or as a change of state in the network as a whole. Put colloquially, cognition is neither reducible to place nor an abstract process floating free from it. (195–96)

Freud's *Project for a Scientific Psychology,* often read as a prepsychoanalytic neurological work, becomes differently significant when Wilson restores to Freud's work its "mediation of the impossible space between biology and psychology" (184). Wilson shows how Freud's conception of the trace may turn out to have been contemporary with connectionism and, in turn, how connectionist theories can be shown to be deconstructively psychoanalytic. But Wilson is not interested in turning neurology into psychoanalysis, or

biology into deconstruction. She is committed instead to having them transform one another with the ultimate goal of restoring to feminist theories
of gender a conception of overdetermination that is not reduced by relying
on the rejection of science. She stresses over and over that her account
of the potential in connectionist theories is only potential and that work
in neurocognitive science drifts, perhaps inevitably, in a more reductionist
direction. She continues throughout to lament the assumption among constructionists that biology requires supplementation by a notion of culture
that then becomes the ultimate determinant of "the body." In one of her
provocations to neurocognitive scientists, she suggests that "the facilitating
movements and effects of neurocognitive breaching are libidinal." She then
draws out the conceptual implications of this claim:

> The flow of activation across a neural network is an affective move-
> ment that could be described in terms of microintensities, tensions,
> repetitions, and satisfactions. "Pain," Freud reminds us, "passes along
> all pathways of discharge" (1895, 307). So rather than considering the
> vicissitudes of libidinal force (sexuality) to be secondary effects or
> "constructions" around, after, or upon the materiality of cognition or
> neurology, they could more acutely be taken to be the very stuff of
> cognition or neurology. One strategic reversal that would be worth
> considering in this context is that sexuality is not just one manifestation
> of cognitive functioning; instead, cognitive functioning is one manifes-
> tation of the sexualized breaching of neurocognitive matter. (204)

In her welcome efforts to challenge the often unthoughtful ways in
which something called "culture" has become determining in the first and
last instance for many constructionists, Wilson leaves questions about
the openness of psychic systems to social systems. Despite Wilson's own
objections to Butler's putative linguistic determinism, it is here in the in-
terpenetration of psychic and social systems that Butler's work on gender
and sexuality would be required, if not as a supplement, then as a kind of
rerouting. Still, Wilson's critique of "culture" understood as the necessary
supplement to an otherwise inert or infinitely malleable biology provides
a helpful challenge to current trends in cultural studies, with its "academicizing" and paradoxically scientistic claims. Wilson's work opens gender theory and theories of sexuality onto discursive worlds it has either
excluded or ignored, demonstrating in the process that the science onto
which it is opened is itself a richer, more mobile metaphoric field than

many social constructionists, not to mention many cognitive and neuro-scientists, have ever permitted themselves to imagine. Such openings do not necessarily lead to theories more adequate to Truth in the traditional sense. Finding ways to make apparently opposed or mutually exclusionary discursive domains converge does have the potential, however, for challenging doxa, enlivening our languages, and generating theory that is more adequate than available accounts of discursive construction for understanding complexity.

Wilson's work is salutary not only because of its overt and effective assault on the opposition between gender theory and science but also because it introduces nonpsychoanalytic scholarly work in psychology into psychoanalytic and deconstructionist debates that have become tiresomely arrogant with their assertions that there is nothing intellectually interesting in the field of psychology, in nonpsychoanalytic psychology, or even in psychoanalysis in the United States, whether in academic or clinical domains. Given the sorry state of mental health care coverage in the United States and the accompanying decline of clinical approaches other than the stabilizing combination of drug and behavioral therapies; given, too, the political consequences of an economic imperative to stabilize and control rather than treat, even heal, it seems crucial that we shift our focus from the often dogmatic theoretical debates within or between disciplines and intervene from informed positions open to the range of practices that might be usefully brought to bear on shared questions. The field of psychology is obviously but one example of a domain in transition both in and outside the university.

IF FEMINIST STUDIES OF GENDER are to remain vital, or even take the lead in reorganizing our approaches to knowledge and learning, we have to recognize and resist defensive refusals to be moved out of entrenched positions, whether disciplinary or political. Where in our universities and in our professional worlds is the *not known* treated creatively? Where do we find curiosity, risk, and a sense of responsibility to Thought? Where does Thought appear to unsettle dogma or to set aside disciplinary turf wars, yet remain engaged in the risk of the political? Where, when, and under what conditions does the demand for excellence and visibility give way to an effort to interact and build the intellectual connections, with all their pleasures, that women's studies once promised and, at times, has even delivered?

I am not confident that we can find or instill curiosity or risk in many of our women's studies programs, and I do not believe that women's studies as now institutionalized can become the site for the kinds of interdisciplinary intellectual interactions that will compel the imaginations of our faculties and students. Questions about women and gender have to become part of larger and less organized mixes in order to effectively identify and distinguish themselves again. As long as feminist analysis is excluded, even prohibited in our primary and secondary schools and in the culture as a whole, however, university education in women's studies remains absolutely vital. Does the provision of feminist education require freestanding women's studies programs? I think the answer to that question will depend on conditions on specific campuses. It would be naive and dangerous to think that the work of women's studies, or of feminism, is over. The question is whether the work can be done in the context of the programs and intellectual formations we have established and institutionalized. Perhaps the work cannot go on in the absence of the placeholder we call women's (or gender) studies even when much of the liveliest scholarship and teaching is conducted outside its official parameters. At the very least, let us begin discussions that enact the interactions, or to use Readings's terms, the cultures and communities, that we tell ourselves we are only studying.

NOTES

1. I am indebted to Trevor Hope for this formulation that he has used to characterize my objections to specific theoretical critiques of the subject.

2. For an exemplary analysis of the dangers of delimiting "proper objects," see Butler, "Against Proper Objects."

3. Again, the work of Judith Butler is exemplary of such sophistication and has had far-reaching consequences. See, in particular, *Gender Trouble*.

4. I could not help but think of Bill Readings's argument while I watched an interview on CBS with Mike Wallace prior to the airing of his *Sixty Minutes* report on queer studies in the university. Wallace was asked how he responded to his "adventure" into the world of queer studies. His first line of defense against the interviewer's obvious skepticism and critical amusement was to say: "You know, there are really first-rate, excellent people involved in this." The *Sixty Minutes* report itself, in the moments when it entertained the potential legitimacy of queer studies, lingered over George Chauncey's commentary on a truly excellent American, Abraham Lincoln, who shared a bed with a male friend but could not be said definitively to have been homosexual or queer ("Sexuality 101"). Alumni/alumnae

calls to universities on the Monday morning after the show demonstrated that ideological battles or culture wars are not entirely over, but the discourse of excellence, about which the comedian Mike Meyers has produced the "most excellent" commentary, does have significant purchase given its capacity to evacuate substance. Still, according to Readings, we should consider that the discourse of excellence creates opportunities and openings that the discourse of culture has not. I would add that we should probably treat the premium on "excellence" with a little less cynicism than Readings does, despite ample evidence of its negative effects.

5. I am indebted to Ron Hoy, Professor of Neurobiology and Behavior, for the discussions that helped me generate this characterization. He bears no responsibility for any inaccuracies.

6. Brown extends the force of this analysis to the specific question of women's studies in "The Impossibility of Women's Studies," a chapter in this book.

7. See Butler's critique of Žižek in "Arguing with the Real," chapter 7 of *Bodies That Matter*.

Abdo, Geneive. *No God but God: Egypt and the Triumph of Islam.* New York: Oxford University Press, 2002.

Abdo, Geneive, and Jonathan Lyons. *Answering Only to God: Faith and Freedom in Twenty-First Century Iran.* New York: Henry Holt, 2004.

Ahmed, Leila. *Women and Gender in Islam: Historical Roots of a Modern Debate.* New Haven: Yale University Press, 1992.

Alam, Fareena. "Enemy of Faith." *New Statesman* 24 July 2006: 54–55.

Alloula, Malek. *The Colonial Harem.* Minneapolis: University of Minnesota Press, 1986.

Althusser, Louis, and Étienne Balibar. *Reading Capital.* London: New Left, 1970.

Amara, Fadela. *Ni putes ni soumises.* Paris: La Découverte, 2004.

Amara, Fadela, and Mohammed Abdi. *Ni putes ni soumises, le combat continue.* Paris: Seuil, 2006.

Asad, Talal. "Ethnography, Literature, and Politics: Some Readings and Uses of Salman Rushdie's *The Satanic Verses.*" *Cultural Anthropology* 5.3 (1990): 239–70.

———. *Formations of the Secular: Christianity, Islam, Modernity.* Stanford: Stanford University Press, 2003.

Atwood, Margaret. "A Book Lover's Tale: A Literary Life Raft on Iran's Fundamentalist Sea." *Amnesty International Magazine* (fall 2003). http://www.amnestyusa.org/magazine/fall_2003/.

Bahdi, Reem. "Iraq, Sanctions, and Security: A Critique." *Duke Journal of Gender, Law, and Policy* 9.1 (summer 2002): 237–52.

Bahramitash, Roksana. "The War on Terror, Feminist Orientalism, and Oriental Feminism: Case Studies of Two North American Bestsellers." *Critique: Critical Middle Eastern Studies* 14.2 (2006): 223–37.

Bell, Susan Groag, and Mollie Schwartz Rosenhan. "A Problem in Naming: Women Studies—Women's Studies?" *Signs: Journal of Women in Culture and Society* 6 (1981): 540–42.

Bellil, Samira. *Dans l'enfer des tournantes.* Paris: Gallimard, 2003.

Benard, Cheryl. *Civil Democratic Islam: Partners, Resources, Strategies.* Pittsburgh: Rand Corporation, 2003.

Berger, Joseph. "Muslim Woman's Critique of Custom." *New York Times* 25 March 2006: B7.

——. "Scholars Attack Campus 'Radicals.'" *New York Times* 15 Nov. 1988: 22.

Bin Laden, Carmen. *Inside the Kingdom: My Life in Saudi Arabia.* New York: Warner, 2004.

Boddy, Janice. *Civilizing Women: British Crusades in Colonial Sudan.* Princeton: Princeton University Press, 2007.

Bordo, Susan. *Unbearable Weight: Feminism, Western Culture, and the Body.* Berkeley: University of California Press, 1993.

Bornstein, Kate. "Her Son/Daughter." *New York Times, Sunday Magazine* 19 Jan. 1997: 70.

Bowles, Gloria, and Renate Duelli Klein, eds. *Theories of Women's Studies.* Boston: Routledge, 1983.

Brooks, Geraldine. *Nine Parts of Desire.* New York: Anchor, 1995.

Brown, Wendy. *Regulating Aversion: Tolerance in the Age of Identity and Empire.* Princeton: Princeton University Press, 2006.

——. *States of Injury: Power and Freedom in Late Modernity.* Princeton: Princeton University Press, 1995.

——. "Suffering Rights as Paradoxes." *Constellations* 7.2 (2000): 208–29.

Butler, Judith. "Against Proper Objects." *Feminism Meets Queer Theory,* ed. Elizabeth Weed and Naomi Schor. Bloomington: Indiana University Press, 1997. 1–30.

——. *Bodies That Matter: On the Discursive Limits of "Sex."* New York: Routledge, 1993.

——. *Gender Trouble: Feminism and the Subversion of Identity.* New York: Routledge, 1990.

——. "Imitation and Gender Insubordination." *Inside/Out: Lesbian Theories, Gay Theories,* ed. Diana Fuss. New York: Routledge, 1991. 13–31.

——. *Undoing Gender.* New York: Routledge, 2004.

Cheah, Pheng. "Mattering." *Diacritics* 26.1 (1996): 108–39.

Chew, Huibin Amee. "Occupation Is Not (Women's) Liberation." *Znet* 24 March 2005. http://www.zmag.org/ (visited 26 Aug. 2006).

Collins, Patricia Hill. *Black Feminist Thought*. New York: Routledge, 1981.

Coughlin, Ellen K. "In Face of Growing Success and Conservatives' Attacks, Cultural-Studies Scholars Ponder Future Directions." *Chronicle of Higher Education* 18 Jan. 1989: 4–5, 12.

Crenshaw, Kimberle. "Demarginalizing the Intersection of Race and Sex: A Black Feminist Critique of Antidiscrimination Doctrine, Feminist Theory, and Antiracist Politics." *University of Chicago Legal Forum* (1989): 139–66.

Crossette, Barbara. "Militancy: Living in a World without Women." *New York Times* 4 Nov. 2001, sec. 4: 1.

Dabashi, Hamid. "Native Informers and the Making of the American Empire." *Al-Ahram Weekly On-line*, 1–7 June 2006. http://weekly.ahram.org.eg/2006/ (visited 24 Aug. 2006).

"Dark Secrets: A Critic of Islam." *Economist* 10 Feb. 2007: 88.

Deeb, Lara. *The Pious Modern*. Princeton: Princeton University Press, 2006.

Denning, Michael. "'The Special American Conditions': Marxism and American Studies." *American Quarterly* 38 (1986): 356–80.

Derrida, Jacques. "Women in the Beehive: A Seminar." *subjects/objects* (1984): 5–19. [Rpt. in *Men in Feminism,* ed. Alice Jardine and Paul Smith. New York: Methuen, 1987. 189–203; rpt. in *differences: A Journal of Feminist Cultural Studies* 16.3 (2005): 138–57.]

Djavann, Chahdortt. *Bas les voiles!* Paris: Nouvelle revue française, 2003.

Dobkin, Alix. "The Emperor's New Gender." *Off Our Backs* 30.4 (2000): 14.

Douglas, Ann. *The Feminization of American Culture*. New York: Avon, 1977.

DuBois, Ellen Carol, Gail Kelly, Elizabeth Kennedy, Carolyn Korsmeyer, and Lillian Robinson. *Feminist Scholarship: Kindling in the Groves of Academe*. Urbana: University of Illinois Press, 1987.

Ehrenreich, Barbara. "The New Macho Feminism." *New York Times,* 29 July 2004: 19.

Evans, Dylan. "Desire." *An Introductory Dictionary of Lacanian Psychoanalysis*. London: Routledge, 1996. 37.

Farnham, Christie. *The Impact of Feminist Research in the Academy*. Bloomington: Indiana University Press, 1987.

Feldman, Noah. "The Way We Live Now: The Only Exit Strategy Left." *New York Times* 30 July 2006: 9.

Ferguson, Margaret. "Teaching and/as Reproduction." *Yale Journal of Criticism* 1.2 (1988): 213–22.

Fernando, Mayanthi. "'French Citizens of Muslim Faith': Islam, Secularism, and the Politics of Difference in Contemporary France." Ph.D. diss., University of Chicago, 2006.

Findlay, Heather. "Losing Sue." *Butch/Femme: Inside Lesbian Gender*, ed. Sally Munt. London: Cassell, 1998. 133–45.

Foucault, Michel. *The History of Sexuality: An Introduction.* Vol. 1. Trans. Robert Hurley. New York: Vintage, 1990. 3 vols., 1978–1986.

———. "Two Lectures." *Power/Knowledge: Selected Interviews and Other Writings 1972–1977,* ed. Colin Gordon. New York: Pantheon, 1980. 78–108.

Freccero, Carla. "Notes of a Post-Sex War Theorizer." *Conflicts in Feminism,* ed. Marianne Hirsch and Evelyn Fox Keller. New York: Routledge, 1990: 305–25.

Friedman, Thomas. "The Kidnapping of Democracy." *New York Times* 14 July 2006: 19.

Furman, Nelly. "French Studies: Back to the Future." *Profession* 1998: 68–80.

Gallop, Jane. *Reading Lacan.* Ithaca: Cornell University Press, 1985.

Ghoreishi, Ahmad. "Where Is Iran Headed?" *Strategic Insights* 1.7 (Sept. 2002). http://www.ccc.nps.navy.mil/si/sep02/ (visited 7 March 2007).

Giroux, Henry, David Shumway, Paul Smith, and James Sosnoski. "The Need for Cultural Studies: Resisting Intellectuals and Oppositional Public Spheres." *Dalhousie Review* 64 (1984): 472–86.

Glass, Charles. "What Osama Said." *London Review of Books* 28.2 (March 2006): 14–18.

Gole, Nilufer. *The Forbidden Modern: Civilization and Veiling.* Ann Arbor: University of Michigan Press, 1996.

Green, Jamison. *Becoming a Visible Man.* Nashville: Vanderbilt University Press, 2004.

Green, Michael. "The Centre for Contemporary Cultural Studies." *Re-Reading English,* ed. Peter Widdowson. London: Methuen, 1982. 77–90.

Grewal, Inderpal, and Caren Kaplan. "Warrior Marks: Global Womanism's Neo-Colonial Discourse in a Multi-cultural Context." *Camera Obscura* 39 (Sept. 1996): 5–33.

———. "Transnational Feminist Practices and Questions of Postmodernity." Introduction. *Scattered Hegemonies: Postmodernity and Transnational Feminist Practices,* ed. Inderpal Grewal and Caren Kaplan. Minneapolis: University of Minnesota Press, 1994. 1–33.

Gubar, Susan. "Feminist Misogyny: Mary Wollstonecraft and the Paradox of 'It Takes One to Know One.'" *Feminism beside Itself.* Ed. Diane Elam and Robyn Wiegman. New York: Routledge, 1995. 133–54.

———. "What Ails Feminist Criticism?" *Critical Inquiry* 24.4 (1998): 878–902.

Guy-Sheftall, Beverly. Preface. *Words of Fire: An Anthology of African-American Feminist Thought.* New York: New Press, 1995. xiii–xx.

Haeri, Shahla. "Temporary Marriage and the State in Iran: An Islamic Discourse in Female Sexuality." *Social Research* 59.1 (1992): 201–23.

Halberstam, Judith. "Transgender Butch: Butch/FTM Border Wars and the Masculine Continuum." *GLQ: A Journal of Lesbian and Gay Studies* 4.2 (1998): 287–310.

Hale, Jacob C. "Consuming the Living/Disremembering the Dead." *GLQ: A Journal of Lesbian and Gay Studies* 42.2 (1998): 311–48.

Hall, Stuart. "Cultural Studies and the Centre: Some Problematics and Problems." *Culture, Media, Language: Working Papers in Cultural Studies, 1972–79*. London: Hutchinson, 1980. 15–47.

——. "The Emergence of Cultural Studies and the Crisis in the Humanities." *October* 53 (1990): 11–23.

Halley, Janet. "Sexuality Harassment." *Directions in Sexual Harassment Law*, ed. Catharine MacKinnon and Reva Siegel. New Haven: Yale University Press, 2002. 182–200.

——. "Reasoning about Sodomy: Act and Identity in and after *Bowers v. Hardwick*." *Virginia Law Review* 79 (1993): 1721–80.

Hampton, Adriel. "Transsexual Ousted from Shelter Shower for Sexual Orientation." *San Francisco Independent* 10 Feb. 2004.

Hausman, Bernice. "Recent Transgender Theory." *Feminist Studies* 27.2 (2001): 465–90.

Hersh, Seymour. "Annals of National Security: The Iran Plans." *New Yorker* 17 April 2006: 30–37.

——. "Annals of National Security: Watching Lebanon." *New Yorker* 21 Aug. 2006: 28–33.

Hirschkind, Charles, and Saba Mahmood. "Feminism, Taliban, and the Politics of Counterinsurgency." *Anthropological Quarterly* 75.2 (2002): 339–54.

Hirsi Ali, Ayaan. *The Caged Virgin: An Emancipation Proclamation for Women and Islam*. New York: Free Press, 2006.

——. *Infidel*. New York: Free Press, 2007.

Hitchens, Christopher. "Dutch Courage: Holland's Latest Insult to Ayaan Hirsi Ali." *Slate* 22 May 2006. http://www.slate.com/ (visited 28 Aug. 2006).

Hodgson, Marshall G. S. *The Venture of Islam: Conscience and History in a World Civilization. The Classical Age of Islam*. Vol. 1. Chicago: University of Chicago Press, 1974.

Hoodfar, Homa, and Samad Assadpour. "The Politics of Population Policy in the Islamic Republic of Iran." *Studies in Family Planning* 31.1 (2000): 19–34.

hooks, bell. *Yearning: Race, Gender, and Cultural Politics*. Boston: South End, 1990.

Hull, Gloria, Patricia Bell-Scott, and Barbara Smith, eds. *All the Women Are White, All the Blacks Are Men, But Some of Us Are Brave: Black Women's Studies*. Old Westbury, N.Y.: Feminist Press, 1982.

Hurtado, Aida. "Relating to Privilege: Seduction and Rejection in the Subordination of White Women and Women of Color." *Signs: Journal of Women in Culture and Society* 14.4 (1989): 833–54.

Jameson, Fredric. *The Political Unconscious: Narrative as a Socially Symbolic Act*. Ithaca: Cornell University Press, 1981.

Jehlen, Myra. "Archimedes and the Paradox of Feminist Criticism." *Feminisms: An Anthology of Literary Theory and Criticism*, ed. Robyn Warhol and Diane Price Herndl. New Brunswick: Rutgers University Press, 1991. 73–96.

Johnson, Richard. "What Is Cultural Studies Anyway?" *Social Text* 16 (1986–87): 38–80.

Kamuf, Peggy. "Replacing Feminist Criticism." *Diacritics* 12.2 (1982): 42–48.

Kaplan, Caren, and Inderpal Grewal. "Transnational Feminist Cultural Studies: Beyond the Marxism/Post-structuralism/Feminism Divides." *Between Women and Nation: Transnational Feminisms and the State*. Ed. Caren Kaplan, Norma Alarcón, and Minoo Moallem. Durham: Duke University Press, 1999. 349–63.

Keshavarz, Fatemeh. *Jasmine and Stars: Reading More Than Lolita in Tehran*. Chapel Hill: University of North Carolina Press, 2007.

Khouri, Norma. *Forbidden Love: A Harrowing Story of Love and Revenge in Jordan*. New York: Random, 2002. [Rpt. as *Honor Lost: Love and Death in Modern-Day Jordan*. New York: Simon and Schuster, 2003.]

King, Katie. *Theory in Its Feminist Travels: Conversations in U.S. Women's Movements*. Bloomington: Indiana University Press, 1994.

Knodt, Eva. Foreword to Niklas Luhmann, *Social Systems*. Stanford: Stanford University Press, 1995. ix–xxxvi.

Koch, Tony, and Paul Whittaker. "With Friends in High Places, Khouri to Defend Her Honour." *The Australian* 10 Aug. 2004: 1.

Kremmer, Janaki. "A 'True Life' Memoir of an Honor Killing Unravels in Australia." *Christian Science Monitor* 3 Aug. 2004: 1.

Kuper, Simon. "Of All Things European: Guru of the Week—Big Thoughts in Brief—Ayaan Hirsi Ali." *Financial Times Weekend Magazine* 27 March 2004. http://search.ft.com/ (visited 8 March 2007).

Lalami, Laila. "The Missionary Position." *The Nation* 19 June 2006. http://www.thenation.com/ (visited 2 Sept. 2006).

Larson, Janet. "Iran: A Model for Family Planning." *Globalist* 3 Aug. 2003. http://www.theglobalist.com/ (visited 20 Jan. 2006).

Lavie, Smadar, and Ted Swedenburg, eds. *Displacement, Diaspora, and Geographies of Identity*. Durham: Duke University Press, 1996.

Lazreg, Marnia. *The Eloquence of Silence: Algerian Women in Question*. New York: Routledge, 1994.

"Leaders and Revolutionaries." *Time* 18 April 2005. http://www.time.com/ (visited 7 March 2007).

Lee, Rachel. "Notes from the (Non)Field: Teaching and Theorizing Women of Color." *Women's Studies on Its Own*, ed. Robyn Wiegman. Durham: Duke University Press, 2002. 82–105.

Legge, Kate. "Hoaxer So Hard to Read." *Weekend Australian* 31 July 2004: 1.

Leila. *Mariée de force*. Paris: OH! Editions, 2004.

Levitt, Laura. *Jews and Feminism: The Ambivalent Search for Home*. New York: Routledge, 1997.

"Living with Islam: The New Dutch Model." *Economist* 2 April 2005: 24–26.

Lowe, Lisa. "The International within the National: American Studies and Asian American Critique." *Cultural Critique* 40 (fall 1998): 29–47.

Luhmann, Niklas. *Social Systems*. Stanford: Stanford University Press, 1995.

MacKinnon, Catharine. *Feminism Unmodified: Discourses on Life and Law*. Cambridge: Harvard University Press, 1987.

——. *Only Words*. Cambridge: Harvard University Press, 1996.

MacLeod, Arlene. "Hegemonic Relations and Gender Resistance: The New Veiling as Accommodating Protest in Cairo." *Signs: Journal of Women in Culture and Society* 17.3 (1992): 533–57.

Mahmood, Saba. *Politics of Piety: The Islamic Revival and the Feminist Subject*. Princeton: Princeton University Press, 2005.

——. "Secularism, Hermeneutics, and Empire: The Politics of Islamic Reformation." *Public Culture* 18.2 (2006): 323–47.

Mani, Lata. *Contentious Traditions: The Debate on Sati in Colonial India*. Berkeley: University of California Press, 1998.

Manji, Irshad. "Don't Be Fooled by the Fanatics." *Times Online* 5 Aug. 2006. http://www.timesonline.co.uk/ (visited 30 Aug. 2006).

——. "How I Learned to Love the Wall." *New York Times* 18 March 2006: A15.

——. *The Trouble with Islam: A Muslim's Call for Reform in Her Faith*. New York: St. Martin's, 2004.

Marcus, Jana. "Transfigurations: The Making of a Man." San Francisco Cameraworks Gallery, Nov. 2005. www.jlmphotography.com/.

Marech, Rona. "Nuances of Gay Identities Reflected in New Language: 'Homosexual' Is Passé in a 'Boi's' Life." *San Francisco Chronicle* 8 Feb. 2004: A1.

Martin, Biddy. *Femininity Played Straight: The Significance of Being Lesbian*. New York: Routledge, 1996.

McCalman, Iain. "The Empty Chador." *New York Times* 4 Aug. 2004: A17.

Mearsheimer, John, and Stephen Walt. "The Israel Lobby." *London Review of Books* 28.6 (2006). http://www.lrb.co.uk/v28/no6/ (visited 1 Aug. 2006).

Meliane, Loubna. *Vivre libre!* Paris: OH! Editions, 2004.

Mernissi, Fatima. *The Veil and the Male Elite: A Feminist Interpretation of Women's Rights in Islam*. Reading, Mass.: Addison-Wesley, 1991.

Minnich, Elizabeth, Jean O'Barr, and Rachel Rosenfeld, eds. *Reconstructing the Academy: Women's Education and Women's Studies*. Chicago: University of Chicago Press, 1988.

Moallem, Minoo. "Women of Color in the US: Pedagogical Reflections on the Politics of the Name." *Women's Studies on Its Own*, ed. Robyn Wiegman. Durham: Duke University Press, 2002. 341–67.

Moghissi, Haideh. "Fiminizm-ipupulistiva 'fiminizm-iIslami': naqdibargirayish'ha-yi muhafizah'kar dar mian-i fiminist'ha-yi danishgahi" [Populist Feminism and

'Islamic Feminism': A Critique of Neo-Conservative Tendencies among Iranian Academic Feminists]. *Kankash* 13 (1997): 57–95.

Mohanty, Chandra Talpade. "On Difference: The Politics of Black Women's Studies." *Women's Studies International Forum* 6 (1983): 243–47.

Mojab, Shahrzad. "Dawlat, fiminizm, va huviyat-i 'zan-i musalman'" [State, Feminism, and Identity of 'Muslim Woman']. *Arash* 60 (1997): 23–26.

Mooney, Carol J. "Conservative Scholars Call for Movement to 'Reclaim' Academy." *Chronicle of Higher Education* 23 Nov. 1988: 11, 13.

Moors, Annelies. "Submission." *ISIM Newsletter* 15 (2005): 8–9. http://www.isim.nl/files/review_15/ (visited 19 Jan. 2007).

Morris, Meaghan. "Politics Now (Anxieties of a Petty-Bourgeois Intellectual)." *The Pirate's Fiancée: Feminism, Reading, Postmodernism*. London: Verso, 1988. 173–86.

Mydans, Seth. "A Friendship Sundered by Muslim Code of Honor." *New York Times* 1 Feb. 2003: A4.

Nafisi, Azar. *Reading Lolita in Tehran*. New York: Random, 2003.

Najmabadi, Afsaneh. "Feminism in an Islamic Republic." *Islam, Gender, and Social Change*, ed. Yvonne Haddad and John Esposito. New York: Oxford University Press, 1998. 59–84.

———. "'Salha-yi usrat, salha-yi ruyish': nigarish' ha-yi zanvaranah dar jumhuri-i Islami-i Iran" ['Years of Hardship, Years of Growth': Feminist Reinterpretations in the Islamic Republic of Iran]. *Kankash* 12 (1995): 171–206.

———. "Secular, Feminist, and Muslim?" Institute for Research on Women and Gender, Columbia University, 26 Oct. 1995.

———. "'Years of Hardship, Years of Growth': Feminisms in an Islamic Republic." *Islam, Gender, and Social Change*, ed. Yvonne Haddad and John Esposito. New York: Oxford University Press, 1998. 59–84.

Namaste, Viviane. *Invisible Lives: The Erasure of Transsexual and Transgendered People*. Chicago: University of Chicago Press, 2000.

Northrop, Douglas. *Veiled Empire: Gender and Power in Stalinist Central Asia*. Ithaca, N.Y.: Cornell University Press, 2004.

Nussbaum, Martha. *Cultivating Humanity: A Classical Defense of Reform in Liberal Education*. Cambridge, Mass.: Harvard University Press, 1997.

———. "The Professor of Parody." *New Republic* 22 Feb. 1999: 37–45.

———. *Sex and Social Justice*. New York: Oxford University Press, 1999.

Ohmann, Richard. *English in America: A Radical View of the Profession*. New York: Oxford University Press, 1976.

———. *Politics of Letters*. Middletown, Conn.: Wesleyan University Press, 1987.

———. "Thoughts on CS in the U.S." *Critical Studies* 3.1 (1991): 5–15.

Okin, Susan. *Is Multiculturalism Bad for Women?* Princeton: Princeton University Press, 1999.

Parada, Carlos. "Muses." *Greek Mythology Link.* 1997. http://homepage.mac.com/cparada/gml/ (visited 13 Nov. 2002).

Pease, Donald E., Jr., and Robyn Wiegman. "Futures." *The Futures of American Studies*, ed. Robyn Wiegman and Donald E. Pease Jr. Durham: Duke University Press, 2002. 1–42.

Pollitt, Katha. Introduction. *Nothing Sacred: Women Respond to Fundamentalism and Terror.* Ed. Betsy Reed. New York: Nation Books, 2002. ix–xviii.

Porterfield, Todd. "Western View of Oriental Women in Modern Painting and Photography." *Forces of Change: Artists of the Arab World*, ed. Salwa Mikdadi Nashashibi. Washington: The National Museum of Women in the Arts, 1994. 58–71.

Prosser, Jay. *Second Skins: The Body Narratives of Transsexuality.* New York: Columbia University Press, 1998.

Rafkin, Louise. "Gender Warrior." *San Francisco Chronicle* 22 June 2003: CM8.

Ramphele, Mamphela. "Whither Feminism?" *Transitions, Environments, Translations: Feminisms in International Politics*, ed. Joan W. Scott, Cora Kaplan, and Debra Keates. New York: Routledge, 1997. 334–40.

Readings, Bill. *The University in Ruins.* Cambridge, Mass.: Harvard University Press, 1996.

Rich, Adrienne. "Notes toward a Politics of Location." *Blood, Bread, and Poetry: Selected Prose, 1979–85.* New York: Norton, 1986. 210–31.

Riley, Denise. *"Am I That Name?" Feminism and the Category of "Women" in History.* Minneapolis: University of Minnesota Press, 1988.

Robbins, Bruce. "The Politics of Theory." *Social Text* 18 (1987–88): 3–18.

Rooney, Ellen. "Going Farther: Literary Theory and the Passage to Cultural Criticism." *Works and Days* 3.1 (1985): 51–72.

——. "Marks of Gender." *Rethinking Marxism* 3.3–4 (fall/winter 1990): 190–201.

——. "What Is to Be Done." *Coming to Terms: Feminism, Theory, Politics*, ed. Elizabeth Weed. New York: Routledge, 1989. 230–39.

Rose, Gillian. *Love's Work: A Reckoning with Life.* New York: Schocken, 1995.

Rubin, Gayle S. "The Criminalization of Sadomasochism and the Legacy of Anti-Porn Feminism: Two Decades of Panic." University of California Humanities Research Institute Group, fall 1998.

——. "Thinking Sex: Notes for a Radical Theory of the Politics of Sexuality." *Lesbian and Gay Studies Reader,* ed. Henry Abelove, Michèle Aina Barale, David M. Halperin. New York: Routledge, 1993. 3–44.

Rupp, Leila. *Worlds of Women: The Making of an International Women's Movement.* Princeton: Princeton University Press, 1997.

Saadawi, Nawal, al-. "An Unholy Alliance." *Al-Ahram Weekly* 22–24 Jan. 2004. http://weekly.ahram.org.eg/2004/ (visited 9 March 2007).

Said, Edward. *Orientalism.* New York: Vintage, 1978.

Salamon, Julie. "Author Finds That with Fame Comes Image Management." *New York Times* 8 June 2004: EI.

Sánchez-Eppler, Karen. *Touching Liberty: Abolition, Feminism, and the Politics of the Body.* Berkeley: University of California Press, 1993.

Scott, Joan Wallach. "The Evidence of Experience." *Critical Inquiry* 17 (summer 1991): 773–97.

———. *The Politics of the Veil.* Princeton: Princeton University Press, 2007.

———, ed. *Feminism and History.* Oxford Readings in Feminism. Oxford: Oxford University Press, 1996.

"Sexuality 101." Narr. Mike Wallace. *Sixty Minutes.* CBS. 22 March 1998.

Shaheed, Farida. "Networking for Change: The Role of Women's Groups in Initiating Dialogue on Women's Issues." *Faith and Freedom: Women's Human Rights in the Muslim World,* ed. Mahnaz Afkhami. Syracuse: Syracuse University Press, 1995. 78–103.

Sheridan, Susan, ed. *Grafts: Feminist Cultural Criticism.* London: Verso, 1988.

Shumway, David. "Interdisciplinarity and Authority in American Studies." Unpublished ms.

———. "Transforming Literary Studies into Cultural Criticism: The Role of Interpretation and Theory." *Works and Days* 3.1 (1985): 79–89.

Souad, Marie-Thérèse Cuny. *Brûlée vive.* Paris: OH! Editions, 2003.

Spade, Dean. "Remarks at Transecting the Academy Conference, Race and Ethnic Studies Panel." 4 Dec. 2006. http://www.makezine.org/transecting.html.

Spender, Dale. *Men's Studies Modified: The Impact of Feminism on the Academic Disciplines.* Oxford: Pergamon, 1981.

Spivak, Gayatri. "Can the Subaltern Speak?" *Marxism and the Interpretation of Culture.* Ed. Cary Nelson and Lawrence Grossberg. Urbana: University of Illinois Press, 1988.

———. "In a Word. Interview." With Ellen Rooney. *differences: A Journal of Feminist Cultural Studies* 1.2 (1989): 124–56.

———. *In Other Words: Essays in Cultural Politics.* New York: Routledge, 1998.

———. Letter to the Editor. *New Republic* 19 April 1999: 43.

———. "The Political Economy of Women as Seen by a Literary Critic." *Coming to Terms: Feminism, Theory, Politics,* ed. Elizabeth Weed. New York: Routledge, 1989. 218–29.

Steady, Filomena Chioma, ed. *The Black Woman Cross-Culturally.* Cambridge, Mass.: Schenkman, 1981.

Stone, Sandy. "The Empire Strikes Back." *Body Guards: The Cultural Politics of Gender Ambiguity,* ed. Kristina Straub and Julia Epstein. New York: Routledge, 1991. 280–304.

Stryker, Susan. "Transgender Studies: Queer Theory's Evil Twin." *GLQ: A Journal of Lesbian and Gay Studies* 10.2 (2004): 212–15.

Stryker, Susan, and Stephen Whittle, eds. *The Transgender Studies Reader*. New York: Routledge, 2006.

Sullivan, Andrew. "Decent Exposure." *New York Times Book Review* 25 Jan. 2004: 10.

Thomas, Kendall. "The Eclipse of Reason: A Rhetorical Reading of *Bowers v. Hardwick*." *Virginia Law Review* 79 (1993): 1805–51.

Tohidi, Nayereh. "'Fiminizm-i Islami': chalishi dimukratik ya charkhishi ti'ukratik?" ['Islamic Feminism': A Democratic Challenge or a Theocratic Reaction?]. *Kankash* 13 (1997): 96–149.

Tompkins, Jane. *Sensational Designs: The Cultural Work of American Fiction, 1790–1860*. New York: Oxford University Press, 1985.

Treichler, Paula A., Cheris Kramarae, and Beth Stafford, eds. *For Alma Mater: Theory and Practice in Feminist Scholarship*. Urbana: University of Illinois Press, 1985.

Valentine, David. "The Calculus of Pain: Violence, Anthropological Ethics, and the Category of Transgender." *Ethnos* 66.1 (2003): 27–48.

Vitello, Paul. "The Trouble When Jane Becomes Jack." *New York Times* 20 Aug. 2006, sec. 9: 1.

Walker, Jamie, and Thomas Hedley. "Clues Written in Sands of Hindsight." *Courier Mail* (Queensland, Australia) 31 July 2004: 1.

Walther, Wiebke. *Women in Islam: From Medieval to Modern Times*. Princeton: Markus Wiener, 1993.

Weed, Elizabeth, ed. *Coming to Terms: Feminism, Theory, Politics*. New York: Routledge, 1989.

Whittle, Stephen. "Where Did We Go Wrong? Feminism and Trans Theory—Two Teams on the Same Side?" *The Transgender Studies Reader*. Ed. Sandy Stone and Stephen Whittle. New York: Routledge, 2006. 144–58.

Wiegman, Robyn. "Feminism's Apocalyptic Futures." *New Literary History* 31.4 (2000): 805–25.

——. "What Ails Feminist Criticism? A Second Opinion." *Critical Inquiry* 25.1 (1999): 362–79.

——, ed. *Women's Studies on Its Own*. Durham: Duke University Press, 2002.

Wilchins, Riki. *Read My Lips: Sexual Subversion and the End of Gender*. New York: Firebrand, 1997.

Williams, Patricia J. *The Alchemy of Race and Rights*. Cambridge: Harvard University Press, 1991.

Williams, Robert A., Jr. "Taking Rights Aggressively: The Perils and Promise of Critical Legal Theory for Peoples of Color." *Law and Inequality* 5.1 (1987): 103–34.

Wilson, Elizabeth. *Neural Geographies: Feminism and the Microstructure of Cognition*. New York: Routledge, 1998.

Wise, Gene. "'Paradigm Dramas' in American Studies: A Cultural and Institutional History of the Movement." *American Quarterly* 32 (1979): 293–337.

Women's Studies Group of the Centre for Contemporary Cultural Studies, eds. *Women Take Issue: Aspects of Women's Subordination.* London: Hutchinson, 1978.

Žižek, Slavoj. *The Abyss of Freedom/Ages of the World: F. W. J. von Schelling.* Ann Arbor: University of Michigan Press, 1997.

WENDY BROWN teaches political theory at the University of California, Berkeley. Her books include *States of Injury: Power and Freedom in Late Modernity* (1995); *Politics Out of History* (2001); *Left Legalism / Left Critique*, coedited with Janet Halley (2002); *Edgework: Essays on Knowledge and Politics* (2005); and *Regulating Aversion: Tolerance in the Age of Identity and Empire* (2006).

BEVERLY GUY-SHEFTALL is the Anna Julia Cooper Professor of Women's Studies and the founding director of the Women's Research and Resource Center at Spelman College in Atlanta, Georgia. She is the editor of *Words of Fire: An Anthology of African American Feminist Thought* (1995); coeditor, with Rudolph P. Byrd, of *Traps: African American Men on Gender and Sexuality* (2001); and coauthor, with Johnnetta Betsch Cole, of *Gender Talk: The Struggle for Women's Equality in African American Communities* (2003).

EVELYNN M. HAMMONDS, a professor of the history of science and of African and African American studies at Harvard University, became Harvard's first Senior Vice Provost for Faculty Development and Diversity in July 2005. In this role Dr. Hammonds directs Harvard's institutional policies and transformation, university-wide, in areas of faculty growth and diversity. Dr. Hammonds's scholarship focuses on the intersection of scientific, medical, and sociopolitical concepts of race in the United States. She is the author of *Childhood's Deadly Scourge: The Campaign to Control Diphtheria in New York City, 1880–1930* (1999). She coedited, with Barbara Laslett, Sally G. Kohl, and Helen Longino, *Gender and Scientific Authority* (1996) and she is completing two new books on the history of race in science and medicine.

SABA MAHMOOD is an associate professor of anthropology at the University of California, Berkeley. She is the author of *Politics of Piety: The Islamic Revival and the Feminist Subject* (2005). She is currently working on issues of secularism in the postcolonial Middle East.

BIDDY MARTIN is a professor of German studies and the university provost at Cornell University. She is the author of *Femininity Played Straight: The Significance of Being Lesbian* (1997) and *Women and Modernity: The Lifestyles of Lou Andreas Salomé* (1991).

AFSANEH NAJMABADI teaches history and studies of women, gender, and sexuality at Harvard University. Her most recent book, *Women with Mustaches and Men without Beards: Gender and Sexual Anxieties of Iranian Modernity* (2005), received the 2005 Joan Kelly Memorial Prize from the American Historical Association. She is an associate editor of the six-volume *Encyclopedia of Women and Islamic Cultures* (2004–2008) and is currently working on "Sexing Gender, Transing Homos: Configurations of Sexuality and Gender in Contemporary Iran."

ELLEN ROONEY is the chair and a professor of modern culture and media and a professor of English at Brown University. She is the editor of the *Cambridge Companion to Feminist Literary Theory* (2007) and is currently at work on a new book project called "A Semiprivate Room." She is the coeditor of *differences: A Journal of Feminist Cultural Studies*.

GAYLE SALAMON is an assistant professor of English at Princeton University. Her areas of specialization are phenomenology, psychoanalysis, and feminist and gender theory, and she is currently completing a manuscript on embodiment and trans subjectivity. Recent articles include "'Boys of the Lex': Transgenderism and Rhetorics of Materiality" (*GLQ*, Sept. 2006), "'The Place Where Life Hides Away': Merleau-Ponty, Fanon, and the Location of Bodily Being" (*differences: A Journal of Feminist Cultural Studies*, fall 2006), and "Sameness, Alterity, Flesh: Luce Irigaray and the Place of Sexual Undecidability," forthcoming in *Luce Irigaray and "The Greeks"*.

JOAN WALLACH SCOTT is the Harold F. Linder Professor of Social Science at the Institute for Advanced Study. The author of the now classic *Gender and the Politics of History*, her most recent book is *The Politics of the Veil* (2007).

ROBYN WIEGMAN is a professor of women's studies and literature at Duke University, where she directed the Women's Studies program from 2001 to 2007.

She has published *American Anatomies: Theorizing Race and Gender* (1995), *Who Can Speak: Identity and Critical Authority* (1995), *Feminism beside Itself* (1995), *AIDS and the National Body* (1997), *The Futures of American Studies* (2002), and *Women's Studies on Its Own* (2002). She is currently completing two book projects. "Being in Time with Feminism" examines the history of institutionalization of feminism in the U.S. academy; "Object Lessons: The U.S. Knowledge Politics of Identity" pays attention to relations of identification and affect in the constitution of identity as a domain of academic inquiry.

Gender (*cont.*)

122–24; transgenderism and, 10–11, 115, 127, 129–36; women's studies and, 115, 163–64, 173

Gogh, Theo van, 110 n. 12

Green, Jamison, 131

Green, Michael, 147

Gubar, Susan, 40

Halberstam, Judith, 127

Hall, Stuart, 139, 141, 143, 147

Hanafi, Hasan, 107

Hausman, Bernice, 127

Hill, Anita, 165

Hirsi Ali, Ayaan, 87–88, 98, 110 n. 12; *The Caged Virgin*, 88

Historically black colleges: curriculum in, 157; feminism and, 158; gender as topic in, 157; women's studies in, 156. *See also* Black women's studies

Hitchens, Christopher, 88

Homosexuality: legal production of, 27–28; mutability debate and, 28; normalization of, 120, 124, 127–28; transgenderism and, 123. *See also* Lesbian and gay studies; Lesbians

Honor killings, 96–99

Howard University, 157, 161

Humanities: future of, 176–87; science and, 173–75, 191–92; university crisis and, 175–77

Hussein, Saddam, 100

Hybridization, 70, 77–78

Identity: black women's studies and, 158–60; categories and, 69–78; Muslim women and, 9–10, 76–77, 80 n. 13; postmodern, 121; specificity of, 31; transgender, 120; in

women's studies, 9–10, 57, 59–61, 69–78, 117–18. *See also* Subjects

Identity politics, 158–60, 181

Identity studies, 58–61, 65 n. 13

Imperialism, 99–104; feminism and, 81–82, 102–4, 108; liberalism and, 103, 107–8; religio-political, 90; U.S., 90, 107. *See also* Colonialism

Individualism: feminism and, 105; ideology of, 4; liberalism and, 10; secularism and, 104; transgenderism and, 11; transgender studies and, 115

Inside the Kingdom (Carmen Bin Laden), 86, 101–3

Institutionalization of women's studies: accomplishment of, 3, 34, 40, 43; assessments of, 8–9, 11–12, 18, 35–36, 53–54, 161, 169–70, 196; crisis of, 20–21, 41, 49, 51, 54–56, 178–79; examination of, 60–61; in historically black colleges, 161–62; paradox of, 1–2; process of, 5–6; rejection of, 63 n. 1, 149–50; subject construction and, 122

Interdisciplinarity, 58–59, 170–71, 192–96

International Cross-Cultural Black Women's Studies Institute, 163

Intersubjectivity, 188–89

Iran, 71, 73–74, 91–93

Iraq, 90, 100, 102

Irigaray, Luce, 182

Islam: in anti-Islamic contexts, 74–75; authentic, 73, 75–76; in autobiographies of Muslim women, 83–99, 101–3; dissent in, 75–76; European sentiment against, 82, 86–88, 98, 100; feminism and, 76–77; fundamentalism and, 82, 99, 106; Golden

Age of, 75; Iran and, 73–74; reform proposals for, 104–8; scholarship and teaching concerning, 73–77; single-voiced, 75; U.S. sentiment against, 82, 88, 96, 100; women and, 10, 73–77, 81–108

Islamic Salvation Front (FIS), 75

Islamist movement, 99, 113 n. 44

Israel, 89, 110 n. 18

Jameson, Fredric, 187; *The Political Unconscious*, 148

Johnson, Richard, 142

Khouri, Norma, 97–98

Knodt, Eva, 191

Knowledge production: cultural studies and, 141–45, 147–48; feminism and, 52–53; identity and, 58; organization of, 170–71 (*see also* Universities: disciplinary logic of); politics of, 141–43, 147–48; in universities, 58, 142, 146–47; the unknown and, 195; women's studies and, 11

Law: feminist use of, 55; subject production and, 26–30, 55

Lawrence v. Texas (2003), 122

Leila, 87

Lesbian and gay studies, 120, 122

Lesbians, and transgenderism, 116, 124–29, 134

Lewis, Bernard, 90, 93

LGBT, 120, 122

Liberalism: anti-Muslim sentiment and, 83–84, 90, 104–8; democracy and, 82; feminism and, 82; imperialism and, 103, 107–8; individualism and, 10; Muslims and, 107; secularism and, 104–8

Literary studies, 23, 183–84

Lolita (Nabokov), 91, 94

Luhmann, Niklas, 191

L Word, The (television show), 124

MacKinnon, Catharine, 50

Macy, William H., 94

Mani, Lata, 104

Manji, Irshad, 85–86, 89–90

Man-on-woman homicide, 96–97, 99

Marcus, Jana, 130–31

Mariée de force (Leila), 87

Marriage debates, 122

Marx, Karl, 28

Masculinity: black, 165; transgenderism and, 126–36

McLaughlin, Andreé, 163

Meliane, Loubna, 87

Mernissi, Fatima, 75

Michigan Womyn's Music Festival, 124

Middle East Media Research Institute (MEMRI), 89, 110 n. 17

Middle East Partnership Initiative, 98

Million Man March, 165

Mohanty, Chandra, 157

Morris, Meaghan, 140

Ms., 89–90

Mud (Rodriguez), 134–35

Multiculturalism, 178

Muslim women: autobiographies of, 10, 83–99, 101–3; identity and, 9–10, 76–77, 80 n. 13; Islam and, 10, 73–77, 81–108; Islamic movement supported by, 102–3, 105; "liberation" of, 81–83, 94–97, 99, 101–5

Muslim World Outreach, 106–7

Nabokov, Vladimir, 91, 94

Nafisi, Azar, 85, 91–95

National Association of Scholars, 139–40

National Commission for Women (Jordan), 98

National Security Council (U.S.), 106

Neoconservatism, 83, 88–90

Neural Geographies (Wilson), 192–95

Neurobiology, 174

Neurocognitive science, 194

Neurology, 192–94

New Yorker, 94

New York Times, 90, 124–30

New York University, 157

Nietzsche, Friedrich, 25

Nine Parts of Desire (Brooks), 73

Ni putes ni soumises (Amara), 86, 109 n. 7

Nonnormative genders. *See* Transgenderism

Nussbaum, Martha, 40, 53, 55, 62; *Cultivating Humanity*, 180–87; "The Professor of Parody," 42, 46–52

O'Donnell, Rosie, 127

Ohmann, Richard, 140, 149

Orientalism, 70, 83–84, 88, 90, 93, 94

Orientalism (Said), 70

Other: education and, 185; Muslims as, 87; relations with, 188–89; scholarship and teaching concerning, 74–75

Palestinians, 89

Patriarchy, in black communities, 164–65

People's Party for Freedom and Democracy (Holland), 88

Pipes, Daniel, 89, 90, 110 n. 18

Politics: academic feminism and, 47–48, 53–54; cultural studies and, 140–42, 144–48, 150, 180; knowledge production and, 141–43, 147–48; Muslim women in, 87–88; nineteenth-century women and, 44–46; theory versus, 33–35, 40–42, 47–54; universities and, 4–5, 139–40, 150; women's studies and, 33–35, 40, 142, 145–46, 158–59

Pollitt, Katha, 104

Postcolonialism, 70, 72

Poststructuralism, 42, 47–50

Power: analysis of, 32; authenticity and, 76; how it works, 25–26; law and, 30; subject construction and, 24–27, 30–32, 55

Price, Glenda, 158

Problem-based learning, 170, 181

Prosser, Jay, 131

Psychoanalysis, 174, 195

Psychology, 192, 195

Queer theory, 20, 120–21

Qur'an, 73, 75, 76

Race: black women's studies and, 159–60; curriculum and, 18; primacy of, for African Americans, 166; women's studies and, 18, 30–31, 56, 65 n. 16, 158, 160, 166. *See also* African Americans; Black women's studies; Historically black colleges

Racism, 29, 164

Ramphele, Mamphela, 164–65

Reading Lolita in Tehran (Nafisi), 85, 91–95

Readings, Bill, 176–80, 184–87

Real, 188–89

Reason, 182, 184–87

Regulation of subjects, 25

Religion: feminist opposition to, 99, 104–5; as model for educational community, 185; role of, 10; secularism and, 104–8. *See also* Islam

Rich, Adrienne, 144

Riley, Denise, 39, 122

Robbins, Bruce, 144

Rodriguez, Lily, *Mud*, 134–35

Rose, Gillian, 188; *Love's Work*, 186

Rubin, Gayle, 127

Rushdie, Salman, 84, 88

Said, Edward, 70

Saudi Arabia, 101–2, 107

Science, humanities and social sciences in relation to, 173–75, 191–92

Second Skins (Prosser), 131

Secularism, 104–8

Sensational Designs (Tompkins), 45

Sentiment: academic feminism and, 33–35, 53–54, 56; women in nineteenth century and, 44–46

Sexuality: black women's studies and, 160; cultural studies and, 173; gender and, 120, 122–24; neuroscience and, 194–95; Nussbaum on study of, 181–83

Shaheed, Farida, 76

Silber, John, 139

Simmons, Ruth, 158

Sisters in Islam, 76

Social constructionism, 172–73, 187–88, 192, 194–95

Social movements, 35, 43

Social science, and science, 173–75, 191–92

Sontag, Susan, 95

Soroush, Abdolkarim, 107

Souad, Marie-Thérèse Cuny, 87

South Africa, 164

Spade, Dean, 122

Spelman College, 156–58, 160–62

Spivak, Gayatri, 144, 146

Stasi commission (France), 86

Steady, Filomena, 163

Steven Barclay Agency, 85

Stewart, Donald, 158

Stone, Sandy, 121

Stonewall, 125–26

Stryker, Susan, 120–21, 124

Subjects: complexity of, 24–25, 30–32, 119; hybrid, 70, 77–78; institutionalism and, 50; positioning of, 69–78; production of, 24–32, 55, 118–19; transgender, 117, 131–36; women as, 2. *See also* Identity

Sullivan, Andrew, 90

Teena, Brandon, 125–26

Theory, 143–44, 148, 150. *See also* Feminist theory; Knowledge production

Thomas, Clarence, 165

Time, narrative construction of, 71–72

Time (magazine), 47, 88

Tompkins, Jane, 45

Transgenderism: difference of, 120, 122, 129; feminism and, 115–16, 128; gender concept and, 10–11, 115, 127, 129–36; identity and, 120, 131–36; individualism and, 115; lesbians and, 116, 124–29, 134; *New York Times* article on, 124–30; origins of, 125; photography and, 128–35; restrooms and, 123; surgery and, 127–33; as threat, 124–26, 129; violence and, 116, 123–28; women's studies and, 10–11, 115–19

Transgender studies: aim of, 121; disciplinary identity of, 116, 117, 119; and lesbian and gay studies, 120, 122; postmodernism and, 121; singular character of, 117; and women's studies, 115–17

Transmen, 124–36

Transnational citizenship, 183

Transnational studies, 181

Transwomen, 123, 130

Trouble with Islam, The (Manji), 85–86, 89–90

United States: anti-Muslim sentiment in, 82, 88, 96; imperialism of, 90, 107; neoconservatism in, 88–90; wars on Muslim nations and, 81–83, 89, 100

Universities: concept of, 4; crisis in, 175–87; culture and, 178–80; disciplinary logic of, 58, 142–43, 146–50, 170–71; economic and technological imperatives in, 176–78; identity in, 58; knowledge production in, 58, 142, 146–47; politics and, 4–5, 139–40, 150; reimagining, 176–87; women in, 2; women's studies in, 1–4, 12, 33–35, 146

University in Ruins, The (Readings), 176–80, 184–87

University of California, Santa Cruz, 18–21

University of Maryland, 162

University of Michigan, 162

University of Texas, 166

U.S. Department of State, 106–7

Vanity Fair, 94

Veil, 77–78, 86, 103, 105

Veil and the Male Elite, The (Mernissi), 75

Victim studies, 159

Violence, and transgenderism, 116, 123–28

Vitello, Paul, 128

Vivre libre (Meliane), 87

Vogel, Lisa, 124

Vogue, 94

Wadud-Muhsin, Amina, 76

Walther, Wiebke, 73–74

White, Fran, 161

White House National Security Council, 106

Wilchins, Riki, 120, 130

Wilson, Elizabeth, 192–95

Wollstonecraft, Mary, 46

Women: in academia, 2; as category, 39–40, 45–46, 49, 52, 54, 56–57, 60, 62, 117, 121–22, 171–73, 179; democracy and, 99–104; in Iran, 93; in Iraq, 100; Islam and, 10, 73–77, 81–108; socioeconomic status of, 99–101; as subjects, 2; violence against, 96–97, 99, 164. *See also* Muslim women

Women in Islam (Walther), 73–74

Women Living under Muslim Law, 76

Women of Algiers (Delacroix), 93

Women of color. *See* African Americans; Black women's studies; Race

Women's studies: attacks on, 4, 6, 17; conservatism of, 21, 33, 54, 118; courses in, 22–23; critique of, 8, 18, 61, 185; cultural studies and, 141; curriculum of, 18–23, 54, 56–57; decline of, 17; differences overlooked by, 171–72; exclusions made by, 171; faculty of, 19–20, 22, 34, 57; feminism and, 145–46, 196; feminist scholarship and, 33–35;

Joan Wallach Scott is the Harold F. Linder Professor
of Social Science at the Institute for Advanced Study.

Library of Congress Cataloging-in-Publication Data
Women's studies on the edge / edited by
    Joan Wallach Scott.
p. cm.
Includes bibliographical references and index.
ISBN 978-0-8223-4252-6 (cloth : alk. paper)
ISBN 978-0-8223-4274-8 (pbk. : alk. paper)
1. Women's studies. I. Scott, Joan Wallach.
HQ1180.W6878 2008
305.4—dc22   2007053027